This is the sixth volume in a series of book
documentation and analysis of music in Asia.
first in the series to be dedicated to the music
more narrowly focused than the past, the essays in the present volume
continue the tradition established by Laurence Picken of publishing
'studies of musical documents from the field of Asian music' and 'studies
of sound-producing devices and of musical instruments'.

Musica Asiatica
6

EDITORIAL BOARD
J. Condit
F. Liebermann
E.J. Markham
A.J. Marett
D.R. Widdess
R.F. Wolpert

Musica Asiatica
6

Edited by Allan Marett

Cambridge University Press

CAMBRIDGE
NEW YORK   PORT CHESTER
MELBOURNE   SYDNEY

CAMBRIDGE UNIVERSITY PRESS
Cambridge, New York, Melbourne, Madrid, Cape Town, Singapore, São Paulo

Cambridge University Press
The Edinburgh Building, Cambridge CB2 8RU, UK

Published in the United States of America by Cambridge University Press, New York

www.cambridge.org
Information on this title: www.cambridge.org/9780521390507

© Cambridge University Press 1991

This publication is in copyright. Subject to statutory exception
and to the provisions of relevant collective licensing agreements,
no reproduction of any part may take place without the written
permission of Cambridge University Press.

First published 1991
This digitally printed version 2008

A catalogue record for this publication is available from the British Library

ISBN 978-0-521-39050-7 hardback
ISBN 978-0-521-07218-2 paperback

Contents

Preface   *page* ix

SONG BANG-SONG
Koguryo instruments in Tomb No. 1 at Ch'ang-ch'uan, Manchuria   1

RILEY LEE
Shakuhachi honkyoku notation: written sources in an oral tradition   18

ANDREAS GUTZWILLER and GERALD BENNETT
The world of a single sound: basic structure of the music of the Japanese flute shakuhachi   36

CHENG YINGSHI (translated by Coralie Rockwell)
A report on Chinese research into the Dunhuang music manuscripts   61

DAVID WATERHOUSE
Where did Toragaku come from?   73

GREGG W. HOWARD
Musico-religious implications of some Buddhist views of sound and music in the Śūrangama Sūtra   95

HUGH DE FERRANTI
Composition and improvisation in Satsuma biwa   102

Glossary of Chinese, Japanese and Korean terms   128
Contributors to this volume   133
Notes for authors   134

Preface

In an editorial note to the previous volume of *Musica Asiatica*, Richard Widdess foreshadowed that future volumes of *Musica Asiatica* would explore specific themes. This is the first such volume, dedicated to the music of East Asia. Just as its contents were being finalised, we heard of the death of a member of our Editorial Board, Yōko Mitani. This volume is dedicated to her memory. It will stand, I trust, as a lasting monument to her scholarship and to the generosity and support she showed to all of us who were privileged to call her a friend and colleague.

Laurence Picken, founding editor of this journal, has written the following tribute to Dr Mitani:

> The death of Professor Yōko Mitani at the age of 53, after a painful wasting illness of three years' duration, has deprived the members of the Tang Music Project of a greatly valued, scholarly colleague, and a dear friend. It was in the mid-seventies, during her tenure of a position as Visiting Scholar at Clare Hall, University of Cambridge, that Yōko-san was drawn into our group – largely of graduate-status – and, as *koto*-player and singer, shared with us the excitement of bringing to life in sound, playing from copies of Japanese manuscripts of the 11th to 13th centuries, music not heard for more than a thousand years. How great was the difference between what she helped to vivify and what has become the practice of those who perform *tōgaku* in Japan, she was perhaps more fully aware than any of us. She was a lovely person to be with, warm and kind, generous in every way, and treating us all, regardless of age, as colleagues of equal status.
>
> After her years as a student at Ochanomizu Women's University, she had spent a year at Columbia University, New York, prior to returning to Tokyo University in 1964, where she obtained her Master's Degree with a thesis on *kumiuta* – the song-suites that form part of the *koto*-repertory. Her doctoral work, under the direction of her friend and teacher, Professor Shiego Kishibe, was a wide-ranging, comprehensive study of zithers of east Asia, and in particular of *kin/qin* and *sō* or *koto/zheng*. We remember with affection the supremely modest way in which she adopted our interpretations of the finger-techniques for *gakusō*, as set out by Fujiwara no Moronaga in *Jinchi-yōroku*, notwithstanding their marked divergence from standard, modern, *zokukoto* practice; and especially we remember her pure, unaffected, 'natural' voice, as she sang, to the accompaniment of *gakusō* and *gakubiwa*, and *saibara* songs given new life in the reconstructions of Elizabeth Markham. Her openness of mind was plainly revealed by her confessing that she found the Heian versions of *saibara* – songs such as Ise no umi and Koromogae – much more beautiful than any of the six surviving items from that repertory, as performed in the versions extant today.
>
> Her gift to us lay not only in her musicianship and friendship, but in the fact that she acted, for all of us, as a living link with Japanese culture. She personified for us so much that remains precious and unforgettable.

To Dr Picken's remarks I would like to add my own acknowledgement of the role played by Yōko Mitani as a friend and mentor during my periods in Japan. Not only did she support my work and assist in the often complicated process of gaining access to people and resources, but also she offered me and my family hospitality and support at the times we needed it most. Although in later years she visited us in Australia, I feel that I was never able to fully repay her kindness.

The essays in the present volume, although more narrowly focused than in the past, continue the tradition established by Laurence Picken of 'publishing studies of musical documents from the fields of Asian music' and 'studies of sound-producing devices and of musical instruments'. The paper by Chen Yingshi on Chinese research into the Dunhuang scores obviously falls within the first area; in a sense though it also represents a new departure in that it celebrates the re-emergence of Chinese musical scholarship since the Cultural Revolution. The isolation of Chinese scholars from research undertaken in the West is clearly reflected in the paper; it is hoped that new contacts between scholars such as Professor Chen and their colleagues in the West marks a new phase in the scholarship of East Asian music.

I would like to thank Jim Franklin for his assistance at all stages in the preparation of this volume. I am also grateful to Charle Reimer for her care and patience in word processing the text.

Department of Music
University of Sydney
Australia

Allan Marett

Koguryŏ instruments in Tomb No. 1 at Ch'ang-ch'uan, Manchuria

SONG BANG-SONG

This paper investigates paintings of musical instruments contained in a fifth century Koguryŏ tomb at Ch'ang ch'uan. A report on the tomb prepared by Chinese local government officials is critically examined and more extensive examination of the evidence is undertaken in the light of Chinese and Korean literary sources and of recent archeological evidence from other Koguryŏ tomb excavations.

1 Introduction

In August 1970, the Chinese government repaired an ancient Koguryŏ tomb near the mid-Yalu riverside at Ch'ang-ch'uan, Chi-an Prefecture of Chi-lin Province, Manchuria. A general report on this ancient tomb, called Tomb No.1 at Ch'ang-ch'uan, was published in 1982 in a Chinese archeological journal, *Tung-pei k'ao-ku yü li-shih* (Chi-an-hsien wen-wu pao-kuan-so 1982),[1] by government officials of Chi-an Prefecture. Tomb No.1 is located about 20 kilometers northeast of Chi-an Town, Chi-lin Province. According to the general report, it is believed to have been constructed by Koguryŏ people around the late fifth century.[2]

The murals of Tomb No.1 at Ch'ang-ch'uan contain ten examples of musical instruments, including new instruments previously undiscovered in Koguryŏ tomb excavations. Of the ten instruments, all of which are depicted in the front room of the tomb, seven appear in the ceiling paintings and three in wall paintings. The general report on Tomb No.1 at Ch'ang-ch'uan gives only simple descriptions and commentaries on the musical instruments, but even these contain probable errors. This paper is an attempt to correct those mistakes and to provide a more extensive examination of the evidence in the light of recent archeological evidence from other Koguryŏ tomb excavations.

2 A general description of musical instruments in Tomb No.1

The general report identifies only eight of the ten instruments depicted in the murals of the front room, as follows: six instruments on the east, south and north sides of the ceiling painting; two instruments in the wall painting on the

---

[1] The romanization is based upon the Wade-Giles system for Chinese, the McCune-Reischauer system for Korea, and the Hepburn system for Japanese. Korean, Chinese and Japanese names are spelled in their indigenous fashion, namely, with the family name first.

[2] The Japanese scholar, Nishitani Tadashi, estimates the date for the construction of Tomb No.1 at Ch'ang-ch'uan as around the early fifth century (*Kyŏnghyang sinmun* (Seoul) 24 April, 1984).

north side (Chi-an-hsien wen-wu pao-kuan-so 1982: 163-68). The deva musicians on the east side of the ceiling are shown in figure 1 (upper panel): there are three distinguishable figures, all of which are apparently playing instruments. The general report considers these instruments to be a transverse flute (*heng-ti*), a round-bodied lute (*yüan-hsien*), and a zither (*ch'in*). As shown in figure 2 (upper panel), there are three deva musicians playing musical instruments on the north side of the ceiling. According to the general report, the three instruments are identified as a long horn (*ch'ang-chio*), a round-bodied long-necked lute (*yüan-hsien*), and a long vertical flute (*shu-ti*).

The general report describes the wall paintings on the north and south sides of the front room, which depict the folk customs of Koguryŏ. Although the painting on the south side has not been well preserved and is mostly erased, that on the north side is relatively clear (see figure 5; figure 4 is a detail from this painting). In the latter painting there are, according to the general report, two interesting instruments: one is evidently a zither (*ch'in*) played by a female musician to accompany a dance (figure 5), and the other, a five-stringed zither (*wu-hsien-ch'in*) carried by a female servant following a noble lady (figures 4 and 5).

The simple descriptions and commentaries in the report contain several mistakes. First, the south side of the ceiling (figure 3) appears to show a deva musician playing a vertical wind instrument. The general report, however, considers the flying deva musician not to be playing a vertical wind instrument, but to be holding a cylindrical stick (1982: 168). In view of the performing position of deva musicians on the east and north sides of the ceiling, however, it is unquestionable that the deva musician on the south side is playing a vertical wind instrument, which seems to be a double-reed pipe (*p'iryul* or *p'iri*) like that recorded in Chinese historical records of Koguryŏ.[3]

A second mistake in the general report concerns the round-bodied long-necked lute (*yüan-hsien*) identified on the east side of the ceiling (figure 1). The painting on the north side of the ceiling (figure 2) clearly depicts a deva musician playing a round-bodied lute (*yüan-hsien*) with four pegs. The lute in the east side of the ceiling painting is unlikely to be a *yüan-hsien* but another type of lute. Secondly, paintings at contemporary sites such as that at T'ung kou (see p.10) show that *yüan-hsien* would consist of four strings with four pegs (figure 11). The lute in figure 1, however, has five pegs. It is therefore reasonable to presume that this is not a *yüan-hsien* but the five-stringed lute known as *ohyŏn* (*wu-hsien* in Chinese) or *ohyŏn-pip'a* (*wu-hsien-p'i-p'a*).

Thirdly, the general report describes the zither depicted on the east side of the ceiling painting (figure 1) as a *ch'in*. It is more likely, however, that the zither is a prototype of the four-stringed zither known as *kŏmun'go* in Korean or *hyŏn'gŭm* in Sino-Korean. The zither depicted in figure 1 appears to be identical with the four-stringed zither (figure 6) in the mural of the Tomb of the Dancers (*Muyongch'ong*). This view will be supported below by literary evidence.

Fourthly, the general report describes the zither played by a female musician (figure 5) depicted on the northern wall as a *ch'in*. This zither may also, however, be explained as a prototype of the *kŏmun'go*, since the performing position is similar to the traditional performing position of present

---

[3] *Pei-shih*, chüan 94.8a6 (hereafter *Pei-shih*, 94.8a6); and *Sui-shu*, 81.2a10. In this paper, the Kan-lung edition (1739) of *Erh-shih-wu-shih* (Taipei: Yee Wen Publishing Co., 1956, 50 volumes) is referred to.

Figure 1: Transverse flute (*Hoengjŏk*), five-stringed lute (*Ohyŏn-pip'a*), and zither (*Kŏmun'go*) on the east side of the ceiling painting

Figure 2: Long horn (*Taegak*), round-bodied lute (*Wanham* or *Yüan-hsien*), and long vertical flute (*Changso*) on the north side of the ceiling painting

Figure 3: Double-reed pipe (*P'iri* or *P'iryul*) on the south side of the ceiling painting

kŏmun'go player.[4]

Finally, the wall-painting of folk customs on the north side (figure 5) clearly depicts a large drum carried by two persons which has not been mentioned in the general report. It is in the top centre of the painting. According to Chinese literary sources,[5] this kind of suspended drum found in Koguryŏ music was called *tamgo*, literally meaning 'bearing drum'. In summary, a careful examination of the paintings leads us to conclude that not eight but ten musical instruments can be recognised from the murals of Tomb No.1 at Ch'ang-ch'uan. These are summarised in table 1.

Table 1: Ten musical instruments of Tomb No.1 at Ch'ang-ch'uan

Front Room of Tomb No. 1		Musical Instruments	Chinese Report	Author's Examination
Ceiling Painting	East side	transverse flute	*heng-ti*	*hoengjŏk* or *hoengch'wi*
		five-stringed lute	*yüan-hsien*	*ohyŏn-pip'a* or *ohyŏn*
		zither	*ch'in*	*kŏmun'go* or *hyŏn'gŭm*
	North side	long horn	*ch'ang-chio*	*taegak*
		round-bodied lute	*yüan-hsien*	*wanham*
		long vertical flute	*shu-ti*	*changso*
	South side	double-reed pipe	-	*p'iryul* or *p'iri*
Wall Painting	North side	five-stringed zither	*wu-hsien-ch'in*	*ohyŏn'gŭm* or *ohyŏnakki*
		zither	*ch'in*	*kŏmun'go* or *hyŏn'gŭm*
		large suspended drum	-	*tamgo*

3 An historical examination of the musical instruments in Tomb No.1

It was King Kwanggaet'o (r. 391-413) who vigorously pursued the task of adding new domains to Koguryŏ by conquest. The great military campaigns of this king are recorded in detail on the huge stone stele which still stands at his tomb in Kungnaesŏng, then the capital of Koguryŏ. Kwanggaet'o was succeeded by King Changsu (r. 413-491), who continued his father's enterprises and brought Koguryŏ to its height. In 427 he transferred the Koguryŏ capital to P'yŏngyang, creating a new epicenter for the nation. With its greatly expanded frontiers, Koguryŏ adopted a policy of friendly relations with the more distant Chinese states and military confrontation with those closest to its borders. Thus the bitter struggle with the nearby Northern Dynasties of China

---

[4] For the traditional performing position of present *kŏmun'go* players, see Chang 1969: pl.69; Pratt 1987: 71.

[5] *Sui-shu*, 15.33b6; *Chiu-T'ang-shu*, 29.11a4; and *T'ang-shu*, 21.12b2.

Figure 4: Five-stringed zither (*Ohyŏn'gŭm* or *Ohyŏnakki*) in the northern wall painting

Figure 5: Five-stringed zither (*Ohyŏn'gŭm* or *Ohyŏnakki*), zither (*Kŏmun'go*), and suspended drum (*tamgo*) in the folk customs of Koguryŏ, northern wall painting

continued, while Koguryŏ at the same time sought diplomatic contact across the sea with China's Southern Dynasties. Koguryŏ also formed ties with the nomadic peoples on China's northern frontier as a further means of holding China at bay (Lee Ki-baik 1984: 38-39).

Already in 372 Koguryŏ had established a National Confucian Academy (*T'aehak*) at which Confucianism was taught. The widely used date for the initial acceptance of Buddhism is the year 372, when the monk Sundo came to Koguryŏ from the Earlier Ch'in (then in control of northeastern China) and transmitted images of the Buddha and Buddhist sutras. In all Three Korean Kingdoms, the principal initiative for the acceptance of Buddhism came from the royal houses. The best known paintings of the Three Kingdoms period are, of course, the murals of the old tombs of Koguryŏ. The Koguryŏ tombs are customarily named after the theme of the paintings that adorn their walls: for example, the Tomb of the Dancers (*Muyongch'ong*), the Tomb of the Four Spirits (*Sasinch'ong*), and the like. Tomb No.1 at Ch'ang-ch'uan is a tomb in the area of Kungnaesŏng, then the capital of Koguryŏ, on the Manchurian side of the mid-Yalu River.

From the historical point of view, the ten musical instruments in the ceiling- and wall-paintings of Tomb No.1 can be divided into two groups: one comprises Koguryŏ instruments from before the fifth century; the other, new Koguryŏ instruments from the fifth century. The pre-fifth century instruments are: the zither (*hyŏn'gŭm* or *kŏmun'go*) on the east side of the ceiling-painting; the long horn (*taegak*), round-bodied lute (*wanham* or *yüan-hsien*) and vertical flute (*changso*) on the north side of the ceiling painting; the zither and suspended drum (*tamgo*) on the northern wall-painting. New Koguryŏ instruments from the fifth century are: the transverse flute (*hoengjŏk* or *hoengch'wi*) and five-stringed lute (*ohyŏn* or *ohyŏn-pip'a*) on the east side of the ceiling painting; the double-reed pipe (*p'iri* or *p'iryul*) on the south side of the ceiling painting; the five-stringed zither (*ohyŏn'gŭm* or *ohyŏnakki*) on the northern wall painting.

Koguryŏ instruments from before the fifth century

Of the Koguryŏ instruments from before the fifth century, the zither (*kŏmun'go*) and long horn (*taegak*) are considered by Korean musicologists to have originated in Koguryŏ; these instruments are recorded in Korean and Chinese literary sources.[6] The wall paintings of musicians in such Koguryŏ tomb excavations as Tomb No.3 at Anak (A.D. 357), Hwanghae Province,[7] suggest however, that one may be able to trace the origin of the other three instruments to China and Central Asia.

Let us now turn to historical evidence from literary sources and recently excavated archeological sites.

According to the Korean history, *Samguk sagi* (1145)[8] by Kim Pu-sik

---

[6] *San-kuo-chih*, 30.42b5; *Samguk sagi*, 32.6a1-7a8. This study is based upon the facsimile *Chŏngdŏk* edition of *Samguk sagi*, Seoul: Minjok munhwa ch'ujinhoe, 1973.

[7] For an intensive study of musical instruments in the murals of Tomb No.3 at Anak, see Lee Hye-ku, 1967: 1-31, 463-83 ('Musical Paintings in a Fourth Century Korean Tomb', trans. by Robert C. Provine).

[8] *Samguk sagi*, 32.6a8-6b4. For an English translation of its text, see Song 1980: 26-28.

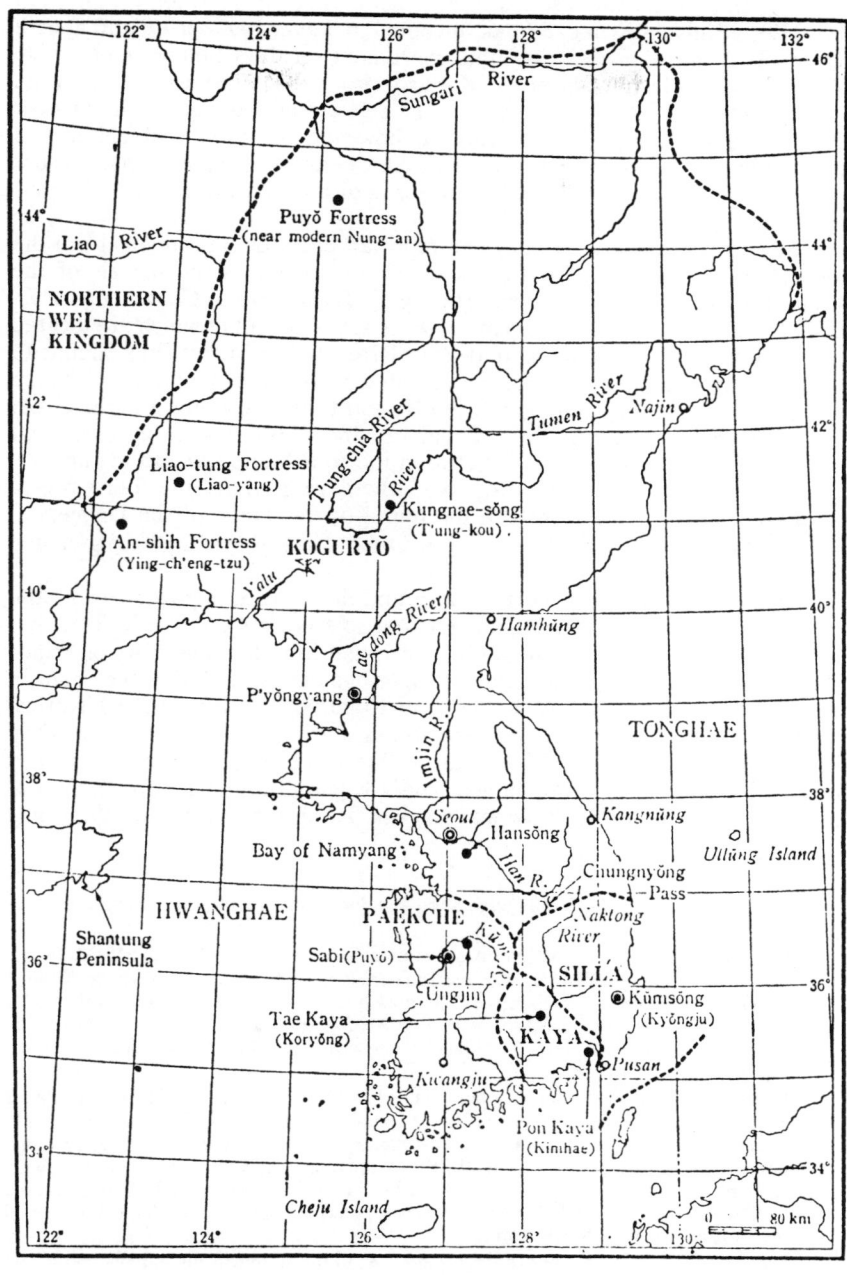

Map: Korea at the height of Koguryŏ expansion in the fifth century (Lee Ki-baik 1984: 46)

(1075-1151), and the Chinese historical record, *San-kuo-chih*[9] by Ch'en Shou (233-279), Minister Wang San-ak invented a *kŏmun'go* during the fourth century. It is said that he based this instrument on the Chinese *ch'in*, which had been officially introduced to Koguryŏ from the Eastern Chin State (317-419) (Song 1986: 5-15), and a zither that already existed in the ancient tribal states of Korea. It is uncertain, however, what type of zither was invented by the Minister. Whether the instrument was similar to the present *kŏmun'go* or whether it was like the zithers depicted in several Koguryŏ tombs is a matter of speculation.

Several zithers have so far been reported in historical remains from the Koguryŏ Kingdom (B.C. 37-A.D. 668). These appear in the murals of the Tomb of the Dancers at T'ung-kou (figure 6), Tomb No.4 at Chi-an (figure 7), Tomb No.12 at T'ung-kou, and Tomb No.17 at Chi-an, all of which are located on the Manchurian side of the mid-Yalu River. Other instruments similar to the above-mentioned zither are represented in the wall paintings of Tomb No.3 at Anak County, Taesŏngni Tomb No.1 at Kangsŏ County, and the Great Tomb at Kangsŏ County, South P'yŏngan Province.[10] It has been suggested that these Koguryŏ tombs were built between the fourth and seventh centuries.[11] The best examples of ancient Koguryŏ zithers are perhaps the four-stringed zither with more than ten frets in the mural of the Tomb of the Dancers at T'ung-kou (figure 6), or the five-stringed zither of Tomb No.1 at Ch'ang-ch'uan (figure 4) which will be discussed later.

In the early Koguryŏ period, horn and drum were important wind and percussion instruments, playing an essential role not only on battle fields but also in court ceremonies. This can be confirmed from the love story of Prince Hodong of Koguryŏ and the princess of Nangnang State during the reign of the third King Taemusin (A.D. 18-43) of Koguryŏ,[12] and from the historical record concerning court ritual ceremonies during that of the first King Tongmyŏng (37-20 B.C.).[13] In addition to literary evidence, there are similar horns depicted in the murals of such early Koguryŏ tombs as Tomb No.3 at Anak County, Hwanghae Province; Kamsin Tomb (ca. 4th C.) at Yonggang

---

[9] *San-kuo-chih*, 30.42b5. For an annotation and discussion of its text, see Song 1985: 156-58 and Song 1986: 6.

[10] For bibliographical information on old Koguryŏ tombs, see Song 1985: 319-32. In this essay, discussion of recent archeological materials from North Korea relies on *Koguryŏ munhwa*, 1975. For the illustrations of the *kŏmun'go* in the murals of Tomb No.12, Taesŏngni Tomb, Tomb No.17, Tomb No.3, see *Koguryŏ munhwa* 1975: 67 (pl.5-8), 154 (pl.100-3); Lee Hye-ku 1967: 24; Umehara Sueharu 1966: pl.16-30 and Song 1985: pls.7, 22, 23.

[11] Different opinions about the estimated dates for the construction of old Koguryŏ tombs are held by Korean scholars. For instance, Tomb No.17 at Chi-an, Manchuria, is thought to have been constructed around the sixth century by Chu Yŏng-hŏn and Chang Sa-hun, but around the early seventh century by Kim Wŏn-yong (Chu 1972: 151 (Table 29); Chang 1969: pl.17; Kim Wŏn-yong 1960: 54-5). This study will be based upon the date presented by Chu Yŏng-hŏn, for Chu's work contains a great number of archeological reports of recent excavations in North Korea.

[12] *Samguk sagi*, 14.6a2-6b2. For the legendary story of the automatically sounding drum and horn in an English translation, see Song 1980: 14-15.

[13] According to Yi Kyu-bo 1982: 3.7a5-7, drum and horn were essential instruments particularly for military processions (*koch'wi* in Sino-Korean, and *ku-ch'ui* in Chinese) from an early stage of the Koguryŏ Kingdom. *San-kuo-chih*, 30.26b1 and *Hou-Han-shu*, 85.6a7-9 state that *koch'wi* musicians were sent to Koguryŏ during the reign of Emperor Wu Ti (B.C. 140-87) of the Han Empire. It is uncertain, however, what kind of percussion and wind instruments might have been introduced to Koguryŏ from the Han period.

Figure 6: Four-stringed zither (*Kŏmun'go*) in the mural of Tomb of the Three Dancers at T'ung-kou, Manchuria

Figure 7: Four-stringed zither (*Kŏmun'go*) in the mural of Tomb No.4 at Chi'an, Chi-lin Province, Manchuria

County, South P'yŏngan Province; Tŏkhŭngni Tomb (407 A.D.) at Taean City, South P'yŏngan Province; the Tomb at P'yŏngyang Station (ca. 4th C.) (figure 10); the Tomb of the Dancers (ca. 4th-5th C.) at T'ung-kou, Manchuria; Susanni tomb (ca. 5th C.) at Kangsŏ County, South P'yŏngan Province; Yaksuri Tomb (ca. 4th-5th C.) at Kangsŏ County; and P'alch'ŏngni Tomb (ca. 5th C.) at Taedong County (figure 9), South P'yŏngan Province.[14] From the available historical records and early archeological remains it may be safe to conclude that the long horn played a continuously important role in the ancient society of Koguryŏ before the fifth century.

The lute known as *yüan-hsien*,[15] an example of which is preserved at the Shōsōin, Nara, Japan, has a distinctive round body and slender neck with four pegs and strings (see figure 12). The Chinese *yüan-hsien* seems to have been very popular in the musical life of Koguryŏ society before the introduction of the *p'ip'a* from Central Asia around the fifth century,[16] since the *yüan-hsien* of Tomb No.1 at Ch'ang-ch'uan closely resembles the other *yüan-hsien* painted in Tomb No.3 at Anak County (figure 8); Tŏkhŭngni Tomb (407 A.D.) at Taean City; P'alch'ŏngni Tomb (ca. 5th C.) at Taedong County, South P'yŏngan Province (figure 9); and the 'Three Chambers' Tomb (ca. 5th-6th C.) at T'ung-kou (figure 11), Manchuria.[17]

The long vertical flute (*changso*) of Tomb No.1 at Ch'ang-ch'uan is very similar to that of Tomb No.3 at Anak County (figure 8). The vertical flute is likely to have been an important wind-instrument in the Han period and in the period of the Northern Dynasties of China.[18] The long vertical flute may also have played a significant role in the musical life of Koguryŏ society before the fifth century, before being gradually replaced by the transverse flute. This may be the reason why the vertical flute (*hsiao* in Chinese and *so* in Sino-Korean) was recorded as one of the Koguryŏ instruments in early Chinese historical documents,[19] but was not recorded in later Korean historical records.

The suspended drum (*tamgo*) was one of the most important percussion instruments in the processional music known as *koch'wi* in Sino-Korean or *ku-ch'ui* in Chinese (see above, p.8, n.13). The *tamgo* painting of Tomb No.1 at Ch'ang-ch'uan is quite similar to that of Tŏkhŭngi Tomb (407 A.D.) at Taean City (figure 13), South P'yŏngan Province, in which a large drum is suspended

---

[14] For the illustrations of long horns depicted in the murals of Koguryŏ tombs, see *Koguryŏ munhwa* 1975: 156 (pl.101-2), 160 (pls.104-1,2,3); Kim Ki-ung 1982: 86; Ikeuchi 1940: pl.28-1; Chang 1969: pl.14; Song 1985: pls.7,8,11,16, 19; Pratt 1987: pls.73 and 108.

[15] The *yüan-hsien* (*wanham* in Sino-Korean) was also called *ch'in-p'ip'a* or *ch'in-han-tzu* in olden times in China. Because the instrument was frequently played by Yüan Hsien, one of Seven Convivial Worthies of the Bamboo Grove (*Chu-lin ch'i-hsien*) during the Chin (265-419) period, it was later known as *yüan-hsien* (Tu Yu 1959: *chüan* 144, *szu* 5; Hayashi Kenzō 1973: 319).

[16] Before the discovery of the murals of Tomb No.1 at Ch'ang-ch'uan, it was believed that the *p'ipa* might have been introduced to Koguryŏ around the sixth century. For an essay on the Korean *p'ipa*, see Song 1973.

[17] See *Koguryŏ munhwa* 1975: 168 (pl.108-1); Ikeuchi 1940: pl.60-1; Lee Hye-ku 1967: 24; Chang 1969: pl.13; Kim Ki-ung 1982: 260; Song 1985: pls.7,9,15; Song 1984a: pls.2 and 6.

[18] For bibliographical information, see Lee Hye-ku 1967: 480. For illustrations of a long vertical flute, Yi Hang-sŏng 1962: 100; Song 1985: pl.41.

[19] The *hsiao* (*so* in Sino-Korean) is recorded as one of the Koguryŏ instruments in such Chinese histories as *Pei-shih*, 94.8a6; *Sui-shu*, 15.33b5, and 81.2a10; *T'ang-shu*, 21.12b1; and *Chiu-T'ang-shu*, 29.11a3. Although it is unclear whether the *hsiao* or *so* is a kind of panpipe or a kind of vertical flute, according to archeological evidence and other literary sources it is likely to have been a kind of vertical flute. For details, see Song 1985: 16-8.

Figure 8: Zither (*Kŏmun'go*), round-bodied lute (*Wanham* or *Yüan-hsien*), and long vertical flute (*Changso*) in the murals of Tomb No.3 at Anak, Hwanghae Province

Figure 9: Long horn (*Changso*), suspended drum (*Tamgo*), and round-bodied lute (*Wanham* or *Yüan-hsien*) in the murals of P'alch'ŏngni Tomb at Taedong County, South P'yongan Province

Figure 10: Standing drum and long horn (*Taegak*) in the mural of the Tomb at P'yŏngyang Station, South P'yŏngan Province

from a long bent pole and carried by two walking musicians (Pratt 1987: pl.21; Song 1985: 21). Tomb No.3 at Anak County (357 A.D.) contains a similar mural, in which there are drums, each requiring a performer and two carriers (Lee Hye-ku 1967: 13; Chang 1969: pl.9; Pratt 1987: pl.20). Besides those of Tŏkhŭngi Tomb and Tomb No.3 at Anak, *tamgo* paintings are also found in Susanni Tomb (ca. 5th C.) at Kangsŏ County, South P'yŏngan Province; Tomb No.1 at Anak County (ca. 4th C.), Hwanghae Province; P'alch'ŏngni Tomb (ca. 5th C.) at Taedong County (figure 10), South P'yŏngan Province (*Koguryŏ munhwa* 1975: 157 (pl.102-5), 168 (pl.108-1); Kim Ki-ung 1982: 226; Song 1985: pls.16, 20, 21; Pratt 1987: pls.21 and 22). From the early Koguryŏ period onward, the *tamgo* seems to have played an important role and to have been an essential percussion instrument in the Koguryŏ *koch'wi* band. This may be the reason why the *tamgo* was mentioned subsequently in Chinese histories.[20]

In short, before the fifth century, Koguryŏ music was represented by such instruments as zithers (*kŏmun'go* or *hyŏn'gŭm*), the long vertical flute (*changso*), the round-bodied lute (*wanham* or *yüan-hsien*), the long horn (*taegak*), and the suspended drum (*tamgo*). With our extensive examination, it is possible to conclude that the *kŏmun'go* and *taegak* might have originated in Korea, and the other instruments might have been imported from China and Central Asia via the Silk Road in the northwestern region of China.

New Koguryŏ instruments from the fifth century

As stated earlier (p.6), new Koguryŏ instruments from the fifth century shown in Table 1 were the transverse flute (*hoengjŏk* or *hoengch'wi*), the double-reed pipe (*p'iri* or *p'iryul*), the five-stringed lute (*ohyŏn* or *ohyŏn-pip'a*), and the five-stringed zither (*ohyŏn'gŭm* or *ohyŏnakki*). Among the new instruments, the five-stringed zither is thought to have originated in Koguryŏ, for the instrument is unique in terms of its physical features, and has not been reported in the archeological excavations in China. The other three instruments might, however, have been introduced to Koguryŏ from Central Asia by way of the Caravan Route in the northwestern region of China. Let us now consider these new instruments in detail.

In contrast to the prototype of the *kŏmun'go* depicted in old Koguryŏ tombs, the five-stringed zither is characterised by the distinctive five pegs (figure 4) which remind us of those of the lute family. Since this type of zither was no longer in use after the fall of Koguryŏ and no literary sources provide an exact record on it,[21] we have no further information about it at the present. It is hoped that future archeological excavations will provide further evidence.

A similar type of zither with pegs called *shichisengakki* (lit. 'seven-

---

[20] *Sui-shu*, 15.33b6; *T'ang-shu*, 21.12b2; *Chiu-T'ang-shu*, 29.11a4.

[21] In *Sui-chu* 81.2a10 and *Pei-shih* 94.8a5, the *wu-hsien-ch'in* (lit. 'five-stringed zither') is mentioned as one of the Koguryŏ instruments. For two reasons, however, the term *wu-hsien-ch'in* may be divided into two words, *wu-hsien* ('five-stringed [lute]') and *ch'in* ('zither'). First, the term *wu-hsien* (*ohyŏn* in Sino-Korean) is used to indicate a five-stringed lute in *Sui-shu* 15.31b2 (*Hsi-liang-chi*), 32b5 (*Kuei-tzu-chi*), 32b10 (*T'ien-chu-chi*), 33a8 (*Shu-ch'ih-chi*), and 33b2 (*An-kuo-chi*). Secondly, the *hyŏn'gŭm* or *kŏmun'go* was already a Koguryŏ stringed instrument when the *Sui-chu* was compiled by Wei Cheng in 636 and the *Pei-shih* by Li Yen-shou during the reign of T'ai-tsung (627-649). One might expect therefore that the zither would be included in the list of Koguryŏ instruments.

Figure 11: Round-bodied lute (*Wanham* or *Yüan-hsien*) in the mural of the Three Chambers' Tomb at T'ung-kou, Manchuria

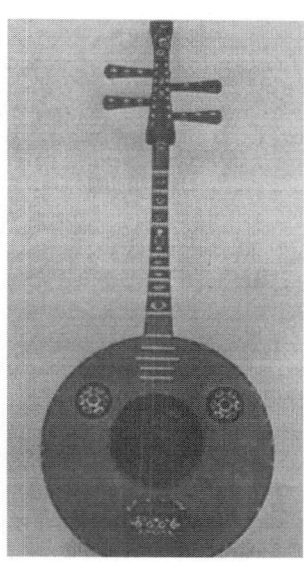

Figure 12: Round-bodied lute (*Yüan-hsien*) in the Shōsōin, Nara, Japan (*Shōsōin jimusho* 1967: pl.17)

Figure 13: Suspended drum (*Tamgo*) in the mural of Tŏkhŭngi Tomb at Taean City, South P'yŏngan Province

stringed zither')[22] has been preserved in the Shōsōin Imperial Treasury of Japan at Nara (figure 14). Two important similarities between the five-stringed and the seven-stringed zither may be noted. First, the five-stringed zither has five pegs, the seven-stringed zither, seven,[23] all at the end of the lower side. Secondly, the overall shape of both zithers is a shallow oblong box with a long, slender shape. It may be postulated therefore, that the seven-stringed zither in Japan is historically related to the five-stringed zither of Koguryŏ. It is impossible, however, to determine any details of performance technique. Since no further historical evidence is available, we can conclude as follows: the five-stringed zither might have been another prototype of the present *kŏmun'go*, like the four-stringed zither with more than ten frets depicted in the murals of Tomb of the Dancers (figure 6), T'ung-kou, Manchuria. Even though the tradition of a five-stringed zither was not transmitted in Korea after the fall of the Koguryŏ Kingdom, Koguryŏ musicians seem to have introduced a similar type of zither to the Nara court of Japan during the Three Kingdoms period (Harich-Schneider 1973: 18-19, 51; Malm 1959: 77; Lee Hye-ku 1976: 164-90; Lee Hye-ku 1985: 219-27; Kikkawa 1965: 33-38; Song 1984a: 75-89). The seven-stringed zither (*shichisengakki*) preserved in the Shōsōin might be an example of it.

Recent archeological excavations in China suggest that the transverse flute, the double-reed pipe, and the five-stringed lute had already been introduced from Central Asia to China during the Northern Dynasties period (386-681). For instance, a transverse flute and a five-stringed lute are found in a pottery relief (figure 15) excavated at An-yang, Honan Province (*Chung-hua jen-min kung-ho-kuo ch'u-t'u wen-wu chan-lan chan-p'in hsüan-chi* 1973: pl.101); a double-reed pipe and a transverse flute are depicted in the ceiling painting of the front room of Stone Cave No.435 at Tun-huang (Tonkō bunbutsu kenkyūsho 1980: Vol.I, pl. 71), and there is a transverse flute in the relief of Stone Cave No.9 at Yün-kang, Shan-hsi Province (*A Pictorial Encyclopedia of the Oriental Arts* 1969: Vol.I, pl. 149).

After the fall of the Han Empire, Koguryŏ continued the military confrontation with the nearby Northern Dynasties, while at the same time seeking close cultural contact with both Northern and Southern Dynasties (Lee Ki-baik 1984: 46). The existence in Koguryŏ paintings of three instruments of Central Asian origin allow us to confirm with a degree of certainty the existence of close cultural contact, particularly with Northern Dynasties, before the fifth century. Chinese literary traditions confirm these contacts.

The three new instruments of Central Asian origin played an important role not only in the Koguryŏ orchestra (*Kao-li-chi*) but also in such Central Asian States' orchestras as those of *Hsi-liang-chi*, *Shu-ch'ih-chi* (Kashgar),

---

[22] See *Shōsōin jimusho* 1967: pls.38-41; Kishibe 1984: 41 (pls.3-4). According to an investigation report in 1948, the length of the *shichisengakki* is 120 cm; its maximum width is 18.6 cm and its minimum width, 17.3 cm; its thickness 3.6 cm. The lengths of the surviving six pegs are from 18.3 cm to 19.1 cm, and their diameters, from 1.05cm to 1.8 cm. The main body of the *shichisengakki* is made from two pieces of paulownia wood; a concave upper piece and a flat lower piece. It is noted in the report that the term 'Tōdaiji', one of the oldest Buddhist Temples, is engraved on the lower piece (*Shōsōin Jimusho* 1967: 92-93). Although Hayashi Kenzō (1973: 741-42) suggests that the *shichisengakki* might have been a measurement for Chinese musical instruments (*shichishun*), his view has not been accepted by Japanese musicologists.

[23] In Figure 14 one can see only six pegs. From *Shōsōin jimusho* (1967: pl. 41), however, it is obvious that one peg is missing from the seven holes, and that only six pegs have survived in the Imperial Treasury of Japan.

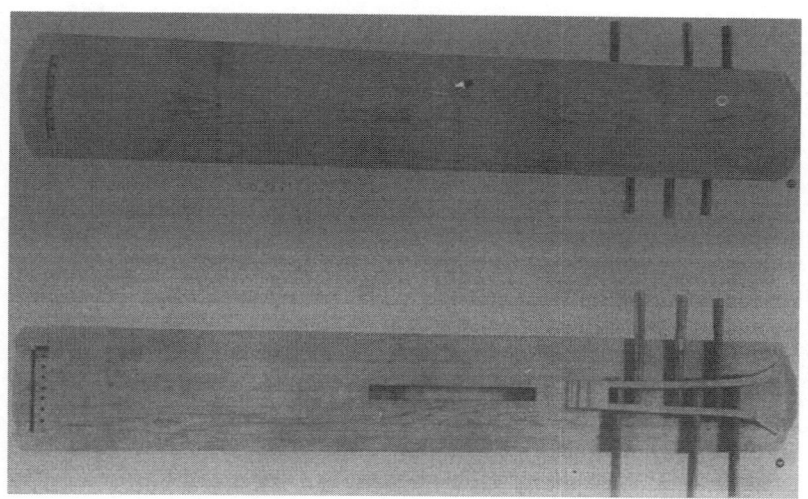

Figure 14: Seven-stringed zither (*Shichisengakki*) in the Shōsōin, Nara, Japan (*Shōsōin jimusho* 1967: pl.41)

Figure 15: Five-stringed lute (*Wu-hsien*) and transverse flute (*Heng-ti*) on a pottery flask from An-yang, Ho-nan Province, China

Kuei-tzu-chi (Kucha), and *An-kuo-chi* (Bukhara) at the Sui court during the K'ai-huang (581-600)[24] and Ta-yeh (605-616)[25] reigns. It must be pointed out here that most instruments of the Koguryŏ orchestra (*Kao-li-chi*) were identical with those of the Hsi-liang orchestra (*Hsi-liang-chi*) (Lee Hye-ku 1957: 195-97). The Hsi-liang state was located in the far northwestern region of China near the upper stream of Huang-ho River. This historical fact affirms the close cultural interrelationship between Koguryŏ and Central Asian states during the Northern Dynasties period.

Chinese literary sources suggest that the date for the importation of Central Asian instruments, including the three new instruments, is around the sixth century (Lee Hye-ku 1957: 206; Song 1973: 465). Their presence in the murals of Tomb No.1 at Ch'ang-ch'uan indicates, however, that the transverse flute, five-stringed lute, and double-reed pipe were already on Korean soil in the fifth century. After the acceptance of Central Asian instruments, Koguryŏ music was enriched in terms of its musical quality and quantity. The new instruments seem to have been an important element in the historical development of Korean music from the fifth century onwards. Without the acceptance of Central Asian instruments, it might have been impossible for the Koguryŏ court not only to send their orchestra to the Sui and T'ang courts in the late sixth and early seventh centuries, but also to send Koguryŏ musicians to the Nara court of Japan during the late Three Kingdoms period (Song 1984b; Song 1985: 2-38).

4 Concluding statements

The study of ancient Korean music history involves a great deal of searching amid Korean and Chinese historical materials, including both literary and archeological remains. Our investigation suggests that one can hardly overstate the importance of the tomb paintings in Tomb No.1 at Ch'ang-ch'uan for the study of the historical development of Korean music.

The ceiling and wall paintings of Tomb No.1 at Ch'ang-ch'uan are evidently a representation of Koguryŏ court music in the fifth century. Seven instruments in the hands of deva musicians are depicted in the ceiling painting of the front room, and three instruments in those of Koguryŏ musicians are painted in the wall painting of the front room. We have been able to suggest identification of ten musical instruments with names and descriptions from Chinese and Korean literary sources. These ten have been divided into two categories, one group from before the fifth century, and the other group of the fifth century. Before the fifth century, Koguryŏ music was represented by such instruments as zithers (*kŏmun'go* or *hyŏn'gum*), the long vertical flute (*changso*), the round-bodied lute (*wanham* or *yüan-hsien*), the long horn (*taegak*), and the suspended drum (*tamgo*). Of these instruments, the *kŏmun'go* and *taegak* seem to have originated in Korea and the other instruments in China and Central Asia.

The Ch'ang-ch'uan Tomb paintings are extraordinary and unique in their representation of new Koguryŏ instruments of the fifth century. The new Koguryŏ instruments in the fifth century were the five-stringed lute (*ohyŏn* or *ohyŏn-pip'a*), the transverse flute (*hoengjŏk* or *hoeng-ch'wi*), the double-reed

---

[24] *Sui-shu*, 15.29b8-10 (*Ch'i-pu-yüeh*).

[25] *Sui-shu*, 15.30b4-5 (*Chiu-pu-chi*), 33b4-6 (*Hsi-liang-chi*), 33a8-9 (*Shu-ch'ih-chi*), 32b5-6 (*Kuei-tzu-chi*), and 33b1-3 (*An-kuo-chi*).

pipe (*p'iri* or *p'iryul*), and the five-stringed zither (*ohyŏn'gŭm* or *ohyŏnakki*). It has been inferred that the five stringed zither was another prototype of the present *kŏmun'go* and that the five stringed zither was introduced by Koguryŏ musicians to Japan during the Three Kingdoms period. The transverse flute, five-stringed lute and double-reed pipe appear to have been introduced from Central Asia via the Silk Road.

The painting of Tomb No.1 at Ch'ang-ch'uan is significant in the historical context of East Asian culture. In contrast to the musical culture of Paekche and Silla Kingdoms, the Koguryŏ Kingdom had established a highly developed music culture by the fifth century. Koguryŏ music was already enriched by new musical instruments of Central Asian origin and had grown into a strong and distinctive music culture in its own right. Thus, during the Three Kingdoms period, the musical river which had flowed from Central Asia to Koguryŏ flowed back to the Chinese courts of the Sui and T'ang dynasties. It also flowed into the waters of the Korea Strait and finally reached Nara, Japan, where some 'bottling' of Korean and Chinese court music took place in the present *gagaku* tradition.

References

A Pictorial Encyclopedia of the Oriental Arts 1969: New York: Crown Publishers Inc.
Chang Sa-hun 1969: *Han'guk akki taegwan*, Seoul: Korean Musicological Society
Chi-an-hsien wen-wu pao-kuan-so 1982: 'Chi'an Ch'ang-ch'uan ihao pi-hua-mu,' *Tung-pei k'ao-ku yü li-shih* No.1, pp.154-73, Peking: Wen-wu ch'u-pan-she
Chu Yŏng-hŏn 1972: *Kōkuri no hekiga kohun*, Tokyo: Gakuseisha
Chung-hua jen-min kung-ho-kuo ch'u-t'u wen-wu chan-lan chan-p'in hsüan-chu 1973: Peking: Wen-wu ch'u-pan-she
Harich-Schneider, Eta 1973: *A History of Japanese Music*, London: Oxford University Press
Hayashi Kenzō 1973: *Higashi ajia gakkikō*, Tokyo: Kawai gakufu
Ikeuchi Hiroshi 1940: *T'ung-kou*, Tokyo: Nichiman bunka kyōkai
Kikkawa Eishi 1965: *Nihon ongaku no rekishi*, Osaka: Sōgensha
Kim Ki-ung 1982: *Han'guk ŭi pyŏkhwa kobun*, Seoul: Tonghwa ch'ulp'an kongsa
Kim Won-yong 1960: 'Koguryŏ kobun pyŏkhwa ŭi kiwŏn e taehan yŏn'gu', *Chindan hakpo* No.21, Seoul: Chindan hakhoe
Kishibe Shigeo 1984: *Tempyō no hibiki*, Tokyo: Ongaku no Tomosha
Koguryŏ munhwa 1975: P'yŏngyang: Sahoe kwahak ch'ulp'ansa
Lee Hye-ku 1957: *Han'guk ŭmak yŏn'gu*, Seoul: Kungmin ŭmak yŏn'guhoe
  1967: *Han'guk ŭmak sōsŏl*, Seoul: Seoul National University Press
  1976: *Han'guk ŭmak nonch'ong*, Seoul: Sumundang
  1985: *Han'guk ŭmak nonjip*, Seoul: Segwang ŭmak ch'ulp'ansa
Lee Ki-baik (trans. Edward W. Wagner) 1984: *A New History of Korea*, Seoul: Ilchogak
Malm, William P. 1959: *Japanese Music and Musical Instruments*, Tokyo: Charles E. Tuttle Co.
Pratt, Keith 1987: *Korean Music: Its History and Its Performance*, London: Faber Music Ltd, and Seoul: Jungeumsa
Shōsōin jimusho (ed.) 1967: *Shōsōin no gakki*, Tokyo: Nihon geizai shinbunsha
Song Bang-song 1973: 'The Korean P'ipa and Its Notation', *Ethnomusicology*, Vol.XVII, No.3, pp.460-93
  1980: *Source Readings in Korean Music*, Seoul: Korean National Commission for UNESCO
  1984a: *Han'guk ŭmak t'ongsa*, Seoul: Ilchogak
  1984b: 'Changch'ŏn ihobun ŭi ŭmaksahakchŏk chŏmgŏm', *Han'guk hakpo*, No.36, pp.2-361, Seoul: Ilchisa
  1985: *Han'guk kodae ŭmaksa yŏn'gu*, Seoul: Ilchisa
  1986: *The Sanjo Tradition of Korean Kŏmun'go Music*, Seoul: Jungeumsa
Tonkō bunbutsu kenkyūsho (ed.) 1980: *Chūgoku sekkutsu: Tonkō bakukōkutsu*, Tokyo: Heibonsha
Tu Yu 1959: *Tung tien*, Taipei: Hsin-hsing-shu-chü
Umehara Sueharu 1966: *Chōsen kobunka sōkan*, Nara: Yōtokusha
Yi Hang-sŏng (ed.) 1962: *Segye misul chŏnjip*, Seoul: Munhwa kyoyuk ch'ulp'ansa
Yi Kyu-bo 1982: *Tongguk isanggukchip*, Seoul: Minjok munhwa ch'ujinhoe

Shakuhachi honkyoku notation: written sources in an oral tradition

RILEY LEE

> This paper is an examination of the relationship between notation and performance in the substantially oral tradition of *shakuhachi honkyoku*. Through a comparison of the notation of the piece *Kokū* with a transcription of a recent performance, four main categories of discrepancies between notation and performance are revealed. It is suggested that the relationships revealed may have implications for historical, document-based studies of primarily oral musical traditions in Europe and Asia.

In recent years a number of studies have been published of early European[1] and Asian[2] notation for traditions which were primarily or partially oral. This paper examines the relationship between notation and performance in a primarily oral tradition that continues to the present, namely that of the *shakuhachi honkyoku* tradition. In this tradition, the relationship between score and sound has been determined largely within the context of oral transmission, which remains dominant within the *honkyoku* tradition despite the existence of notation for at least a century. The ways in which orality influences the relationship between notation and performance will be illustrated by examining in detail the *honkyoku* Kokū, a piece considered representative of the tradition. Certain observations made in the course of this study have clear implications for the study of early records of primarily orally transmitted music.

The *shakuhachi*, Japan's end-blown bamboo flute, is believed to have been first introduced into Japan from China in the eighth century as part of the ensemble of the Chinese court music, *gagaku*. By the eleventh century it was no longer used in *gagaku* performances. After several centuries of obscurity, it resurfaced during the Edo period (1600-1868) in the hands of a group of mendicant Zen Buddhist monks. Calling themselves *komusō* (priests of nothingness), these monks developed a repertoire of pieces for the *shakuhachi* which they performed as part of their religious practices. The pieces composed and performed by the *komusō* are appropriately called *honkyoku* (main or original pieces), today the most venerated music of the *shakuhachi*. The *komusō* considered the *shakuhachi* a religious tool (*hōki*), not a musical instrument (*gakki*). They performed the *honkyoku* as *suizen*, 'blowing Zen'.

---

[1] See for example Treitler 1974.
[2] An example of a study of early Asian notations and their place in oral tradition is Marett 1983. Studies of Japanese music traditions with an emphasis on the elements of orality and literacy, as well as essays concerning those elements in other music cultures can be found in Tokumaru and Yamaguti 1986.

Historically, the present-day *honkyoku* tradition can be traced back at least to the fifteenth century, when the Zen priest Ikkyū (1394-1481) expressed in a collection of *waka* and other poetry his appreciation of the *shakuhachi* as a meditative instrument (Kamisangō 1974: 11). Though the earliest documented notation for a related instrument, the *hitoyogiri*, is dated 1608, *shakuhachi* notation was not widely used until the late 1800s (Lee 1986: 87-88). Even after the adoption of various notation systems became widespread, the *shakuhachi honkyoku* tradition remained fundamentally an oral one. *Shakuhachi* lessons almost always consist of the student playing together with the teacher. A student is never asked to sight-read a new *honkyoku* piece; in fact he is told that this is impossible since *honkyoku* notation is a mere outline of the music at best and frequently is totally unrelated to the actual sounds produced. The transmission of the piece is accomplished orally (or aurally) from teacher to student.

1 *Shakuhachi honkyoku* and theories of orality

In view of the importance of orality in its transmission, any examination of *shakuhachi honkyoku* might benefit from being undertaken in the light of recently developed theories of orality. Theories of orality were originally delineated in the field of epic poetry, notably by Parry (1971) and Lord (1964).

Parry's work began as an analysis of written texts, namely the Homeric epics. In his studies of Homer, Parry advanced the hypothesis that certain features of this written text suggested that it records an oral poetic tradition. He believed that in order to understand how the texts work, it was necessary to identify features of oral poetry and to explicate their functions in the processes of oral composition.

Parry's work was subsequently developed by his student, Albert B. Lord. In *A Singer of Tales* (1964), Lord tested Parry's theories in a contemporary oral context. Lord focused on the sung poetry of performers of a living oral epic tradition of Yugoslavia, that of the *guzla* players. Using Parry's collection of South Slavic texts, both recordings and transcriptions, as well as material gathered from his own extensive fieldwork, Lord set forth a theoretical description of the processes whereby oral narrative poetry was composed. In doing so, he demonstrated that the features postulated by Parry as characteristic of oral composition were indeed present in a living oral tradition.

Lord defined the oral epic song as 'narrative poetry composed in a manner evolved over many generations by singers of tales who did not know how to write; it consists of the building of metrical lines and half lines by means of formulas and formulaic expressions and of the building of songs by the use of themes'. He retained Parry's original definition of formula: 'a group of words which is regularly employed under the same metrical conditions to express a given essential idea'. Formulaic expression was defined as 'a line or half line constructed on the pattern of the formulas'. Finally, theme was defined as 'the repeated incidents and descriptive passages in the song' (1964: 4).

The work of Parry, Lord and others on oral epic has been applied in examining other musical traditions, for example by Treitler (1974, 1975) and Cutter (1976) in their work in Gregorian Chant, and Clunies Ross (1978, 1983) and Clunies Ross and Wild (1984) with respect to Australian Aboriginal music. Treitler, like Parry, bases his study of Gregorian Chant on early written sources.

With early plainchant, as with any oral musical tradition which existed before this century, the written transmission is the principal record of the oral performance as it was at that time. Since the primary source of evidence for the development of pre-twentieth century oral traditions are written records, it is useful to reflect on the roles that notation can play in orally transmitted musical traditions. Marett (1983) has pointed out that in the course of its history, the *tōgaku* tradition of Japanese court music has seen a number of changes in the relationship between notation and performance; in addition, Marett has pointed to difficulties inherent in reconstructing performance practice from notations in traditions that are primarily or substantially oral. This paper examines the relationship between a relatively recently developed notational system and a living oral performance tradition. Contemporary *shakuhachi* practice indicates that in a primarily oral musical tradition, the relationship between notation and performance can be fairly tenuous.

The *shakuhachi honkyoku* tradition, unlike Gregorian Chant, has a relatively short and continuous history. In all likelihood, the main features of the *shakuhachi honkyoku* tradition originated between the mid-sixteenth and mid-seventeenth centuries. During this period, the Fuke sect, a *shakuhachi*-playing religious organization nominally associated with the Rinzai sect of Zen Buddhism, was given exclusive rights to perform and transmit the *honkyoku* tradition as part of their religious practices. After the Meiji Restoration (1868), the Fuke sect was, for various political reasons, banned. Numerous schools or guilds called *ryū* were immediately founded by the leading players of the newly secularized *shakuhachi* (see Sanford 1977). These schools can be classified into two main types: first, those which have emphasized modern, secular music, such as the Tozan school, which has no traditional *honkyoku* in its repertoire, and second, those which derive much of their identity from their *honkyoku* tradition, such as the Kinko and Chikuho schools. It is primarily this second group of *shakuhachi* schools or sects which have transmitted the *honkyoku* tradition to the present time.

Shakuhachi notation has been in evidence for over three centuries (*Hōgaku Hyakka Jiten*, hereafter HHJ, 1984: 888). It is frequently stated in the literature that the typical *honkyoku* notation is skeletal in its representation of the final sound product, an outline or guideline of the actual music performed (Weisgarber 1968: 332; Stanfield 1977: 83; Lee 1986: 127). *Honkyoku* notation is more complex, however, in its relationship with the final performance than the terms 'skeletal' and 'outline' imply. To illustrate this an explanation of the notation is necessary.

The notation system which will be studied in this paper is that of the Chikuho school of *shakuhachi*. This notation system was devised in 1916 by the founder of the school, Sakai Chikuho I, who combined elements of earlier notation systems with innovations of his own, in particular the addition of a relatively precise system of notating duration values of notes and rests. *Honkyoku* scores written in such earlier notation systems date from the mid-1800s. These historical notations, however, are outside the scope of this paper. Although modern *shakuhachi* notation systems differ slightly with each *ryū*, all share the same basic features. They are all tablature notations, using approximately twenty *katakana* (one of two Japanese syllabaries) to symbolize fingering positions of the instrument.

Data presented in this paper is based largely upon the *honkyoku* notation and the performance practices of the Chikuho school of *shakuhachi*. Nevertheless, because the Chikuho school shares a common history with all *shakuhachi* schools until this century and has the largest repertoire of classical *honkyoku* of any single *shakuhachi* school today, I believe that conclusions derived from this data are generally applicable to most of the modern *shakuhachi honkyoku* tradition.

2 The tablature notation of the Chikuho Ryū

Tablature notation called *fu ho u* notation is used in the teaching and performing of all pieces in the Chikuho repertoire, including *honkyoku*. *Fu, ho,* and *u* refer to the first three of twenty *katakana* used to symbolize fingering positions of the instrument (see figure 1). Many symbols are shared with the earliest notation system for the *shakuhachi* family of instruments, a *hitoyogiri* notation system first documented in 1608 in the *Tanteki Hiden Fu* (HHJ: 888). The *hitoyogiri* system had no rhythmic notation other than circles indicating pauses between melodic lines. Notation systems used by the *komusō* (see pp.18), known collectively as Meian notation, incorporated many of the same fingering symbols of the *hitoyogiri* system, adding symbols for upper and lower octaves, simple rhythmic indications, and symbols for various performing techniques and grace notes (HHJ: 888). Katsuura Seizan, a *komusō* of the 19th century, taught the Meian Shimpō Ryū *honkyoku* to Sakai Chikuho I, founder of the Chikuho school, using a version of the old Meian notation systems.[3]

Chikuho Ryū notation, devised by Chikuho I in 1916, incorporates much of the old *hitoyogiri* notation, as well as most of the additional indicators of the old Meian systems, such as those used by Katsuura Seizan. According to the *Hōgaku Hyakka Jiten*, it is the principal existing example of the old *fu ho u* system of shakuhachi notation (HHJ: 888). Chikuho I also used some of the *kana* of notation systems of the newer Kinko and Tozan schools, *ro, tsu, re, chi, ha,* and *ri* or *hi*,[4] to symbolize different fingering positions, as a way of emphasizing one of strengths of his new *ryū*: that it had a repertoire of both the classical *honkyoku* of the Kyoto Meian tradition and the newer repertoire of *gaikyoku* (secular ensemble pieces) such as performed by Kinko and Tozan players, as well as modern compositions by Chikuho himself and others.

According to Chikuho II, the *fu ho u* system was devised when the *shakuhachi* was used almost entirely as a solo instrument to play *honkyoku*. The *katakana* representing main fingerings were chosen because their soft sound – *fu ho u e ya i*, resembled the sound of the blown bamboo. When the newer system was developed however, ensemble pieces were being performed on the *shakuhachi* more frequently, usually with the *koto* and/or the *shamisen*. Percussive attacks are characteristic of both of these stringed instruments. Consequently *katakana* were chosen because of their percussive sounds – *ro tsu re chi ri*. Typically, Chikuho II thought that the *fu ho u* system was superior to the *ro tsu re* system of the rival *ryū*, being older and more closely associated with the venerated *honkyoku*.

---

[3] Shōzan's system is explained in detail in Tomimori Kyozan 1979.

[4] A different set of *katakana* symbols is used by the two larger *shakuhachi* schools, Tozan Ryū and Kinko Ryū. Their systems are based on the *ro tsu re* system devised in the latter 1800s by Araki Kodō II, a Kinko Ryū player. A third major *shakuhachi ryū*, Meian Taizan Ryū also uses a variation of the *ro tsu re* system. As Kinko, Tozan, and Meian Taizan Ryū encompass the majority of *shakuhachi* players in Japan today, almost all present-day *shakuhachi* players are more familiar with the *ro tsu re* than the older *fu ho u* notation system.

Tablature notation, fingering, and pitch

Figure 1 shows the fingering chart for the Chikuho Ryū notation system. Because notational symbols are tablature, the pitch corresponding to each sign depends upon the length of the *shakuhachi* being played and the fingerhole placement. In this paper, the pitches produced by the standard 1.8 *shaku* length flute (approx. 55 cm) will be used in transnotating the Chikuho scores. Thus, as indicated on the fingering chart, the symbol *fu* ⁊ produces the pitch D above middle C, the symbol *ho* ぁ produces the pitch F, etc. The unmodified open-hole notes are ⁊ , ぁ , り , エ , や , イ , and ト . Theoretically, each of these fingering positions may be modified with the symbol ✗ , indicating a technique called *meri*, whereby a pitch is flattened by changing the angle of the blowing edge. In practice, only two of the open-hole note symbols are written with the ✗ symbol, ぁ and や . Thus *ya-meri* ゆ is realised as C flat and *ho-meri* ぁ indicates F flat on the standard 1.8 *shaku* length flute.

In some cases, the *meri* technique is implicit in the meaning of a fingering symbol. Most, but not all, fingering positions of this type require a lower hole to be partially covered and are consequently called 'half-hole' positions. There are two Japanese terms used by *shakuhachi* players to denote the half-hole positions, each emphasizing a different aspect of the same thing. *Hankai* means half-opened and *kazashi*, derived from the verb *kazasu* implies a half-closed position (Simura 1988: 3-4). Thus the symbol *tsu* ツ indicates that the bottom hole is to be partially covered (or partially opened) and the *meri* technique applied. The fingerings of this type are ツ , レ , チ , ハ and ヒ

Some fingering symbols indicate the *meri* technique but without a half-hole finger position. These symbols are ロ , ル , コ , and リ . As with the unmodified open-hole notes, all finger positions in which the *meri* technique is implicit in the symbols may theoretically be further modified by placing the ✗ (*meri*) symbol beside or inside the primary tablature sign, thereby indicating a kind of double flat. Only two of the *meri* symbols are commonly modified with ✗ however: the half-hole fingering *tsu* ツ✗ indicates E double flat and the non-half-hole *ro meri* ロ indicates D double flat. *Tsu meri* does not appear on the fingering chart.

Though there are open-hole, or non-half-hole fingering positions which require a *meri* technique (e.g. *ho meri*, ぁ), there are no half-hole fingering positions which do not incorporate the *meri* technique. This may be due to the primacy of the *meri* technique in *shakuhachi* performance. The *meri* symbol may be further modified by the symbol 大 (*dai*, great or big). Thus 大 (*dai meri*) when written beside the symbol ぁ becomes 大ぁ (*ho dai meri*), which is played using the *meri* technique only, in contrast to ツ , which is played with both the *meri* technique and the 'half-hole' technique. The former may be considered an F-double flat and the latter an E-flat. In practice 大 occurs usually with the symbols ぁ and ロ . The symbol ツ is frequently modified with a ✗ (*meri*) sign, as stated above, which creates a *dai meri* (E-double flat). The symbol 大 is not necessary in this case as one level of *meri* is already implied in the symbol itself.

Three symbols in the fingering chart indicate the technique *kari*, which is opposite to *meri*. Pitch is raised instead of lowered by changing the angle of the blowing edge in the opposite direction from that of *meri*. Though the *kari* technique is symbolized by the sign カ (*ka*), the technique is implicit in the meaning of the symbols ピ (*pi*) # (*i*) and ヒ (*shi no hi*). One fingering

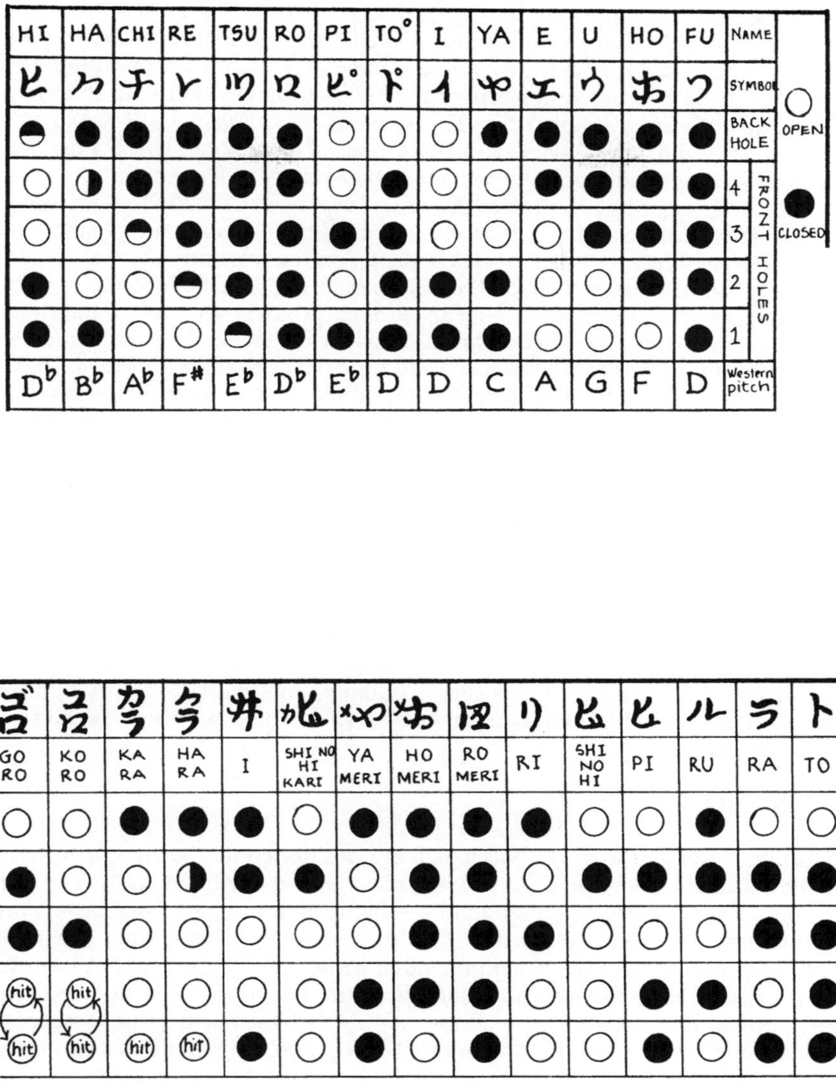

Figure 1: Chikuho Ryū fingering chart (*Chikuho Ryū Shakuhachi no Tebiki*: 28-29)

symbol is modified with the ﬂ symbol, that is ⁿ比 (*shi no hi kari*) which is a kind of double-sharp, and is rarely used. Of the remaining symbols in the fingering chart, ヒ (*pi*) indicates an open-hole and slightly *kari* position and is a rarely used alternative fingering for the fingering position with the same name but different symbol ヒ° . The symbols ヲ (*ha ra*), ヲ (*ka ra*), ヲ (*ko ro*), and ヲ゛ (*go ro*) indicate special combinations of fingering positions and onomatopoeically represent the sounds produced.

Several fingering positions as shown in the official Chikuho Ryū fingering chart differ from those that are taught and used by teachers and members of the sect today. The symbol ヒ (*hi*) is shown on the fingering chart as a half-hole note. In practice, the back hole is opened entirely, that is, the symbol ヒ is presently perceived to mean a *meri* position without a half-hole technique. A possible reason for this discrepancy is the change in construction of *shakuhachi* instruments which occurred over the last several decades. Older instruments produced an incorrect sharp pitch if the back hole was not partially closed when playing ヒ . Most instruments made during the last two decades have been corrected so that ヒ can be played without the half-hole technique. The three other discrepancies between fingering chart and present-day performance practices are ♯ (*i*), ﾊ (*ha*) and ト° (*to*). The modern fingering of ♯ is with the second hole from the bottom closed; ﾊ is usually performed with the first hole from the bottom open and the fourth hole partially opened from the bottom rather than from the side as is implied in the fingering chart. Finally, ト° is usually played with the back hole partially closed. The special fingering combination ヲ (*ha ra*), like ﾊ , is now played with the fourth hole partially opened from the bottom. These discrepancies are indicative of a music tradition continuing to develop more quickly and with more emphasis on oral devices than on written or literary transmission.

Mensural notation

Duration is notated with symbols which are positioned on the right-hand side of the tablature notation. Figure 2 is a chart of the rhythmic symbols of the Chikuho Ryū. Generally, horizontal lines indicate durations of one beat; thus a symbol with one horizontal line つ- is held for one beat while a symbol with three horizontal lines is held for three beats つ≡ . Fingering positions to be held four beats have two horizontal lines on their right-hand side and two long vertical lines below the symbols, thus つ= . Notes with values in excess of four beats are rare and are notated using a combination of the above duration-symbols. Vertical lines to the right of the fingering symbols have similar functions to flags in western staff notation. A single vertical line つ' indicates a duration of half a beat; two vertical lines つ'' indicate a duration of quarter of a beat, etc. Rests of one or more beats in value are notated by one or more ο symbols. Thus a note of one beat followed by a two beat rest would be つ- ο ο . Symbols for rests are modifications of equivalent symbols in western staff notation. Other durations are indicated by various symbols as shown in figure 2.

Other techniques

Besides the symbols for standard finger positions and durations, instructions regarding various performance techniques and other information regarding a particular piece are written on the score. The information is represented by

Figure 2: Chikuho Ryū notation symbols for duration (*Chikuho Ryū Shakuhachi no Tebiki*: 29)

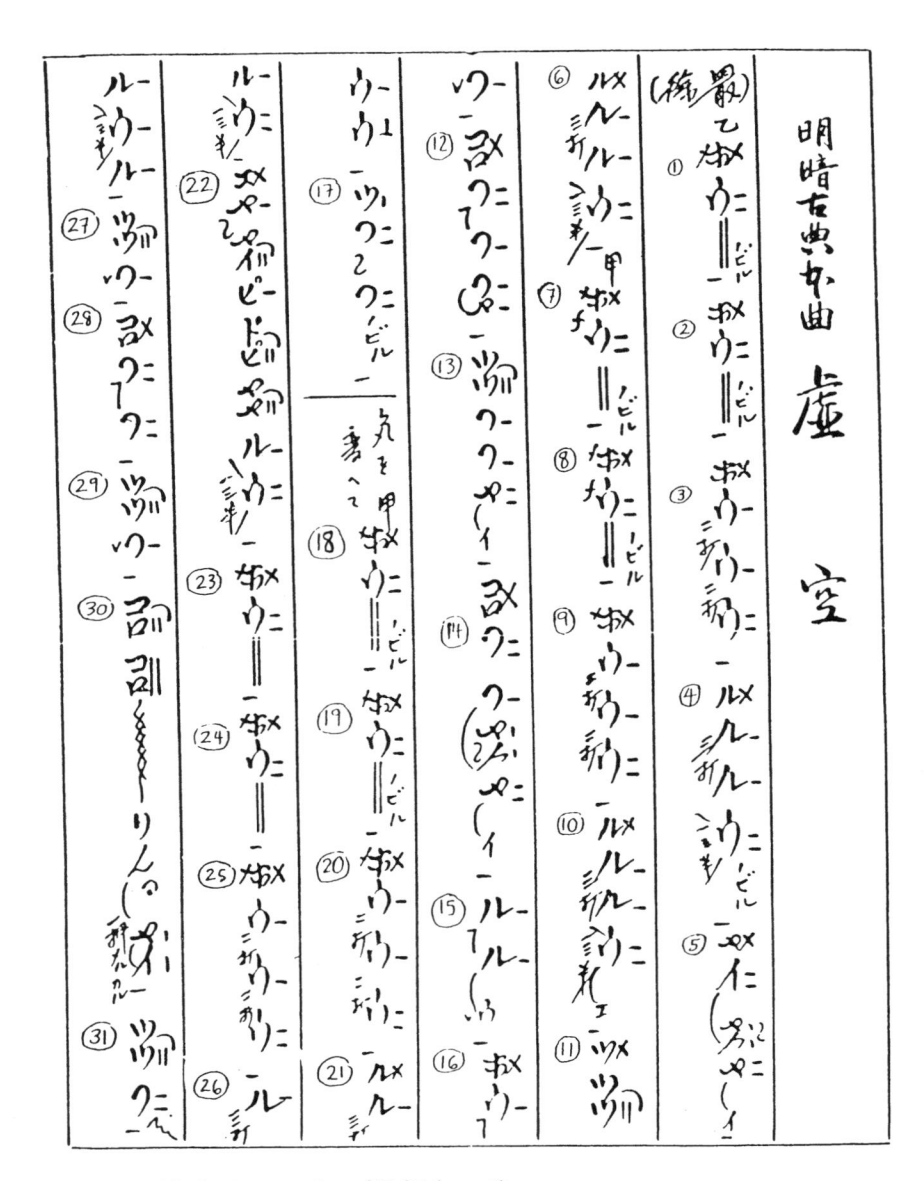

Figure 3: Chikuho Ryū notation of Kokū (page 1)

kanji (Chinese characters), *kana* (Japanese syllabaries), symbols borrowed from western staff notation, graphic symbols, or a combination of these. Frequently in Chikuho notation, the same technique is represented by *kanji* in one instance, *kana* in another, and graphically in a third (Lee 1986: 94). There appears to be no discernable significance in the usage of any particular set of symbols in a given situation. This random use of symbols perhaps represents a common trait of oral tradition, namely a cavalier attitude to written notation.

3 Transnotation of the piece, Kokū

As demonstrated above, the notation of the *shakuhachi honkyoku* is not ambiguous; all of the symbols used in the notation have specific definitions, either as described in the *Chikuhō Ryū Shakuhachi no Tebiki* (Chikuho School beginners manual), or as defined by one's teacher, usually during the early stages of learning the instrument. With only the above information, a literal transnotation of a Chikuho *honkyoku* score is possible. The piece Kokū will be used as our example. Kokū is one of the *San Kyorei*, the three most venerated *honkyoku* in the repertoire (Sanford 1977: 430-31) and deemed representative of the *honkyoku* tradition. Figure 3 depicts page one of the Chikuho score of the piece Kokū. Let us assume that the score of Kokū is a historical document being interpreted in the light of the tables shown in figures 1 and 2 and that we know nothing about the living performance tradition. A literal transnotation of the first twenty phrases of Kokū into staff notation using the principles outlined in the previous section is shown in example 1. This transnotation of Kokū is perhaps equivalent to an interpretation of historical notations in the light of known principles but without reference to a living performance tradition.

4 Differences between transnotation and performance of Kokū

Unlike traditions for which we have historical notations but no access to a performance tradition even remotely contemporary with the notations, conclusions drawn on the basis of the transnotation of the *shakuhachi* notations can be tested against the performance tradition. It will be instructive to see how much the score changes when the living performance tradition is taken into account. Example 2 is a transcription of phrases 1-18 of the piece, Kokū, based upon a performance of Sakai Chikuho II, who was *iemoto* or head master of Chikuho Ryū at the time of the recording. A brief comparison of the first few phrases of the piece with the transnotation immediately reveals discrepancies between the two.

The discrepancies between the notation and performance can be categorized in a number of ways. One possible method of categorization might rely upon differences between the notated and the performed for the three groups of symbols used in the notation, that is pitch, duration, and other technical instructions. I believe a more revealing indication of the differences is permitted by the following four categories:

1. Instances where symbols are consistently given new meanings which are, however, different from their standard meanings. The consistency of these new meanings may apply in a single piece only, or throughout the *honkyoku* repertoire of the *ryū*.
2. Instances where symbols are totally ignored.

Example 1: Transnotation of Chikuho Ryū Kokū

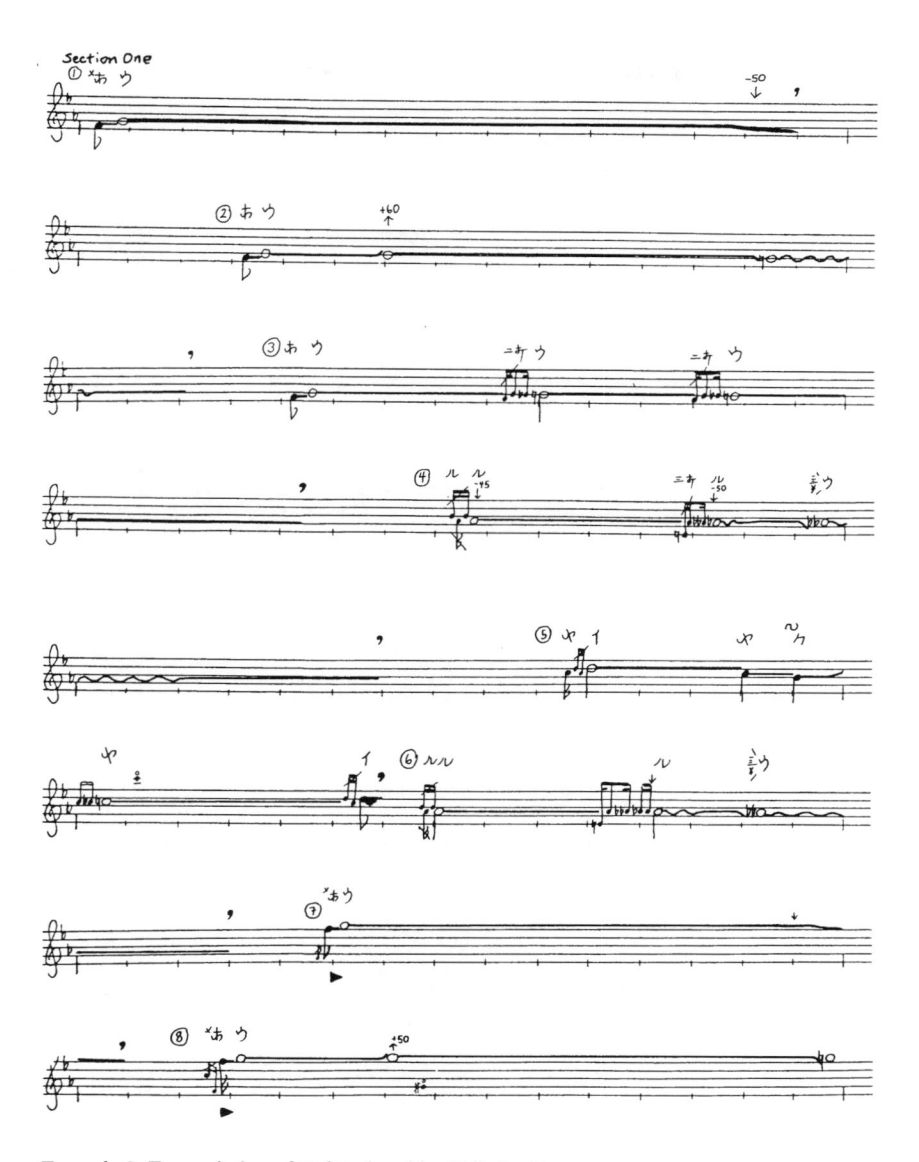

Example 2: Transcription of Kokū played by Chikuho II

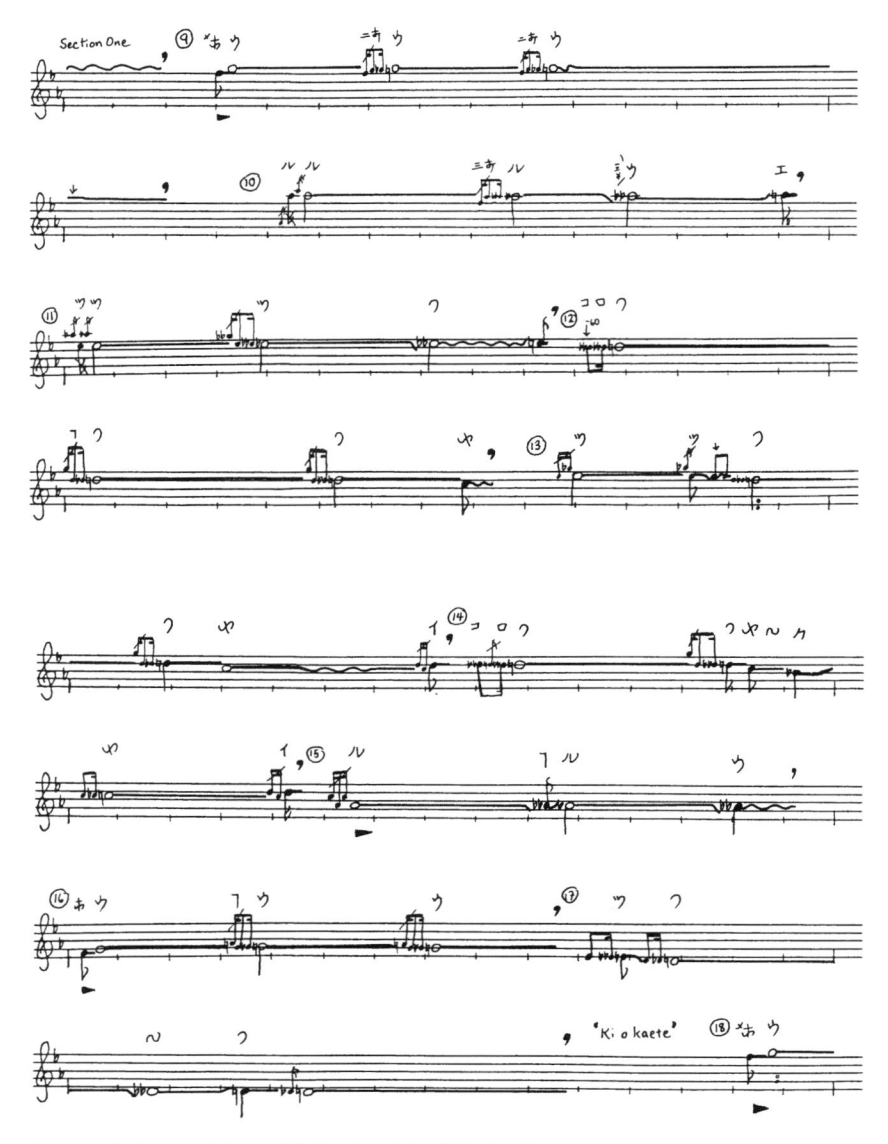

Example 2: Transcription of Kokū played by Chikuho II

Appendix 1: Legend for transcription of Musical Example 2.

1. Vertical dashes on the bottom line of the staff indicate in seconds the elapse of real time in the performance: 1/4 inch = one second (e.g. ⊢—⊢—⊣ = two seconds); one staff line = fifteen seconds.
2. ο = > four seconds. ρ = two to four seconds. ρ = one to two seconds. ϱ = one to one-half seconds. ϱ = < one-half second.
3. Pitches notated in the Chikuho score have downward stems ϱ . Pitches not notated in the Chikuho score have upward stems ♪ .
4. Standards of pitch reference used in pitch measurements are based upon the average pitch of g' being 0 cents on the measuring device, and reflect the adjustment in calibration from A = 440.
5. ↑ or ↓ indicate deviations of fifty cents or more from pitches based on the standard pitch reference (see above). The numerical value is noted near the arrow.
6. ʔ indicate breaths actually taken by the performer. Note that they do not always correspond to the ends of phrases as notated.
7. The beginnings of phrases as notated in original score are indicated with circled numbers above the staff.
8. Solid lines following the notes indicate duration and calibrate the time-line (see no.1, above). They also indicate vibrato and glissando produced by *meri-kari* techniques. These lines are qualitative rather than quantitative symbols, i.e. they do not express dynamic intensity or frequency of vibrato to scale.
9. Non-notated harmonics and multiphonics considered significant are indicated by ˚• . (See example 2, phrase 5.) Note that though frequently unintentional, these harmonics are not necessarily considered mistakes, but rather sounds which are integral to the entire performance and are part of the specific performance.
10. Fingering symbols from the original notation appear above the appropriate note.
11. Unintentional breaks in the sound are indicated with circled numbers above the staff.
12. Short pitches produced by the rapid opening and/or closing of finger holes are indicated with slashes through the beams. Pitches produced with the *meri-kari* or note-bending technique have no slashes.

3. Instances where a pitch, duration or playing technique is performed, but is not notated in the score.
4. Instances where meanings for symbols are inconsistent. For example, a symbol may have the standard meaning in one phrase, but be given one or more different meanings in other phrases.

Illustrations of all of the above categories can be found throughout the *honkyoku* repertoire of Chikuho Ryū. Where possible, however, examples of the categories will be taken from the piece, Kokū. These examples are presented below.

Category 1: symbols are given new meanings

An example where signs are given new meanings may be found in phrase 3 (see examples 1 and 2). The notation calls for the player to articulate the second and third notes of the phrase by hitting the second hole (which if executed would produce a grace note F – see example 1). Instead, Chikuho consistently produces, at least in this phrase, the pitches shown in example 2.

One of the most common examples in this category occurs in the piece, Honte Chōshi, the first *honkyoku* learned by all students in Chikuho Ryū. Whenever the symbol *u* ウ – corresponding to the pitch G and produced with a simple open-holed technique – follows the symbol *ru* ル – producing the pitch A-flat, the pitch G is produced not with the *u* fingering position, but with the *meri* or flattening technique combined with the *ru* fingering position – a kind of A-double flat. This rule is fairly consistent throughout the Chikuho *honkyoku* repertoire.

Category 2: symbols are ignored

Instances where signs are ignored are illustrated in phrases 1, 7, 8, and 9 (see examples 1 and 2). The notation calls for the fingering position *ho* (corresponding to the pitch F) to be flattened (the technique *meri*, symbolized by the mark ✗), producing the pitch E natural. However, as is shown in example 2, Chikuho consistently produces the pitch F instead of the pitch E natural, ignoring the *meri* or flattening symbol.

Category 3: pitch, duration or playing technique is not notated

Examples of the performance of elements not notated in the score can be found in phrases 2 and 8 (see examples 1 and 2), and elsewhere in the piece. The fingering position *u*, producing the pitch G, is notated and performed. Wherever this phrase occurs twice in a row, however, Chikuho consistently raises the pitch midway through the second occurrence. He does this by using the *kari* technique (the reverse of the *meri* or flattening technique). Because he made a point of my doing the same when teaching me this piece, it is reasonable to assume that this non-notated addition to the piece is a deliberate one.

Category 4: inconsistent interpretation of symbols

The most obvious examples of symbols with inconsistent meanings, are all of the duration symbols. Though these symbols are ascribed standard meanings as precise as their counterparts in western staff notation, these standard meanings are not applied in *honkyoku* performance. At best, they are interpreted as only vaguely indicating the duration of a given note. A note in a *honkyoku* score with the symbol corresponding to two beats in the standard chart will, in general, be held longer than a note with the standard symbol for one-half beat. How much longer depends upon the context, the performer, and even the performer's physical and mental condition during a given performance. In the first section of Chikuho's performance of Kokū, notes given the standard value of four beats vary in duration from seven (phrase 32, not shown in examples) to almost fourteen seconds (phrase 2). In the same section, notes given the standard value of one beat vary in duration from one-half second (phrase 14) to almost four seconds (phrase 3) (see examples 1 and 2).

Besides those of duration, examples of other symbols with inconsistent meanings can be found in phrases 12, 15, and 16. The standard realization of the symbol ㄱ is the *furi* (振 ; to shake or sway) technique, a rapid *meri-kari* or bending of the pitch. In phrase 15, Chikuho performs the standard realization of the *furi* symbol. In phrases 12 and 16 however, he performs a different technique (normally notated 之) which is a *furi* (bending the pitch) preceded by a standard re-articulation, in this case a rapid opening and closing of the third hole producing the grace note above the main note. I was not taught a name for this common embellishment.

Another dimension of the inconsistency of interpretation occurs in the teaching method employed in transmitting *honkyoku*, namely where the teacher constantly attributes different meanings to the symbol during different lessons, with different students and/or during different performances, usually with no explanations offered. This final category would not be evident in a transcription of a single performance. A prime example of this category is described by Yokoyama Katsuya, one of the foremost performers of *honkyoku* (Yokoyama 1985). Yokoyama describes being taught the piece San An (Safe Delivery) by his teacher, Watazumi Dōso. Part of the reason it took Yokoyama three years to learn the piece was because of the many changes Watazumi made in playing the piece. He records that by the end of the three years the piece was considerably altered.

Yokoyama states that he is not certain why he spent such a long time on San An with his teacher. He speculates that a possible reason was his own preconceptions. He explains that he had first heard a recording of his teacher, Watazumi, perform the piece a number of years before he actually began studying it. This particular recording was one of his favourites and he consequently listened to it regularly. When Watazumi finally began teaching San An to Yokoyama, the piece had changed considerably from the recording that was by then firmly in Yokoyama's mind. Yokoyama was never satisfied with his own progress in playing the piece. In fact, the more time Yokoyama spent on San An, the less it resembled his cherished version as preserved in the original recording (1985: 116-20). This facinating element of transmission in the *honkyoku* tradition is related to the concepts of creativity, change, and status.

While many more examples illustrating discrepancies between notation and performance can be found in the *shakuhachi honkyoku* tradition, those listed above represent some of the main categories. It is hoped that the point has been made that a transnotation of an original score of *honkyoku* can only be a beginning. Although the *honkyoku* tradition has utilized notation for as long as three centuries, it remains to a large extent an oral tradition. What appear to be gross inconsistencies on paper, frequently become more acceptable in the context of the lesson.

The arguments presented in this paper are not intended to invalidate work already done on the written records of primarily or partly oral traditions in Europe and Asia. Rather the paper follows the tradition of Parry and Lord in exploring an aspect of contemporary oral culture – in this case the relationship between score and performance in present-day *shakuhachi* practice – in order to reveal aspects of oral culture which may help us in interpreting historical documents. Further study of the historical notation of the *shakuhachi* remains a necessary task. At this stage it is not clear what such studies will show. Nevertheless, it is clear that the relationship between performance and score in living *honkyoku* tradition as performed today reflects important aspects of the tradition which must be borne in mind in researching the early sources.

References

Clunies Ross, Margaret 1978: 'The structure of Arnhem Land song-poetry', *Oceania* 49(2): 128-45
　1983: 'Modes of formal performance in societies without writing: the case of Aboriginal Australia', *Australian Aboriginal Studies* 1: 16-26
Clunies Ross, Margaret & S. Wild 1984: 'Formal performance: the relation of music, text and dance in Arnhem Land clan songs', *Ethnomusicology* 28: 209-29
Darbellay, Etienne 1986: 'Traditions and notations in baroque music', *The Oral and Literate in Music*, ed. Tokumaru and Yamaguti: 57-68, Tokyo: Academia Music Ltd
Cutter, Paul F. 1976: 'Oral transmission of the Old-Roman responsories?' *The Music Quarterly*, 62 (2): 182-94
Hōgaku Hyakka Jiten 1984: Encyclopedia of Traditional Japanese Music, ed. Kikkawa Eishi, Tokyo: Ongaku No Tomo Sha
Kamisangō Yūkō 1974: 'Shakuhachi gaku ryakushi: suizen no rikai no tame ni', in descriptive notes from 33 1/3 LP record set KX 7001-3: 9-22, Tokyo: Nippon Columbia
Lee, Riley 1986: *Blowing Zen: Aspects of Performance Practices of the Chikuho Ryū Honkyoku*, Unpublished M.A. Thesis (University of Hawaii)
Lord, Albert B. 1964: *The Singer of Tales*, Cambridge, Mass.: Harvard University Press
Ohmiya, Makoto 1986: 'The lost performance tradition: the notated and the unnotated in European classic music', *The Oral and Literate in Music*, ed. Tokumaru & Yamaguti: 380-92, Tokyo: Academia Music Ltd
Marett, Allan 1977: 'Tunes notated in flute-tablature from a Japanese source of the tenth century', *Musica Asiatica*, 1: 1-59
　1981: '"Banshiki sangun" and "Shōenraku": metrical structure and notation of two Tang-music melodies for flute', *Music and Tradition: Essays on Heian and other music presented to Laurence Picken*, ed. Widdess & Wolpert: 41-68, Cambridge: Cambridge University Press
　1983: 'The role of transmission in the development of the Tōgaku tradition of Japanese Court Music', unpublished manuscript
Parry, Milman 1971: *The Making of Homeric Verse*, edited by Adam Parry, Oxford University Press
Simura Satosi 1988: 'Selections of potential playing techniques on the *shakuhachi*: changes of stylistic needs through periods', unpublished manuscript
Sanford, James 1977: 'Shakuhachi – Zen and Fuke Shu Komuso', *Monumenta Nipponica*, (Fall) 4: 429
Stanfield, Norman Allen 1977: *The Kinko-Ryu and its San Koten Honkyoku*, unpublished M.A. thesis (University of British Columbia)
Tokumaru, Y. & O. Yamaguti (ed). 1986: *The Oral and Literate in Music*, Tokyo: Academia Music Ltd
Tomimori Kyozan 1979: *Meian Shakuhachi Kaisetsu* (An Exposition on the Meian Shakuhachi), Tokyo: Meian Kyozan Bō Dōyūkai
Treitler, Leo 1974: 'Homer and Gregory: the transmission of epic poetry and plainchant', *The Music Quarterly* 60: 333-73
　1975: '"Centonate" Chant: *Übles Flickwerk* or *E pluribus unus?*', *Journal of the American Musicological Society*, 28 (1): 1-23

1986: 'Orality and literacy in the music of the European Middle Ages', *The Oral and Literate in Music*, ed. Tokumaru & Yamaguti: 38-56, Tokyo: Academica Music Ltd.

Weisgarber, Elliot 1968: 'The Honkyoku of the Kinko-ryu: some principles of its organization', *Ethnomusicology* 12 (3): 313-44

Yokoyama Katsuya 1985: *Shakuhachi gaku no miryoku* (The Fascination of the Shakuhachi), Tokyo: Kodansha

The world of a single sound: basic structure of the music of the Japanese flute shakuhachi

ANDREAS GUTZWILLER and GERALD BENNETT

This paper proposes an investigation of the acoustical characteristics of the sound of the *shakuhachi*. We have worked on the hypothesis that a study of this kind would not only provide an exact description of physical phenomena but would also offer a description of the music itself. Our point of departure was the observation that traditional *shakuhachi* music has shown virtually no interest in architectonic formal relationships; on the other hand, highly structured smaller units – what we have called tone cells – clearly have great musical significance. We set ourselves the task of studying these tone cells as the primary vehicle by which musical meaning is conveyed.

In this 'world of a single sound' we found structures whose musical meaning mirrors their physical evolution. As the tone cell stands somewhere between the tone as a physical event and the independent musical phrase, so is our description of its qualities both the representation of physical characteristics and the analysis of music. The Japanese musicologist Tsuge Gen'ichi has said that in Japanese music 'there is a deep-seated attitude towards realization of a self-sufficient musical world within the scope of even a *single* sound' (Tsuge 1981: 110). We hope with this study to contribute to an understanding of this important characteristic of Japanese music.

1 Introduction

In Western musicology there is virtually no connection between musical analysis and the acoustical analysis of instrumental sounds. Musical analysis is concerned with the way music is constructed – how it is put together; it is not concerned with individual tones. On the other hand, the physical analysis of single instrumental tones disregards the music these tones make; it looks only at the acoustical premises for music, at those things which might be called 'pre-musical'.

The reasons for this strict dichotomy are not to be found in the general nature of music itself, but rather in occidental thought which, to put it simply, sees music only where several tones enter into relationship together, either simultaneously or successively. In such a context, interest in a single note will necessarily be restricted to its acoustical characteristics.

In Japanese music we find quite a different situation. 'There is a deep-seated attitude towards realization of a self-sufficient musical world within the scope of even a *single* sound. This is the world in which sounds are created and experienced as organic and free from the instinct to build and form complicated structure' (Tsuge 1981: 110).

Nowhere is this attitude more evident than in the music of the Japanese bamboo flute *shakuhachi* (figure 1). Here the main constitutive element is the tone itself. For this reason it is possible to speak meaningfully about this music by analyzing the physical structure of its individual tones.

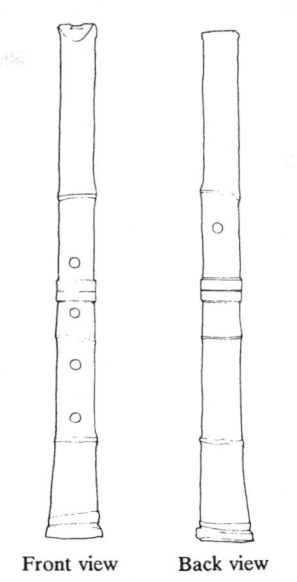

Figure 1

Front view   Back view

All previous attempts to characterize the sound of the *shakuhachi* have tried to define some specific acoustic quality of the instrument.[1] To do so, spectra were made, presumably at the instant of maximum amplitude, of each of a series of single notes. However good this method may be for characterizing the sound of Western instruments (and it is not very good), it is hopelessly inadequate for the *shakuhachi*, for one of the essential features of music is that the sound is never constant for a sufficiently long time, say 10 milliseconds, to permit such an analysis. Single tones taken out of their musical context can portray at best a transitory phase of this movement, not its real nature.

This sonorous movement is essential to *shakuhachi* music. Hence, in order to speak about the musical significance of the movement, it is necessary to analyze the music itself, not merely isolated tones presumed to be characteristic.

For this study, which was carried out at the Institut de Recherche et Coordination Acoustique/Musique (Paris), excerpts from the repertory of the Kinko school (see below) played by one of the authors (Gutzwiller) were recorded and analyzed. Originally, many different tone cells in different registers were recorded; subsequent analysis showed that the important acoustical characteristics varied about as much between tone cells as between different recordings of the same tone cell. Hence, although the study analyzes in detail only a few different tone cells, the authors are convinced that their findings apply to the tone cell as a phenomenon in *shakuhachi* playing, at least as evinced by the Kinko school.

---

[1] See, for example, Nishikawa (1968/1973), quoted in Fritsch (1979). Nishikawa's study is an attempt to establish the acoustical properties of good and bad instruments.

2 The structure of *shakuhachi* music

The music for solo *shakuhachi* is *honkyoku*; it originated between the 16th and the 18th centuries within the Fuke order of Zen Buddhism. Kurosawa Kinko selected 36 pieces from the large repertory of *honkyoku*; this choice was then considered binding for the Kinko school of *shakuhachi* playing, which represented the main stylistic orientation at the principal temples in and around Edo. This repertory was divided into 18 Inner Pieces related to meditation exercises and the rite in the temples, and 18 outer pieces, less strictly associated with the monks' religious practices.[2] The 18 Inner Pieces in particular have a somewhat unusual structure for Japanese music. The rhythmically very free music is organized into 'tone cells' which generally last the length of a breath and are separated from one another by clear rests.[3] Because of the extremely slow tempo, these tone cells rarely fuse into a coherent melody, but rather form relatively independent musical entities.

Most of the tone cells have three parts. They consist of a first phase, the preparatory note, a second phase, the main note, and a third phase, the ending.[4] In this study we shall investigate the evolution of the three parameters, pitch movement, dynamics, and timbral change in each of a tone cell's three phases.

3 Pitch movement within the tone cell

Two different kinds of pitch movement occur within the tone cell: movement between phases and movement within the phases themselves. These two different movements can be seen in the following example of the simple and common tone-cell *tsu-ro*.[5]

Figure 2 shows the movement in time of the fundamental frequency for a typical *tsu-ro* tone-cell. The first phase (0 – 2.9 seconds) corresponds to the note *tsu* (about e flat^4), the second and third phases correspond to the note *ro* (about d^4) and to *ro*'s ending. A clear change of fundamental frequency occurs only between the first and second phases. All other movement of the fundamental frequency is within one tone with unchanged fingering. This pattern is typical for the majority of tone cells in *honkyoku*.[6]

---

[2] For a comprehensive history of this order, its music and of the repertory of the Kinko school, see Gutzwiller (1983).

[3] *Issokuon*, literally 'one-breath-tone'.

[4] We shall be concerned exclusively with this three-part cell which forms the basic musical material of *honkyoku*. In the oldest pieces it accounts for about 65% of the musical material (Gutzwiller 1983: 123). This simplest form of a tone cell can be expanded to longer cells in which the second phase consists of two or three notes. This in no way changes the three-part structure of the tone cell.

[5] Notational symbol:

[6] See Gutzwiller 1983: 122-34. The straight diagonal lines between about sec 8.5 and 10.3 and after about sec 10.5 are artefacts of the pitch extraction analysis; the amplitude here is so low that the program cannot detect any fundamental frequency. See also figure 8.

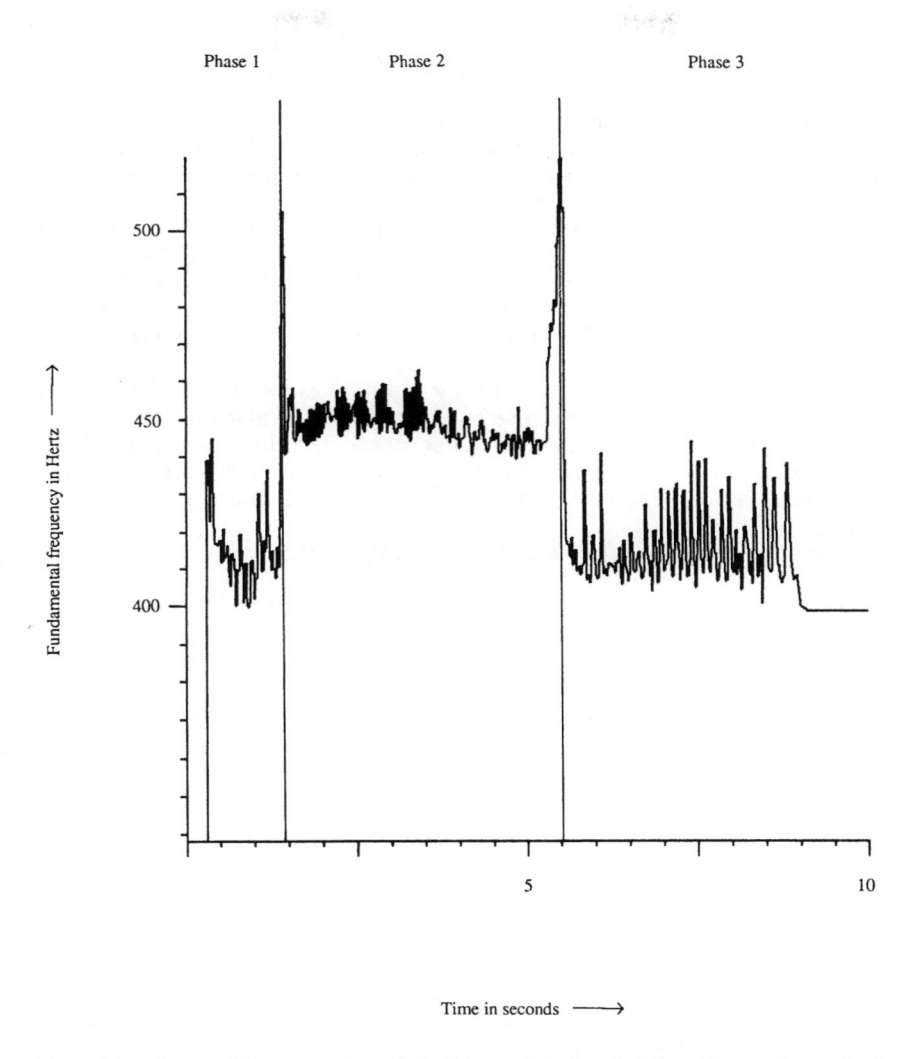

Figure 2: Fundamental frequency of a *shakuhachi* tone plotted against time. The note's perceived pitch moves from e flat^4 to d^4.

3.1 Pitch movement within the first phase

As figure 2 shows, each of the three phases of a tone cell is characterized by a different pattern of pitch movement. The first phase (0 – 2.9 seconds) is introduced by *oshi*, an attack particular to the *shakuhachi*. On the *shakuhachi* a tone is not tongued as on the western flute. Instead, just after the breath attack one of the holes normally covered in the fingering is very briefly opened and closed again.[7] Thus another sound is heard preceding the note of the first phase. This sound is not meant to have an identifiable pitch.[8]

In figure 2 we see that after the *oshi*, where a pitch of 355 Hz (a bit less than a minor third higher than the principal note of the phase) is very briefly reached,[9] a tone of 312 Hz appears for about .4 seconds, which descends and then rises to 325 Hz by the end of the phase.

Taken as a whole, the first phase of the tone cell is quite a complicated event. If we ignore for a moment the *oshi* movement (which is not meant to be perceived as a distinct pitch), the fundamental frequency descends 10 Hz (53 Cents), then rises 23 Hz (123 Cents). This pitch movement is brought about not by a change of fingering, but solely by changing the blowing angle and by raising and lowering the head.

In figure 2 the principal tone of the cell, d^4, lies lower than the pitch of the introductory phase. The relative position of the introductory phase to the principal tone is only of secondary importance for the movement of the fundamental frequency within the first phase. An identical pattern occurs when, as in figure 3, the principal tone a^4 lies above the introductory phase.[10]

3.2 The second phase (principal note) of the tone cell

In contrast to the introductory first phase, the pitch of the second phase is quite stable. It will be shown below (section 4; section 5.4), however, that significant changes of dynamics and timbre occur in the second phase.

---

[7] In this example:

[8] It should be noted that *oshi* is only a part of the *atari* process, to which *shakuhachi* players accord great importance. The process consists of: 1. *kiai*, 'spiritual readiness'; 2. tensing of the abdominal muscles to start the tone; 3. thrusting the chin slightly outward and up; 4. the *oshi* technique described above.

[9] It is essential not to hear *oshi* as a grace note yielding two distinct pitches. Analysis programs seem to feel obliged to find precise values even for imprecise events, a characteristic to be noted in considering computer-aided analysis and transcription.

[10] Principal notes can also be attacked from above or below via the preparatory neighbour tone. For the *shakuhachi*'s lower octave, *honkyoku* admits the following possibilities (the following system can be expanded by combining several neighbour notes in the first phase; we shall not consider these additional possibilities):

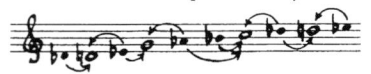

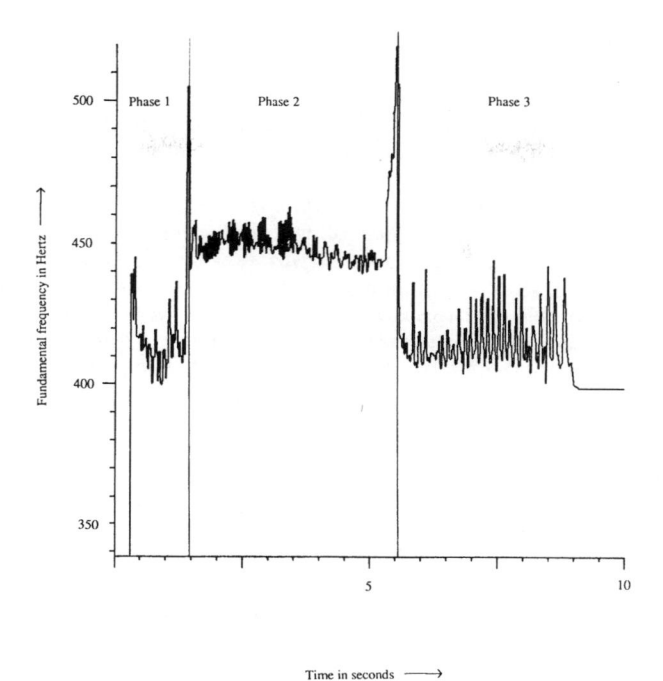

Figure 3: The tone cell *u-chi*, whose principal tone lies above the preparatory phase.

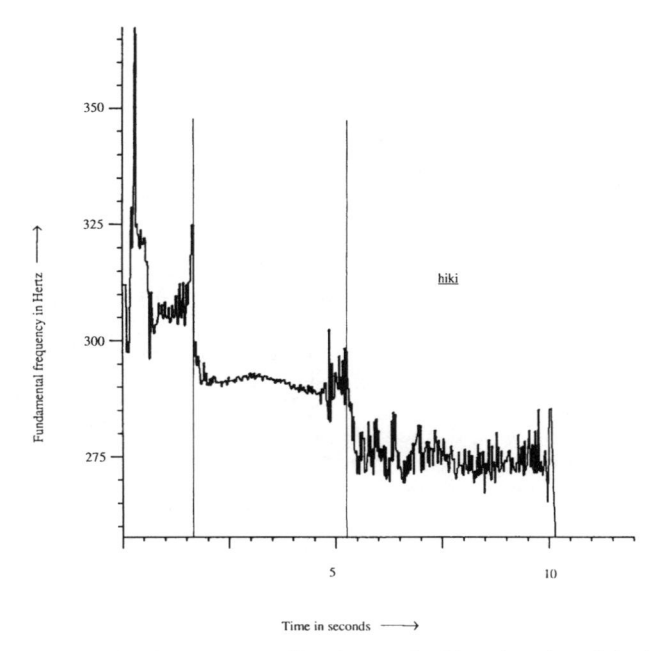

Figure 4: An example showing *hiki*, an ending characterized by a lowering of the fundamental frequency of the principal tone. In addition, the fundamental frequency in *hiki* is much less stable than that of the principal tone.

3.3 Movement of the fundamental frequency within the third phase

The third phase of the example illustrated in figure 2 is characterized by gradual destabilization of the pitch, brought about by the application of *yuri*.[11] *Yuri* is a pure pitch vibrato (frequency modulation) effected by the movement of the head. Normally the head movement is lateral (*yokoyuri*); however, the *shakuhachi* player also employs vertical (*tateyuri*) and circular head movement (*mawashiyuri*). The different kinds of *yuri* influence the pitch differently: *yokoyuri* modulates the pitch upward; *tateyuri*, downward; *mawashiyuri*, in both directions. The transitions from one kind of *yuri* to the other are fluid and not systematically defined. All forms are played slowly, with about two or three pulsations per second. The *yuri* in our example is *yokoyuri* and raises the perceived fundamental pitch by a very small amount. The principal tone of the second phase had a frequency of 293 Hz; the vibrato in the third phase ranges between 289 and 302 Hz or over 76 Cents. Example 2 ends with *ori*, in this case a lowering of the tone by 124 Cents to about 275 Hz. In the example, *ori* is separated from the preceding *yuri* by a break of nearly 2 seconds.[12] *Yuri* with concluding *ori* is but one of several ways to end a tone cell. Another frequently used ending is *hiki*,[13] where, as in *ori*, the tone descends at the end but is held a long time (figure 4). Note that *hiki* is not preceded by *yuri*.

This discussion of fundamental frequency movement in the tone cell of *honkyoku* shows that only one of the three phases, the principal tone, is stable in pitch, whereas both the introductory first and the ending third phases are unstable. In addition, one can say that a U- or V- formed curve is characteristic for the pitch movement of the first phase, whereas various means are at one's disposal in the third phase to conclude the tone cell. The most common of these is pitch destabilization through *yuri* (vibrato) with final *ori*.

4 The dynamic evolution within the tone cell

The dynamics of the tone cell *tsu-ro*, whose pitch evolution was shown as figure 2, are summarized in figure 5.

Here too the three-part structure of the tone cell is clearly visible, consisting of a preparatory phase (0 – 2.9 seconds), the principal tone (2.9 – 6.2 seconds), and the decay in the third phase (6.2 – 12 seconds). The dynamic evolution of the first phase is exactly parallel to the pitch movement, that is, the sound pressure level (SPL) decreases by about 15 dB when the pitch sinks by 56 Cents, and increases by 23 dB when the pitch is raised by 123 Cents. It is also obvious that a dynamic accentuation of the beginning of the first phase accompanies the pitch change in *oshi* (see 3.1.).

In the second phase the pitch is stable while the SPL first increases by 9 dB in 1.6 seconds and then decreases by 3 dB in the same time. Characteristic of the dynamic pattern is that the transitions from one phase to another are accentuated dynamically, thus insuring that the phases remain clearly separated from one another.

The third phase shows a sharply decreasing dynamic curve (a drop of 24

---

[11] Literally 'to shake'.
[12] The rather long rest is characteristic of the Kawase branch of the Kinko school to which the author belongs. Other branches play *ori* immediately after the previous note.
[13] Literally 'to draw in'.

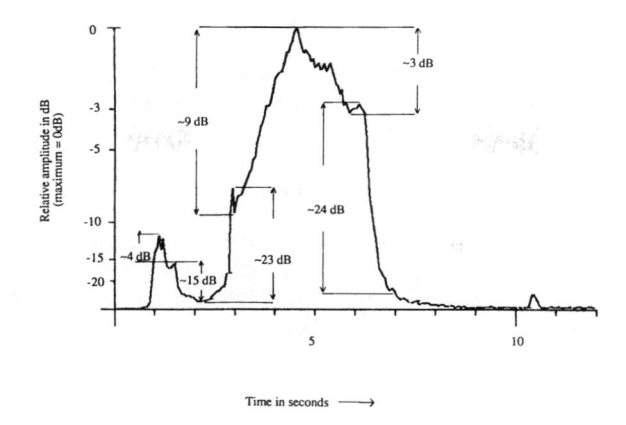

Figure 5: The dynamic evolution of the tone cell *tsu-ro* (cf. Fig. 2).

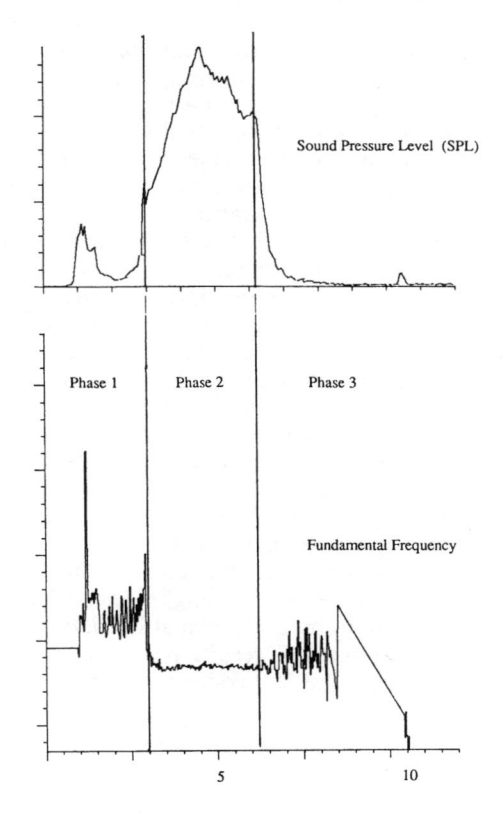

Figure 6: Evolution of SPL (above) and fundamental frequency (below) of the tone cell *tsu-ro* from Figure 2.

dB in the period from 6.2 to 7.2 seconds), which remains uninfluenced by the vibrato (*yuri*) which begins at the same time. The concluding *ori* follows at 10.3 seconds.

In figure 6 the evolution of SPL and fundamental frequency for the tone cell *tsu-ro* are shown one above the other in order to make clear the relationship between these two dimensions.

5 Timbral change within the tone cell

Just as fundamental frequency changes in various ways within the tone cells of *honkyoku*, so too does timbre. We may distinguish two kinds of timbral change: that between two phases on the one hand and that within each of the phases of a tone cell on the other. The timbral changes between phases, especially between the first and the second phase, are accentuated by the techniques of *meri* and *kari*.

5.1 The technique of meri and kari

Meri and *kari* are two notions, or rather two aspects of the same notion, which are basic to the technique of the ancient *shakuhachi* schools.[14] The names designate both a particular technique and its sounding result.

At the technical level, *kari* denotes the 'normal' mode of blowing and 'normal' fingerings, indicates in other words that one blows the instrument with one's head held erect and that the holes are either completely covered or completely open. *Meri*, on the contrary, means that the head is lowered and that one or more holes may be only partially covered. The *meri*-technique influences all three aspects of a tone: it lowers its pitch by as much as a whole tone, it reduces its loudness, and it changes its timbre. Two of these aspects, lowering of pitch and decrease of amplitude, are coupled to a certain degree, for it is technically very difficult to play a *meri* tone as loudly as a *kari* tone. Indeed this is never required in *honkyoku*. On the contrary, this limiting factor is employed as a constructive element of the tone cell structure.[15] As far as the timbral difference between *kari* and *meri* is concerned, it can be precisely measured in 'laboratory tones'. However, such results should be treated with considerable caution because *meri* tones normally constitute the first phase in *honkyoku* tone cells and we have seen that these introductory phases go through certain changes in pitch and loudness which necessarily modify the timbre. If the pitch and dynamics of the first phase of a tone cell can be characterized as unstable, this instability extends to the timbre as well. The second phase also, as we shall see, goes through a particular timbral evolution despite its stability in pitch. For the discussion at hand, this means that we can hardly expect relevant experimental results from either *kari* or *meri* tones played and analyzed outside a musical context.

---

[14] '*Meri-kari* is of special importance. If *meri-kari* is lacking in *shakuhachi* playing it is as if one blows upon a stick and is contemptible.' (Hisamatsu Fūyō: 'Hitori Kotoba', essay written around 1825, translated in Gutzwiller 1983: 164-68).

[15] I have shown elsewhere how in the 19th century such 'disadvantages' stemming from the instrument's construction were exploited to express functional aspects of *insen*, the predominant scale in Japanese chamber music, by using *kari-meri* to articulate the *shakuhachi*'s basic scale. (Gutzwiller 1974: 43-74).

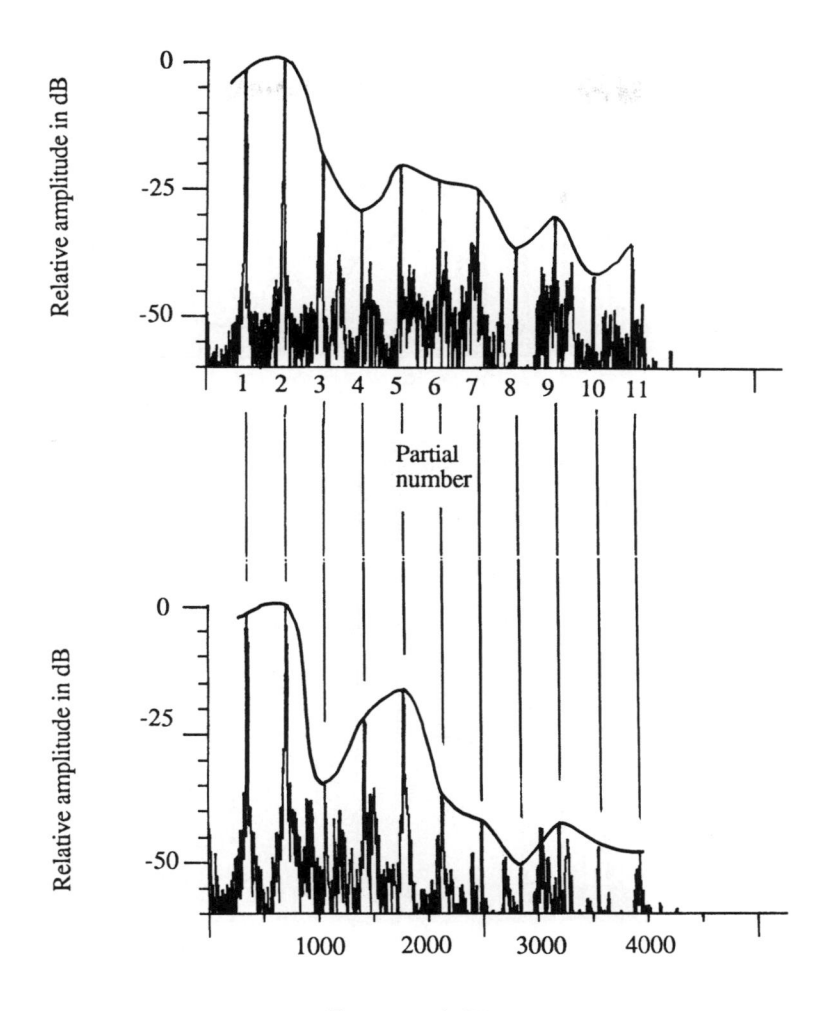

Figure 7a: Spectrum obtained by fast Fourier transformation (FFT) over 4096 points (ca. 160 ms) of a tone played with *kari* technique. The fundamental frequency is 350 Hz. In this and the following examples we have sketched the spectrum's envelope to make the resonances clearer.

Figure 7b: Spectrum obtained by the same analysis of a tone having the same fundamental frequency but played with *meri* technique.

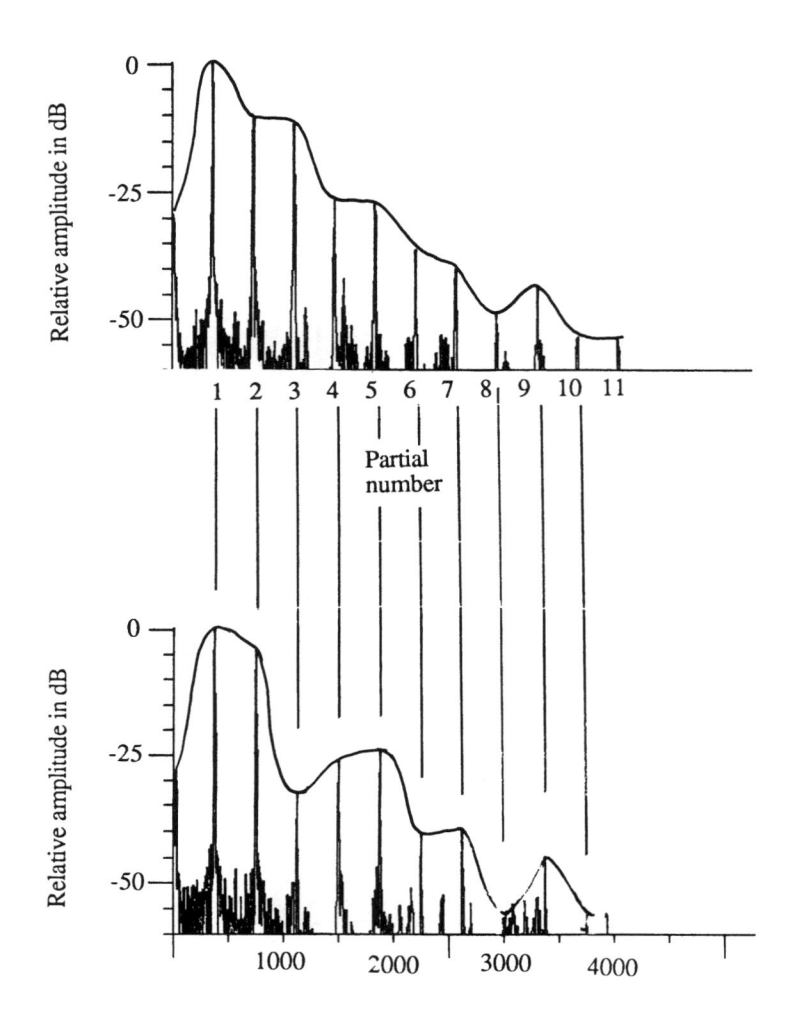

Figure 8a: Spectrum obtained by FFT over 4096 points of a tone played with lowered head but fully covered holes. The fundamental frequency is about 375 Hz.

Figure 8b: Spectrum of the same tone played with the head in normal position and the holes only partially covered.

Let us nonetheless show the spectra of a *meri* and a *kari* tone having the same pitch, mainly to show that they are in fact different, even if we cannot draw any further conclusions from them (figures 7a and 7b).

There are two important differences between the spectra. First, the *meri* tone has much weaker upper partials than has the *kari* tone. Second, the *meri* tone shows more pronounced resonances, or formants, than the *kari* tone particularly between the two lowest partials and partials four and five. Both spectra show considerable noise.

One question which might be asked about the relation of *meri-kari*-technique and timbre is this: what influences timbre more, lowering of the head or partial covering of the holes? The question is only of passing musical interest, since partial covering without lowering the head is not a traditional *shakuhachi* technique. Nonetheless we present for comparison spectra of the same tone lowered by two different techniques: in the first (figure 8a) only the position of the head varies; in the second (figure 8b) only the partial covering of the holes varies from the normal playing mode.

Here we see clearly that lowering the head reduces the amplitude of the upper partials (by 10 to 20 dB above the fifth partial), while partial covering of the holes seems to be responsible both for creating new resonances in the *shakuhachi* (that is, reducing the third partial's amplitude while raising that of partial four and five), and for emphasizing those already present (for instance one around 3300 Hz). These findings are hardly surprising, since lowering the head changes the way the airstream is broken at the mouthpiece of the instrument, specifically the airstream flows more smoothly across the edge of the mouthpiece when the head is lowered. There is less air turbulence, hence less high-frequency energy in the sound. As the high-frequency energy decreases, so does the perceived amplitude.

5.2 Meri-kari movement within the tone cell

Meri-kari is of constitutive significance for the structure of tone cells in *honkyoku*, since, as in the present example of the tone cell *tsu-ro*, the first phase is always *meri*, and the second always *kari*.[16]

Thus, to the pitch movement and dynamic evolution characteristic of the development of a tone cell must be added a specific timbral change from the first (*meri*) to the second phase (*kari*). The third phase returns then to *meri*, and the tone cell concludes either with *ori* after the *yuri* (vibrato), or, as shown in figure 4, with *hiki*. Both *ori* and *hiki* belong to the realm of *meri*, for both are played with lowered head while keeping the fingering of the preceding *kari* tone. Thus the tone cell as a whole consists of a movement from *meri* to *kari* and back to *meri*.

5.3 Timbral change within the meri phases

It is difficult to describe and quantitatively measure the timbral change within *meri* phases, particularly during the first phase. Since *meri*-technique influences not only pitch, but also amplitude and timbre of the tone, it is hard to

---

[16] Exceptions are to be found in a small group of tone cells which lie completely in the *meri* region. (Gutzwiller 1983: 129-30). However, there are no tone cells consisting only of *kari*-tones.

determine which of these three elements are responsible for which acoustical change.

5.4 Timbral change in the second phase

The second phase carries the principal tone of the tone cell and is characterized by stable pitch and a strong crescendo followed by a weaker decrescendo. The three-dimensional spectra in figures 9a and 9b permit one to follow the evolution of individual partials and thus to form a clearer picture of this second phase.

Although figures 9a and 9b show the entire tone cell *tsu-ro*, we shall only be concerned with the second phase (3 to 6.2 seconds). The non-synchronous dynamic evolution of the individual partials is particularly striking; this evolution is responsible for timbral change within the phase. To make this non-synchronism clear, we have separated the partials of two tone cells and have put their individual dynamic patterns one beneath the other. Figure 10a shows the partials for the principal tone of figures 9a and 9b; figure 10b shows those of the principal tone of another *tsu-ro* tone cell for comparison. In both figures, the SPL in dB has been added for the most important relationships.

The most significant result is that the partials reach their maximal amplitudes at different times. The first partial reaches its maximum very shortly after the beginning of the phase, then decreases in amplitude.[17] The increase in amplitude at 6.2 seconds in figure 10a and 6.1 seconds in figure 10b correspond to the beginning of phase three in each note (see figure 5). Partials two and three reach their maxima when partial one has already begun to lose amplitude. Partial four is delayed even longer; it only reaches its maximum when the lower partials have lost a considerable part of their intensity. The fifth partial rises more quickly; its maximum coincides with that of partials two and three.

We should point out that the accent between phases one and two and that between two and three do not appear in the same partials. The accent at the beginning of phase two is found mainly in partials one to three, while that at the beginning of phase three is found in partials one and two and again in five and higher.

Thus, the most important result for the timbral development within the second phase is that the individual partials do not evolve in synchronous fashion, but rather that each pattern, particularly that of partials one to four, is staggered relative to the others so that the upper partials seem to increase in intensity as the lower partials become softer.

One must not confuse this phenomenon of increasing brightness and acuteness within phase two of the tone cell with what occurs in an attack where the individual partials enter almost simultaneously. In such an attack, delays are measured in hundredths of a second. The full development of, say, the fourth partial in figure 10b, however, takes two seconds.

Figures 11a and 11b show a crescendo and decrescendo played on a transverse flute (the pitch is d^4). Despite the jittery curves, it is clear that here the partials move more synchronously than those of the *shakuhachi* in the second phase of a tone cell in *honkyoku*.

---

[17] The double maxima of the first partial in figure 10a seem atypical. Configurations of this type are not present in other recordings of the same tone cell.

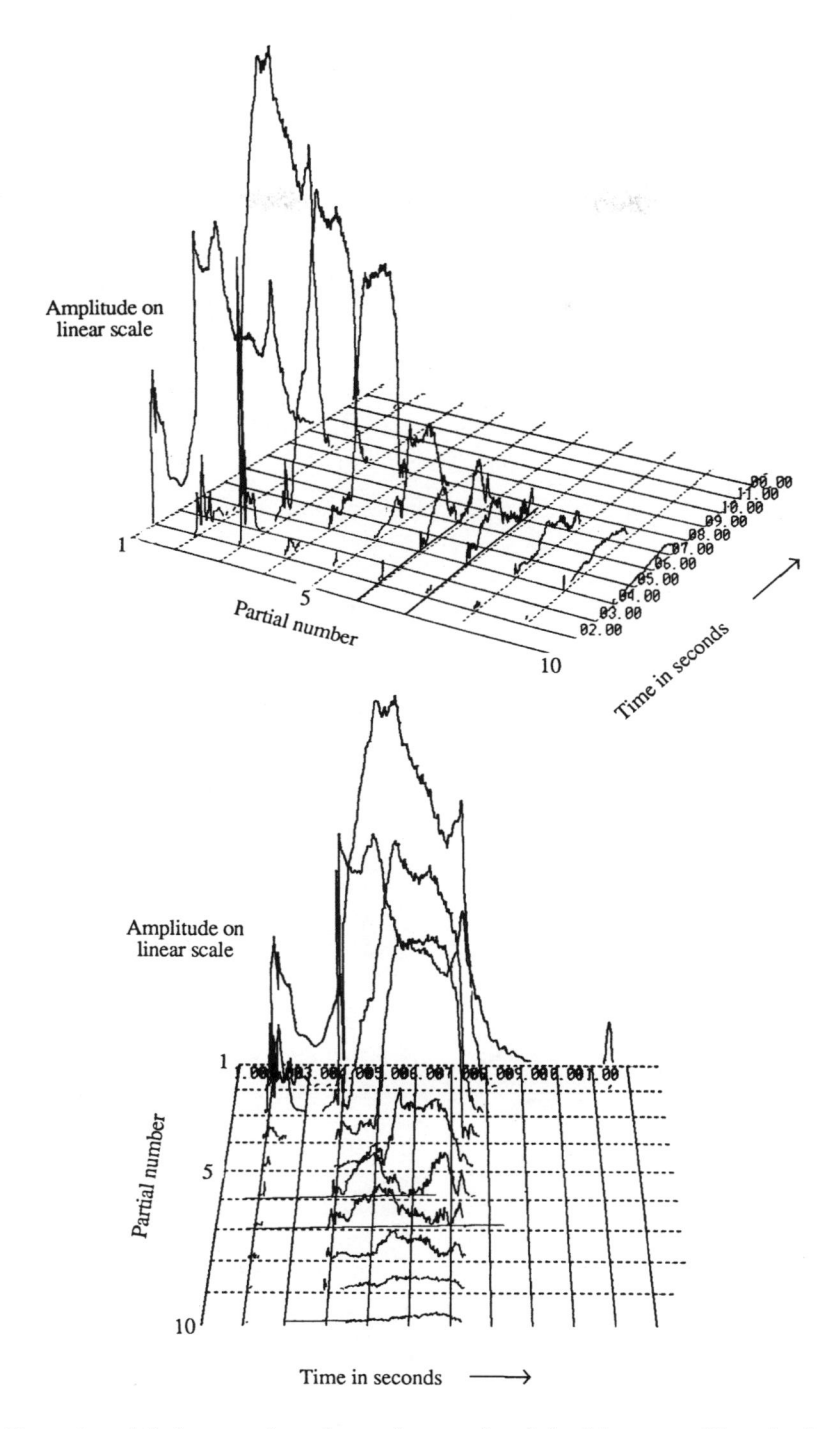

Figures 9a and 9b show two views of a pseudo-spectral analysis of the *tsu-ro* cell by a simulated vocoder. The signal was run through digital filters centered on its partials. The illustrations show the output of those filters.

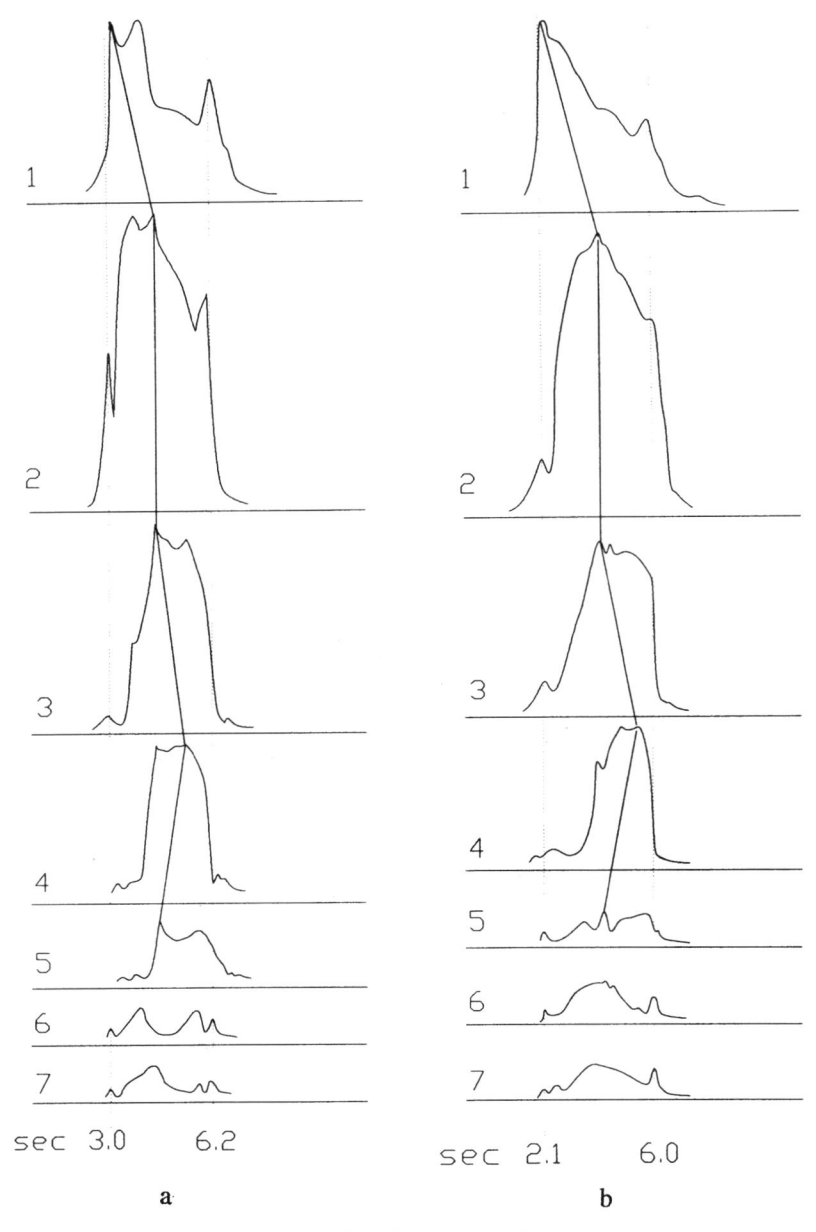

Figure 10a shows the amplitude evolution of each of the first 7 partials of the *tsu-ro* cell of Figure 9. The line connecting the maxima of partials 1 to 5 helps to illustrate the order in which the partials reach their respective maxima.

Figure 10b shows the amplitude evolution of another *tsu-ro* tone cell.

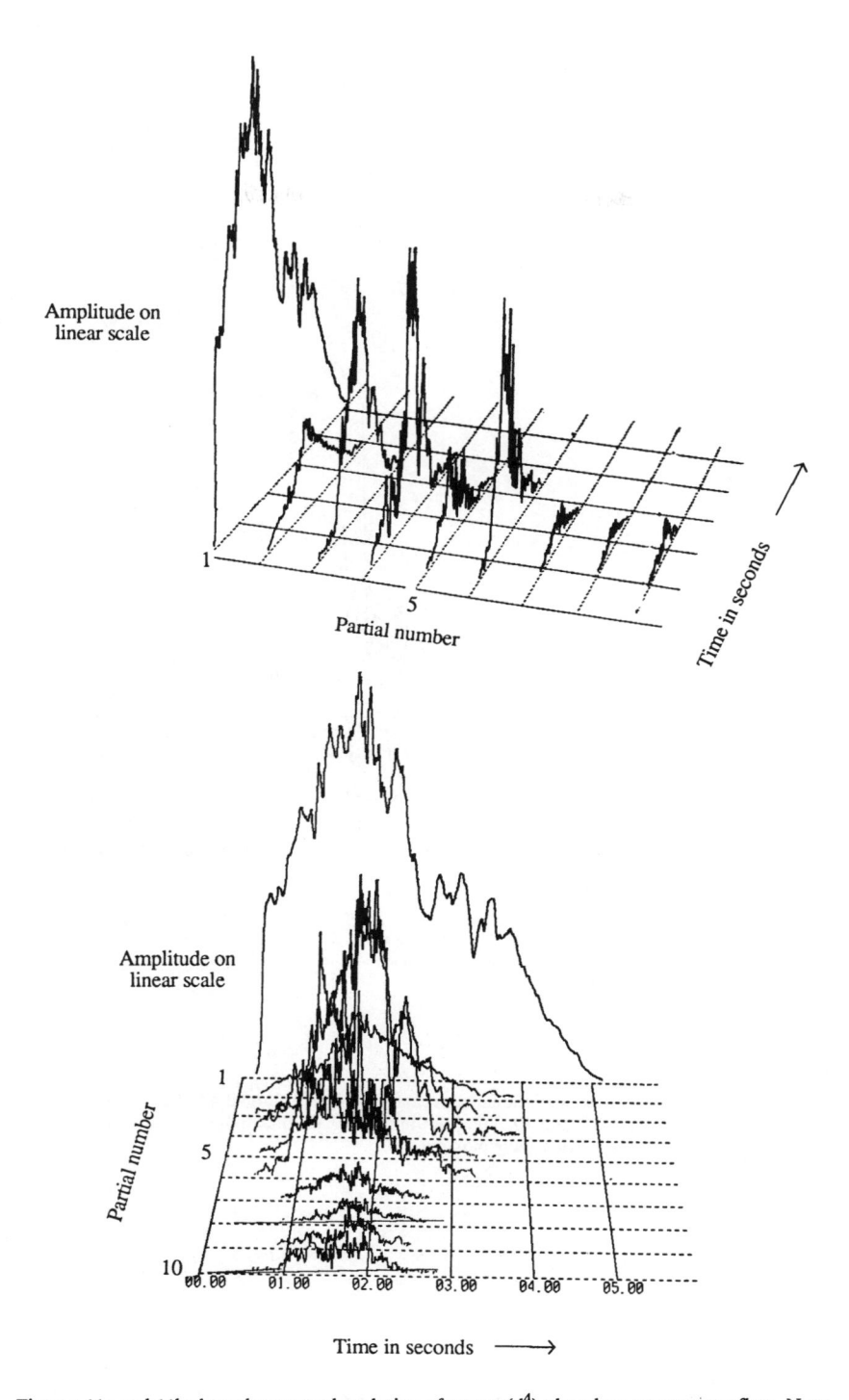

Figures 11a and 11b show the spectral evolution of a tone (d^4) played on a transverse flute. Note the relative synchronicity of the dynamic evolution of the partials.

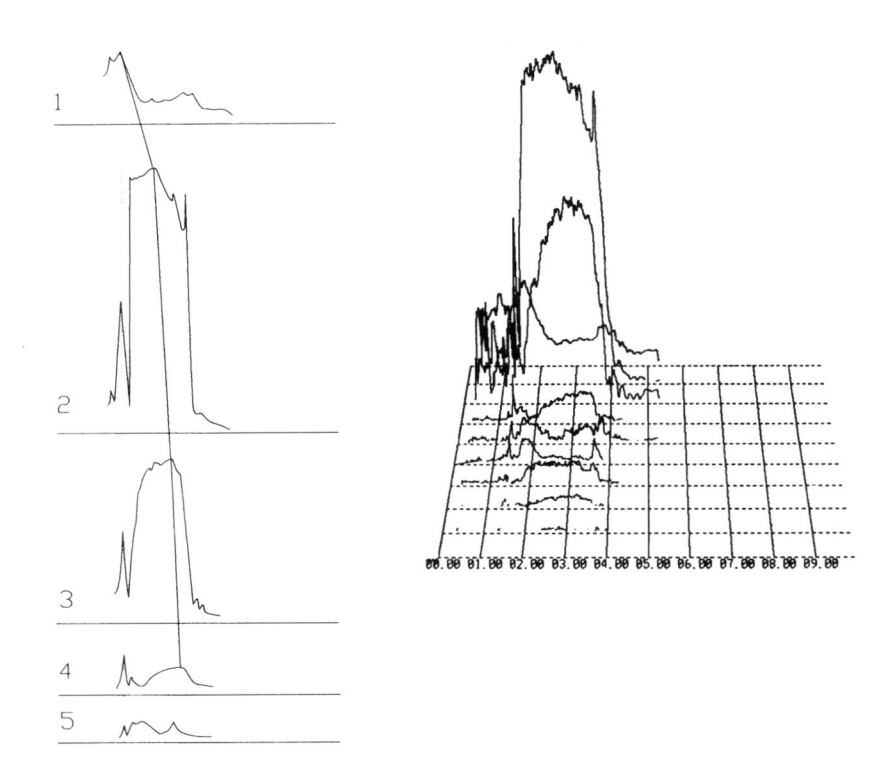

Figure 12a: A *shakuhachi* tone with the fundamental frequency of about 440 Hz, analyzed in the manner of Figure 9 and 10. The line linking the partials helps to show the order in which the partials reach their maxima.

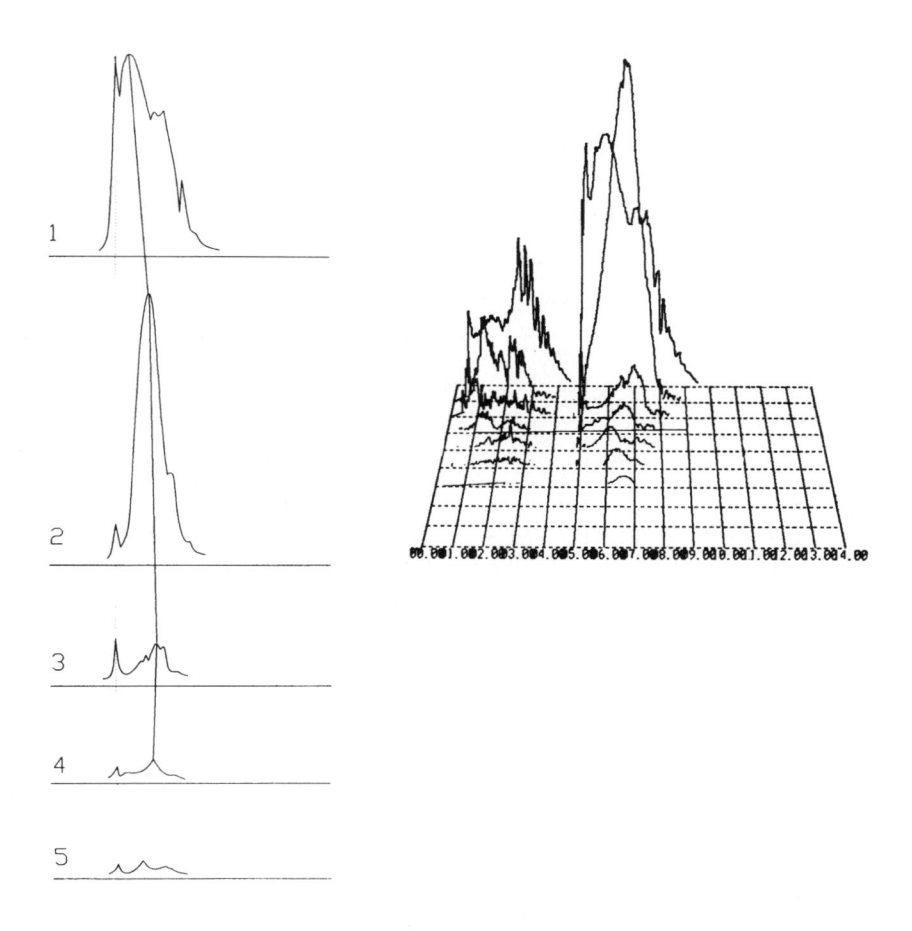

Figure 12b: A *shakuhachi* tone with the fundamental frequency of about 585 Hz, analyzed in the manner of Figure 9 and 10.

Finally, we may ask whether the non-synchronicity of partials just described is particular to the tone cell *tsu-ro*. Figure 12a shows the evolution of the principal tone (pitch a^4) of the second phase of the tone cell *u-chi* (see figure 3); figure 12b analyzes the second phase of the tone cell *ha-ra-ro*, the principal tone of which has the pitch d^5. In both figures we see a similar non-synchronicity in the maxima of the partials.

6 Summary

Table 1 summarizes the most important characteristics of the individual phases of a tone cell in *honkyoku*:

	1st phase	2nd phase	3rd phase
P I T C H	Unstable movement in form of v or u; attack with *oshi*	Stable	Unstable destabilization by *yuri* with *ori*
D Y N A M I C S	softer; movement in v or u form	louder; crescendo – descrescendo	softer; dynamics steeply decaying
D Y N A M I C S	Dynamic accentuation of phase transitions		
T I M B R E	*meri*	*kari* timbral change; non-synchronous dynamic evolution	*meri*

Table 1

Thus far we have examined the tone cells in the music of the *shakuhachi* only from the point of view of their acoustic properties. It may now be of use to consider briefly how the *shakuhachi* player perceives the structure of tone cells.

The *shakuhachi* player experiences the playing of *honkyoku* as an absolutely physical event, a gesture referred to the center of the body, *hara*.

This center is at the same time the locus of breathing. In the player's imagination, the *honkyoku* tone cell is seen as circular, ever returning to its point of departure. It has been understood as a manifestation of the principle of *yin/in* and *yang/yō*, a principle of non-dualistic opposition, whose elements come into being apart from one another, yet remain ever intertwined in one another. The breathing process itself represents this principle, where, particularly in the Kawase branch of the Kinko school, inhalation is interpreted as *yin*, and exhalation, the source of energy, as *yang*. The first phase represents a movement from *yin* to *yang*, the second is *yang*, and the third leads back to *yin* (see figure 14). *Yin* and *yang* may be thought of as the aesthetic concept which denotes all aspects of the *meri-kari* technique.

The first phase begins with *oshi*. In figure 15 the line moving towards the player indicates the lowering of pitch with decreasing loudness. The movement away from the player describes the expanding tone in the second phase, which in phase three is drawn inwards towards the player again, with decreasing loudness and destabilized pitch.

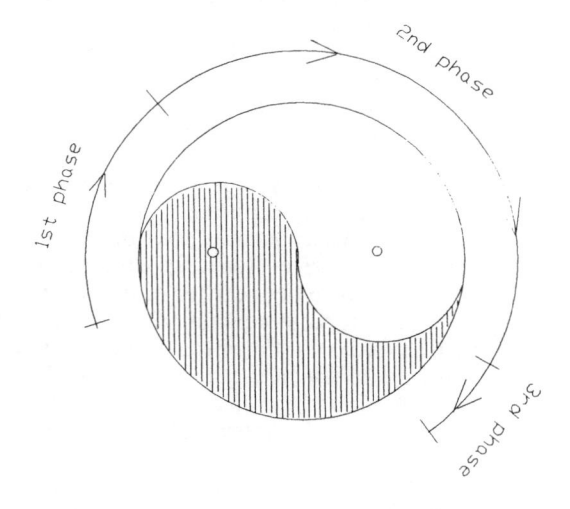

Figure 13: The player imagines the *honkyoku* tone cell as circular and focused on the *hara*.

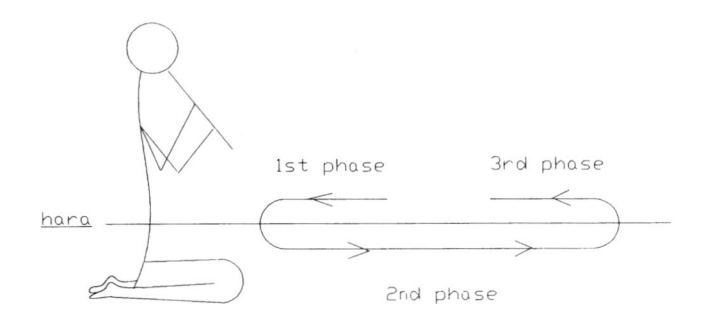

Figure 14: The *honkyoku* tone cell interpreted in relation to the principle of *yin* and *yang*.

7 The tone cell in *honkyoku* as a 'composed tone'

When one considers its tripartite nature, the tone cell as a musical complex seems clearly related to the tone as a physical phenomenon. Just as every instrumental tone with distinct pitch and duration consists of three parts (attack, quasi-stationary phase, and decay) so too does the tone cell. In the tone cell, the tone's physical characteristics become music (see figure 15).

Although source material for the historical development of *shakuhachi honkyoku* is very scarce, by considering the music's function, we can reconstruct with some certainty how these structures arose. *Honkyoku* was played within the Fuke order as a form of *shugyō*, more exactly as *kisoku shugyō*.[18] It seems very probable that in the meditation exercises, originally simple melodies were broken up into the tone cells which so dominate this music, for the emphasis in these exercises lay not on longer melodic phrases, but rather on *tettei on*,[19] the tone in and of itself, the playing of which brings about Enlightenment.[20] One can assume that it was this concentration on the tone itself which led the *shakuhachi* player to elevate the physical qualities of the tone to the rank of music, to 'compose the tone'.

This elevation of the tone leads to the tone cell, which occupies a singular intermediate position between an isolated tone, a pre-musical phenomenon, and a phrase of higher order consisting of several tones. The tone cell possesses on the one hand characteristics of the tone, primarily because of the predominance of the second phase; on the other hand, being made up of various phases, each having a different function, it also demonstrates characteristics of a musical phrase.

It is interesting to compare this concept of the 'tone-phrase' in *honkyoku* with the occidental vision of musical tone. In the context of western composition, a tone is assumed not to be a carrier of musical information, but to be neutral. This permits the tone to remain free for the composition of larger structures. In the framework of European history, composition might well be described as a process in which the musical tone gains ever greater malleability as it loses its individuality by giving up those qualities which are independent of a particular musical context. Pierre Boulez spoke of this process in the framework of serial composition:

> I believe that dialectic in composition is easier to achieve with a neutral object not immediately identifiable, such as a 'normal' tone or a simple aggregate of simple tones which are not characterized by internal changes of dynamics, duration and timbre. Whenever one forms pre-treated figures smacking of a 'formulated' context, one must not forget – if one is not to come to grief – that they have lost all neutrality in order to take on a personality and individuality which make them more or less useless for a generalized dialectic of sound relationships (Boulez 1963: 196).

---

[18] Literally 'spiritual breath-discipline'. See 'Kaisei Hōgo' by Hisamatsu Fūyō (1838) translated in Gutzwiller 1983: 189-94.
[19] Literally 'absolute sound'.
[20] This becomes clear in an aphorism concerning the ultimate goal of *shakuhachi* playing attributed to Kurosawa Kinko, founder of the Kinko school: *Ichion jōbutsu*, 'become Buddha in a single tone', i.e. attain Enlightenment.

a. Tone

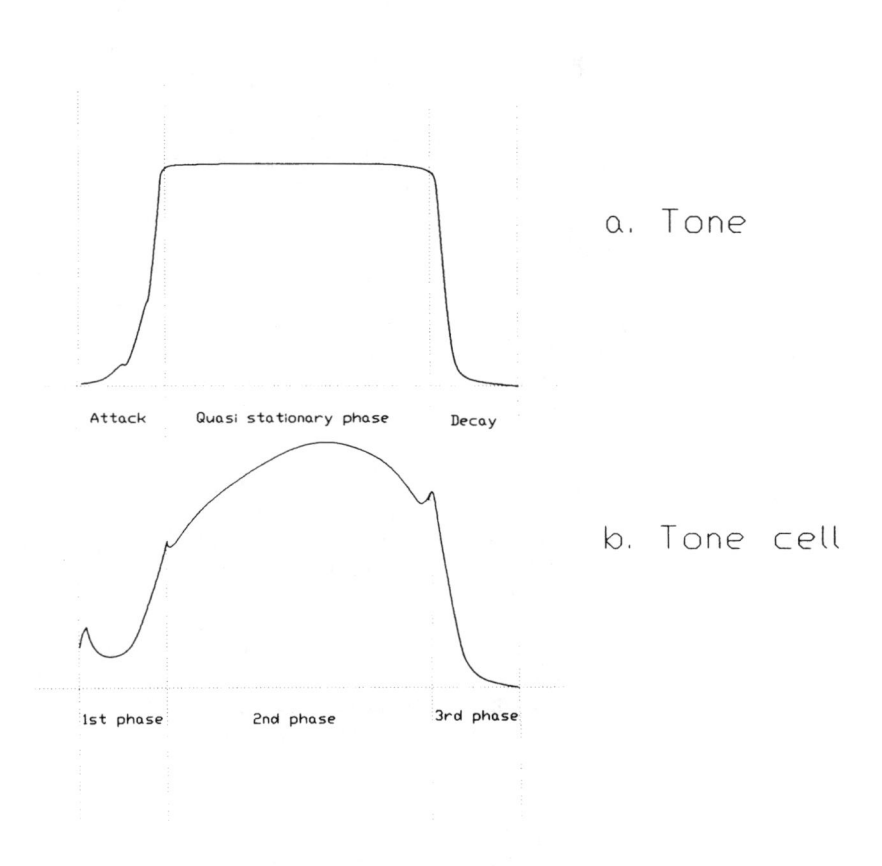

Attack　　Quasi stationary phase　　Decay

b. Tone cell

1st phase　　2nd phase　　3rd phase

Figures 15a and 15b illustrate the structural relationship between any musical tone and a tone cell in *honkyoku*.

The point is that already formed material can be less easily ordered by serial techniques.[21]

Clearly, the tone cell in *honkyoku* is not neutral material, but rather tones which are characterized by internal changes of dynamics, duration, and timbre. Each of the above analyzed elements – pitch movement, dynamics, and timbre – in each of a tone cell's three phases, contributes to the function of the particular phase in question.

Equally clear is that it is very difficult to produce musical structures composed of elements so complexly organized as tone cells while keeping the tone cell subordinate to larger structures.[22] In fact it is extremely difficult to observe higher order formal structure in the pieces of *honkyoku*.

To be sure, the production of 'music', even as 18th century Japan understood the word, was not the goal of practising *shakuhachi honkyoku* within this Buddhist order. Kurosawa Kinko, in his reform of about 1750, purged the *shakuhachi* repertory of the secular elements it was showing signs of adopting. Hisamatsu Fūyō spoke thus of this new repertory in his essay 'Hitori Mondo' of 1823:

> Thirty-six pieces are but one piece;
> one piece is no-piece;
> Emptiness and Nothingness. (Gutzwiller 1983: 179)

8 Conclusions

This paper has proposed an investigation of the acoustical characteristics of the sound of the *shakuhachi*. We have worked on the hypothesis that a study of this kind would not only provide an exact description of physical phenomena but would also offer a description of the music itself. Our point of departure was the observation that traditional *shakuhachi* music has shown virtually no interest in architectonic formal relationships; on the other hand, highly structured smaller units – what we have called tone cells – clearly have great musical significance. We set ourselves the task of studying these tone cells as the primary vehicle by which musical meaning is conveyed.

In this 'world of a single sound' we found structures whose musical meaning mirrors their physical evolution. Just as the tone cell stands somewhere between the tone as a physical event and the independent musical phrase, so too our description of its qualities is both the representation of physical characteristics and the analysis of music.

In the introduction to this paper we quoted Tsuge as saying that in Japanese music 'there is a deep-seated attitude towards realization of a self-sufficient musical world within the scope of even a *single* sound' (Tsuge 1981: 110). We hope with this study to have contributed to an understanding of this important characteristic of Japanese music.[23]

---

[21] It is a moot point whether one can speak of a dialectic of composition where hierarchical dependency defines the relation of structure and material.

[22] Since it has been the goal of this study to describe the basic structure of the tone cell, only simple examples were chosen. The basic form of the three-part cell can be expanded to a certain degree, the first phase by stringing together several *meri* neighbour tones, the second phase by stringing together at most three *kari* principal notes. In the same way variations are possible in the final phase of the tone cell. Weisgarber (1968: 313-44) identified over 300 variants of tone cells in *honkyoku*.

[23] The acoustical studies for this paper were carried out at the Institut de Recherche et de Coordination Acoustique/Musique (IRCAM) in Paris during 1979 and 1980. Sound

References

Boulez, Pierre 1963: *Musikdenken heute*, Darmstädter Beiträge zur Neuen Musik V, Mainz: B. Schotts Söhne

Fritsch, Ingrid 1979: *Die Solo-honkyoku der Tozan-Schule*, Studien zur traditionellen Musik Japans, vol. IV, Kassel: Bärenreiter

Gutzwiller, Andreas 1974: *'Shakuhachi: Aspects of history, practice and teaching'* (Ph.D. dissertation, Wesleyan University), Ann Arbor, Michigan: University Microfilms

    1983: *Die shakuhachi der Kinko-Schule*, Studien zur traditionellen Musik Japans, vol. V, Kassel: Bärenreiter

Nishikawa, Rizan 1968/1973: 'Shakuhachi no neiro no bunseki' (Analysis of the timbre of the shakuhachi), *Gakuho*, July 1968, No. 1973

Tsuge, Gen'ichi 1981: 'Symbolic techniques in Japanese *koto-kumiuta*', *Asian Music* 12.2: 109-132

Weisgarber, Eliott 1968: 'The *honkyoku* of the *Kinko-ryū*: some principles of its organisation', *Ethnomusicology*, vol. 12, no. 3: 313-44

    examples were recorded directly in digital form on a PDP 11/34 computer in 16 bit integer format. The sound files were then transferred to a PDP 10 computer, where the analysis was performed. The analysis programs were developed at Stanford University, primarily by James A. Moorer.

A report on Chinese research into the Dunhuang music manuscripts

CHEN YINGSHI

Translated by Coralie Rockwell

This paper is a survey of recent Chinese scholarship into the collection of musical notations, believed to be of tenth century date, discovered at Dunhuang. Following a description of the scores and their contents, the author outlines the views that have been put forward by Chinese scholars concerning the nature of the Dunhuang notations, and concludes that they are tablature-notation for *pipa* (lute). He then examines the tunings that have been adopted in transcribing the notations and discusses Chinese theories concerning the interpretation of rhythm, metre and playing technique. The paper includes four scholars' transcriptions of the piece, Yizhou, from the Dunhuang scores.

Dunhuang, located in the western part of China's Gansu Province, was an ancient holy seat of Buddhism and a strategic place on the Silk Road, the ancient trade route along which eastern and western culture was transmitted. Approximately forty kilometres southeast at Dunhuang is a steep cliff with an average height of seventeen metres where, from the beginning of the fourth century, people dug Buddhist caves (*mogao ku*). A stone inscription made by Li Huairang in 698 states that at that time there were already more than one thousand caves, and for this reason, the Mogao caves have also come to be known as the 'Thousand Buddha caves' (*qianfodong*).

At the beginning of this century, the caretaker of the Mogao caves, a Daoist monk called Wang, unexpectedly discovered another cave through a crack which had opened up. In this cave, which had long been sealed off, were preserved many Buddhist scriptures and other documents, the latest of which date from 1002. In the second year of the Jing You reign period of the northern Song dynasty (1035) the western Xia state attacked Dunhuang. It is popularly believed that a Buddhist monk from a temple at the Mogao caves of the time might, at that time, have assembled the documents in this cave and then sealed it off. If this is the case these documents may be regarded as pre-eleventh century relics.

In 1908 the French sinologist, Paul Pelliot, removed some of the documents to Paris where they were deposited in the Bibliothèque Nationale. On the back of three Buddhist scrolls (catalogued as P 3808, P 3539 and P 3719) were written a number of musical pieces. These musical scores (*yuepu*) are referred to as the *Dunhuang yuepu* (Dunhuang music scores). On the cover of the Buddhist scripture P 3808 is written 'fourth year of the Changxing Period' (933). Most Chinese scholars consider that the Dunhuang scores copied on the Buddhist text P 3808 were written close to this year, and that the music had, for the most part, been passed down from the Tang dynasty and was still popular in the Five Dynasties period.

In 1937, the Japanese scholar, Hayashi Kenzō, discovered a photograph of the back of P 3808 at a friend's place. With the assistance of Hirade Hisao, he took the lead in making a study of this manuscript, comparing it with a similar one, the *Tempyō biwa-fu*, which had been discovered in the Shōsōin in Japan. In 1938 they published a paper entitled 'Biwa kofu no kenkyū (Research into old scores for biwa)' which included discussion of P 3808 and the *Tempyō biwa-fu*. In 1955 Hayashi published a specialised study in English which contained photographs of the notations of the twenty five pieces in this manuscript together with transcriptions into staff notation (Hayashi 1955). After this article was revised, it was translated into Chinese by Pan Huaisu and published in China (Hayashi 1957). In 1969, Hayashi Kenzō revised it again and retranscribed the scores, thus completing his final research on this group of scores (Hayashi 1969: 202-34).

Hayashi's research into the Dunhuang music scores has had an enormous influence in China's academic circles. Beginning from the 1950's, Chinese scholars began to carry out research into the transcription of the Dunhuang scores, based on Hayashi's research. Most Chinese research has consisted of reconsideration and supplementation of his work. The main areas of Chinese research into the Dunhuang scores may be considered under the following headings: the contents of the scores; classification of the notations; the *pipa* tunings; rhythm and metre; technical terms and other symbols.

1 The contents of the scores

The contents of the three scores P 3539, P 3719 and P 3808 are as follows: P 3539 contains a list of twenty different tablature symbols. These are clearly not the notation of a piece. P 3719 comprises an incomplete composition with the title Huan Xisha (Washing by the Stream); P 3808 contains twenty five complete pieces. Research on the Dunhuang music scores has tended, therefore, to focus on the twenty five pieces recorded in P 3808.

The twenty five compositions in P 3808 may be divided into two main categories. The first category, in which the name of a composition is non-programmatic, involves the word *quzi* in the name of the piece. '*Quzi*' is a general term for a short song form in the Later Tang of the Five Dynasties Period (923-936). As can be seen from table 1, the technical terms *you* (repeat), *ji* (fast), *man* (slow), *youji* (repeat fast), *youman* (repeat slow) etc. are added in front of '*quzi*'. In the second category the titles are largely programmatic: Qingbeiyue (Emptying the Cup), Xijiangyue (Moon over the Western River), Xinshizi (Involvement of the Heart), Yizhou (a place name), Shuiguzi (Water Drum Melody), Huxiangwen (The Barbarian Asks), Changshanüyin (The Changsha Maiden), Sajinsha (Scatter the Golden Sand), Yingfu (Seeking Wealth). In some case programmatic titles are preceded by technical terms, for example, *Youmanquzi* Xijiangyue and *Ji* Huxiangwen.

According to Ren Bantang (1982: 165) the compositions in the Dunhuang music scores include seven pieces which were included by the Tang dynasty's Cui Lingqin in his book, *Jiaofangji*, written in the eighth century. The seven pieces are Qingbeiyue, Xijiangyue, Xinshizi, Yizhou, Shuiguzi, *Ji*:Huxiangwen, and Sajinsha. In addition, the present writer has discovered that the piece Huan Xisha (in P 3719) was also in *Jiaofangji*. Rao Zongyi (1960) has also shown that the Dunhuang compositions, Qingbeiyue, Yizhou, Shuiguzi, Changshanüyin etc. are all Tang dynasty pieces. He has also pointed out that the song texts of Qingbeiyue, Xijiangyue, Yizhou, Shuiguzi, etc., can be seen in ancient works still extant.

P 3539	Twenty tablature symbols		
P 3719	Huan Xisha (Washing by the Stream)		
P 3808	First Group	Second Group	Third Group
	1. Pinnong (Tuning piece) 2. Pinnong 3. Qingbeiyue (Emptying the Cup) 4. *Youmanquzi* 5. *Youquzi* 6. *Jiquzi* 7. *Youquzi* 8. *Youmanquzi* 9. *Jiquzi* 10. *Youmanquzi*	11. Title unknown 12. Qingbeiyue 13. *Youmanquzi* Xijiangyue (Moon over the Western River) 14. *Youmanquzi* 15. *Manquzi* Xinshizi (Involvement of the heart) 16. *Youmanquzi* Yizhou (A place name) 17. *Youjiquzi* 18. Shuiguzi (Water drum melody) 19. *Ji*:Huxiangwen (The Barbarian Asks) 20. Changshanüyin (Song of the Changsha maiden)	21. Title unknown 22. Sajinsha (Scatter the Golden Sand) 23. Yingfu (Seeking wealth) 24. Yizhou (A Place name) 25. Shuiguzi (Water Drum Melody)

Table 1: Contents of the Dunhuang music scores

2 Classification of the notations

As early as the 1930's, the Chinese scholar Xiang Da took photographs of the Dunhuang music scores back to China. Wang Zhongmin (1950) and Ren Erbei (1954) have identified the Dunhuang music scores as *gongchepu*, a system of notation found in sources of the Sung period. In 1960, Rao Zongyi, basing his opinion on Hayashi's research and on a study of the four-stringed pipa with four frets dating back to the Tang dynasty, presently housed in the Shōsōin in Japan, questioned the *gongchepu* theory and considered that the Dunhuang music scores should be called *pipa pu* (lute (*pipa*) scores). Yang Yinliu (1964: 270), however, considers that the Dunhuang scores belong to the *gongchepu* system, and has suggested that this kind of musical notation is what people of the Song dynasty referred to as *yanyue banzipu*. Ye Dong's paper 'Research on the Dunhuang music scores' published in 1982 caused controversy in China because, following Hayashi's method, he continued to interpreted the Dunhuang music scores as *pipa*-notations. Supporters of the *gongchepu* theory believed that because some notational characters in the Dunhuang scores appeared similar to those in *gongchepu* of the Song dynasty, or its draft form *suzipu*, the Dunhuang manuscripts were an early form of *gongchepu*. It was already generally accepted, however, that *gongchepu* and *suzipu* were a type of wind music notation. The explanations written at the side of a list of twenty tablature symbols (*ershipuzi*) used in the Dunhuang music score P 3539 (see figure 1), namely 'strike the strings as chord', 'index finger strikes a chord', 'ring finger strikes a chord', 'little finger strikes a chord', show without doubt that these twenty symbols represent 20 finger positions, corresponding to 20 pitches on the four-stringed, four-fretted Tang dynasty pipa, as shown in table 2.

If we examine the twenty symbols in P 3539, the first ten contain six characters (一 久 七 八 九 十), which are related to the characters for numbers (see table 3). Because of the difficulties that arise from writing compound characters as tablature-signs, the latter ten characters do not contain characters for numbers.

	1	2	3	4	5	6	7	8	9	10	11	12	13	14	15	16	17	18	19	20
Numbers	一	二	三	四	五	六	七	八	九	十	十一	十二	十三	十四	十五	十六	十七	十八	十九	二十
Tablature-signs	一	ㄥ	ㄅ	丄	ユ	ス	七	八	几	十	ヒ	マ	フ	て	)	ム	サ	レ	之	ヤ

Table 3: Tablature signs compared with characters for numbers

When the twenty tablature-signs in P 3539 are compared with those in P 3808, it is clear that they are similar. Hayashi (1957: 37) has suggested that differences between the two sets of characters are the result of miscopying; that the position of ㄅ and) is correct, for example, in P 3808, but wrong in P 3539. Chinese scholars consider that his ideas are correct and have adopted them in making transcriptions.

Figure 1: Explanation of notational symbols (P 3539)

String name	I	II	III	IV
Open string	一	ㄥ	小	上
1st fret (index finger)	ユ	ス	七	八
2nd fret (middle finger)	几	十	比	マ
3rd fret (ring finger)	フ	て	丨	尒
4th fret (little finger)	↓	乙	之	也

Table 2: Finger positions on the Tang pipa

P 3539   一乚小上ユス七八几十比マフて丿糸丿之㇝七

P 3808   一乚ケ上ユス七八几十𠃊マフて丿厶サレ㇝メ

Table 4: The character-set in P 3539 compared with that in P 3808

3 Pipa-tunings

A four-stringed, four-fretted *pipa* contemporary with the Tang dynasty still survives today in the Shōsōin in Japan. From this *pipa* we learn the following: the distance between the open string and the first fret is a tone, and the distance between the other frets is a semitone. As a result, once the pitch of any open string is established and the fingerings indicated by the five tablature-signs are applied, the pitches corresponding to each sign can be determined. For the twenty five pieces in the Dunhuang score P 3808, however, there is no indication of the *pipa*-tuning in the score. Thus, even if one selects a tuning-pitch for one of the strings there is no way of determining the pitch of the other three strings.

It was Hayashi Kenzō (1957: 41) who first discovered that three handwriting styles had been used in copying the twenty five pieces in P 3808. He also discovered that for each of the hands the three or four tablature-signs used at the end of each piece were all completely identical. This implies that all pieces in one hand are in the same mode. He therefore divided the twenty-five pieces into three groups according to the handwriting (first group, pieces 1-10; second group, pieces 11-20; third group, pieces 21-25; see table 1), then worked out the *pipa*-tuning for each group. His calculation of the *pipa*-tuning for the three groups of pieces was based on Japanese performance practice viewed in the light of Chinese musical theory. Between 1955 and 1957 he determined three *pipa*-tunings as set out below (1957: 44):

Strings:	I	II	III	IV
First group	B	d	g	a
Second group	A	c	e	a
Third group	A	c#	e	a

Table 5: *Pipa*-tuning according to Hayashi (1957: 44)

From these three *pipa*-tunings we can then work out the pitch yielded by all tablature-signs used in each group:

		Group 1				Group 2				Group 3			
String name		I	II	III	IV	I	II	III	IV	I	II	III	IV
Frets	0	⼀ B	㇄ d	㇉ g	⊥ a	⼀ A	㇄ c	㇉ e	⊥ a	⼀ A	㇄ c#	㇉ e	⊥ a
	1	ス e	七 a	八 b		ユ B	ス d	七 f#	八 b	ユ B	ス d#	七 f#	八 b
	2	几 d	十 f		) c'	几 c		し g	) c'	十 e			
	3	𡈼 f#	? b			𡈼 e				㇀ c#		? g#	㇉ c#'
	4	㇄ g	? c'	㇇ d'		㇇ d		? a	㇇ d'	㇄ f#	? a		

Table 6: Pitches corresponding to tablature-signs in P 3808

When in 1969, Hayashi was revising his 1955-57 transcriptions, he changed the tuning for the first group of ten pieces, from B,d,g,a to E,A,d,a (1969: 209).

Chinese scholars have, in general, accepted the principles used by Hayashi in calculating the *pipa* tunings, but they have differing opinions concerning his changing of the tuning of the first group of pieces. In 1983, Chen Yingshi (1983a) re-examined the whole issue. He considered that while there were problems about the way Hayashi set about calculating the *pipa*-tunings in 1955-57, the results were tenable. He felt, however, that Hayashi's revision of the tunings for the first group of pieces in 1969 was overhasty and not warranted. His reasons were as follows:

First, when Hayashi transcribed the pieces according to the original B,d,g,a tuning, he analysed them as yielding the modes, *biangongdiao* (B C D E F# G A) and *bianzhidiao* mode (F# G A B C D E). Believing that these modes could not possibly have existed in Chinese music of the Tang period, he revised the tuning to E,A,d,a. In fact, however, the modes of the pieces transcribed according to the B,d,g,a tuning were as follows: the first, seventh, eighth, ninth and tenth pieces were typical examples of the pentatonic *juediaoshi* mode. The second, third, fourth, fifth and sixth pieces were also in *juediaoshi* but contained elements of modulation. Chen concludes, therefore, that the original tuning was tenable since all ten pieces were yielded in the *juediaoshi* mode.

A second reason for Hayashi's revision of the tunings of the first group was to match the melodies of two pieces with the same title, Qingbeiyue, which are included in both the first and second groups of pieces (see table 1). After changing the tuning, however, the two versions remained different; there were only some melodic fragments made up for the most part of the eight notational symbols which were held in common. Since, moreover, the Qingbeiyue in the first group comprises 125 notational symbols, but in the second group comprises 130 notational symbols, there is no basis for revising the original tuning on the assumption that they are the same piece.

Thirdly, the *pipa*-arpeggio which terminated all pieces in the second group was c,c,g,c', and the arpeggio in the third group was A,e,a,a that is, they are made up of notes a fifth and an octave apart. When the original tuning, B,d,g,a, was applied to the first group, the final arpeggio was B,e,b,b. Like the final arpeggio in the pieces from the second and third groups it is made up of notes a fifth and octave apart. After changing the tuning to E,A,d,a, however, the final arpeggio became E,B,f#,b, and is thus structured differently from the final arpeggios of the second and third groups.

In 1982, Ye Dong set the tuning for the first group of ten pieces as d,f,g,c', but after the criticisms of Chen Yingshi (1983b: 58) and Ying Youqin (1983) he changed it to d,f,b^b,c' (Ye 1986). This tuning is in fact the B,d,g,a tuning proposed by Hayashi between 1955 and 1957, transposed up a minor third. He Changlin (1987), on the other hand, used the string tuning B,d,g,d' for the first group, thus raising Hayashi's 1955-57 tuning of the fourth string by a perfect fourth. He gave no detailed explanation for this.

Chinese scholars have basically accepted Hayashi's three string-tunings as determined between 1955 and 1957. Only He Changlin raised the pitch of the fourth string by a perfect fourth in the first group of pieces. Thus the fourth string notes transcribed by him are a fourth higher than Hayashi's 1955-57 transcription. Hayashi's 1969 revision of the pipa-tuning for the first group of ten pieces has not been accepted in China.

4 Rhythm and metre

Alongside the tablature signs in the Dunhuang *pipa*-scores are two symbols: ▾ and ◘ . In 1938, Hayashi (1987: 4) explained ▾ as the secondary beat, and ◘ as a drum beat, like the beat marked by the *taiko* drum in Japanese music. In 1957, however, he asserted that ▾ did not imply the secondary beat (1957: 53). In 1969 he interpreted this symbol as meaning a method of plucking the pipa strings upwards (*tiao*) (1969: 216).

Zhang Shibin (1975: 297) has explained ▾ as equivalent to the Japanese biwa stroke, *hōten* (Chinese: *fangdian*) but without explaining what it meant. He also explained ◘ as the simplified form for *ju* (匀), a symbol indicating the beat (*pai*) of the music. He did not agree with Hayashi's interpretation of ▾ as *tiao* (plucking the string upwards), on the grounds that since there was already a sign for *tiao* in the score, there was no need for another symbol for the same thing.

Ye Dong (1982a: 1) adopted Ren Erbai's (1954: 456) interpretation of ▾ and ◘ . Ren transcribed ◘ as *ban* or accented beat, and ▾ as *yan* or unaccented beat (the Chinese *yiban yiyan*, 'one accented beat and one unaccented beat' is like 2/4 time in Western music, while *yiban sanyan*, 'one accented beat and three unaccented beats' is like 4/4 time). He Changlin (1987: 365) basically agrees with Ye Dong's interpretation of ◘ and ▾ , but considers that Ye Dong's transcription of the pattern ◘ ▾ ▾ as 3/4 or 6/8

Example 1: Yizhou as transcribed by Hayashi (1969),
Ye (1982), He (1987) and Zhao (1987)

time in twenty-one of the twenty-five Dunhuang compositions was not consistent with traditional Chinese musical composition since he maintained that in ancient Chinese music it was rare to find *san paizi* or triple metre. Referring to the notation of Xi'an Drum music (*Xi'an guyue*), a form of music that flourished in the Xi'an area in the late Tang and Song periods, he proposed that in actual practice ◘ indicated a duration of two metric beats. He therefore transcribed ◘ ˋ ˙ as four beats (*yiban sanyan*). Zhao Xiaosheng (1987: 16) made a further criticism of Ye Dong's transcriptions. He considered that Ye Dong imposed contemporary Western notational concepts onto the ancient music of the Tang people. In his opinion ˋ and ◘ are analogous to slight pauses in the sentences of classical Chinese, with ˋ indicating a comma and ◘ indicating a full stop. As a result he came up with a quite different type of rhythmic transcription.

As a result of the differing interpretations of ˋ and ◘ , metre and rhythm have been interpreted in four different ways. Example 1 shows a transcription of the piece Yizhou from the third group in P 3808 (see table 1) according to Hayashi (1969), Ye (1982a), He (1987) and Zhao (1987), for which the following tunings were used: Hayashi, A,C#,e,a; Ye, He and Zhao, d,f#,a,d'. Since the intervals between the strings are the same, all transcriptions have been adjusted to the same pitch for ease of comparison. Places where brackets are added to the score refer to symbols which have been added by the transcriber, or which indicate variant transcriptions. The significance of arrows in He Changlin's transcription is not clear.

5 Technical terms and other symbols

In addition to the twenty tablature-signs, and the symbols ˋ and ◘ which indicate rhythm and metre, P 3808 contains a number of technical terms and some symbols for performance techniques. Since the meanings of the technical terms are fairly clear, Chinese scholars in general agree with the interpretations of Hayashi. The first sections of compositions are called *tou* (head), and the final sections are called *wei* (tail). A repeat is indicated by *chong* (repeat) or *dierbian* (second time through). If only part of a piece is to be repeated or if a repeat is to be made from a certain place, the characters *zhu* (住) or *ji* (記), or *wang* (王) or *jin* (今) are written at the point where the repeat is to begin and are followed by separate annotations such as 'repeat from the beginning to the character *zhu* and stop', or 'repeat from the beginning to the character *ji* and stop', or 'repeat to the character *wang* at the end' or 'repeat from the beginning to the character *wang* at the end', or 'repeat from the beginning to the character *wang*' or 'repeat from the end and go to the character *jin*', etc. If only a section is to be repeated, *jin* is placed at the beginning and *he* (合) beside the final tablature sign of that section; then the following instruction is written: 'go from the character *jin* to the character *he*'. Among the technical terms there is another character *huo* (火) meaning 'urgent' or 'pressing'. The character *huo* indicates that the duration of tablature signs should be halved.

Chinese scholars basically agree with Hayashi's explanations of the symbols for performance techniques on the *pipa*. There are two main symbols for performance techniques: ╯ indicates the technique *tiao* (pluck the strings upwards) – the strings indicated by two or more tablature-signs are to be plucked from the lowest to the highest string. The symbol ╱ indicates the technique *tan* (pluck). Strings are to be plucked from higher to lower, the opposite of the plucking method *tiao*. The symbols ⁀╱ and ⁀╯ are compounds of *tiao* and *tan*: the former symbol indicates *tiao* then *tan*, and the latter symbol indicates *tan* then *tiao*. The symbol ⚭ is a compound of *tan*, *tiao*, *tan*. The symbol 丁 (*tanting* (literally 'play, stop') indicates a rest or prolongation. The symbol 彡 was not explained by Hayashi; He Changlin (1987) considers it to be a shortened form of the character 趨, which has the meaning, 'quickly play the lower sound'.

Hayashi did not transcribe technical terms and variant forms of tablature-signs found in the piece, Huang Xisha, from P 3719 (see table 1). In this score the following technical terms appear: 'slow two (*man er*)', 'quick three (*ji san*)', 'slow three (*man san*)', 'quick two (*ji er*)'. Rao Zongyi (1985: 46) considers that they are technical terms for metre used to accompany dancing. As for the character *fu* (復) in this score, Rao Zongyi is of the opinion that it is a technical term (also used for the *guqin*), which indicates a repetition of the previous tablature-sign. This score also contains the tablature sign 么 which Rao Zongyi considers to be a variant form of ㄥ (see p.64). There is another tablature-sign ヽ , which He Changlin (1987: 429) considers to be a simplified form of the character *fu*, indicating a repeat (see above).

6 Conclusion

In the fifty years since Hayashi Kenzō first carried out research into the Dunhuang music scores, no uniform transcription-method has been agreed upon. The principal areas of divergence have been the *pipa*-tunings for the first set of ten pieces in P 3808, and the handling of metre and rhythm in all the pieces. Apart from matters of detail, the main need is thus to concentrate on researching these two aspects. In this way we can achieve transcriptions which truly accord with the original features of the Dunhuang scores. It is our hope that even more scholars will throw themselves into this significant research task.

Finally I wish to thank Dr. Allan Marett for inviting me to write this article, and Ms. Coralie Rockwell for translating the text into English.

References

Chen Yinshi 1983a: 'Lun Dunhuang qupu de pipa dingxian (A discussion of *pipa*-tunings in the Dunhuang music scores)', *Guangzhou Yinyue Xueyuan Xuebao*, pp.25-39
    1983b: 'Ping Dunhuang qupu yanjiu (A critique of research into the Dunhuang music scores)', *Zhongguo Yinyue*, No.1, pp.56-59
Hayashi Kenzō & Hisao Hirade 1938: 'Biwa kofu no kenkyū (Research into old scores for *biwa*)', *Gekkan*, Vol.27, No.1. Translated into Chinese in *Yinyue Yishu*, 1987 (2), pp.1-15
Hayashi Kenzō 1955: 'Study of Explication of Ancient Musical Score of *P'i-p'a* Discovered at Tun'huang, China', *Nara Gakugei Daigaku Kiyō*, 5(1), pp.1-22
    1957: (trans. Pan Huaisu) *Dunhuang pipa pu de jiedu* (Interpretive research into the Dunhuang *pipa* scores), Shanghai Yinyue Chubanshe
    1969: *Gagaku: kogaku-fu no kaidoku*, Tokyo: Ongaku no Tomosha
He Changlin 1987: 'Dunhuang pipa pu zhi kao, jie, yi (An investigation, explanation and transcription of the Dunhuang *pipa* scores)', *1983 nian quanguo Dunhuang xueshu taolunhui zhi ji, Shiku Yishu*, Lanzhou: Gansu Renmin Chubanshe, pp.331-441
Rao Zongyi 1960: 'Dunhuang pipa pu du ji (Study notes on the Dunhuang *pipa* scores)', *Xinya Xuebao*, Vol.4, No.2, pp.249-52
    1985: 'Dunhuang pipa pu *Huan Xisha* canpu yanjiu (Research into the incomplete Dunhuang *pipa* score, *Huan Xisha*)', *Zhongguo yinyue*, No.1, pp.46-7
Ren Bantang 1982: *Tang Shengshi* (Tang poetry for singing), Shanghai: Shanghai Guji Chubanshe
Ren Erbei 1954: *Dunhuangqu Chutan* (Dunhuang Music: Preliminary Explorations), Shanghai Wenyi Lianhe Chubanshe

Wang Zhongming 1950: *Dunhuang Quzi Ci* (The Texts of the Dunhuang Quzi), Shanghai: Shangwu Yinshuguan

Yang Yinliu 1964: *Zhongguo Gudai Yinyue Shigao* (A Draft History of Ancient Chinese Music), Vol.1, Beijing: Yinyue chubanshe

Ye Dong 1982a: 'Dunhuang qupu yanjiu (Research into the Dunhuang music scores)', *Yinyue yishu*, No.1, pp.1-13

 1982b: 'Dunhuang Tangren qupu (The Tang Scores of Dunhuang); *Yinyue Yishu*', No.2, pp.1-5

 1986: *Dunhuang Pipa Qupu* (The Dunhuang Pipa Scores), Shanghai: Shanghai Wenyi Chubanshe

Ying Youqin 1983: 'Yanzhang Dunhuang qupu wei Tang pipa pu (Verification of the Dunhuang scores)', *Yinyue Yishu*, No.1, pp.25-41

Zhang Shibin 1975: *Zhongguo Yinyueshi Lunshugao* (Draft Treatise on the History of Chinese Music), Hong Kong: Union Press Ltd

Zhao Xiaosheng 1987: 'Dunhuang Tangren qupu jiezou lingjie (Another explanation of the rhythm of the Tang Score of Dunhuang)', *Yinyue Yishu*, No.2, pp.16-20

Where did *Toragaku* come from?

DAVID WATERHOUSE

Toragaku is a little-known and long defunct form of Japanese court music, which flourished in the Nara period (710-84) and for a short while thereafter, and which then disappeared, leaving few traces. This paper is the first to be devoted to it in any language, and the first discussion of it which is more than a paragraph in length. After a review of divergent Japanese theories concerning the origin of *Toragaku*, it is argued that it came in the first instance from Chejudo, the large southern island of Korea, but that it also contained elements which link it to regions in Southeast Asia and elsewhere. The names of its dances, and the fragmentary descriptions of them in the sources, suggest that it was strongly tinged with shamanism, but that it also drew on Buddhism and on traditions of Chinese court music practice. An Appendix discusses evidence for the music and dance of Dvāravatī, which currently several Japanese musicologists accept as the source of *Toragaku*.

Through the devoted efforts of a handful of scholars, chiefly French, English and Thai, the ancient Southeast-Asian kingdom of Dvāravatī has been rescued from oblivion. Using evidence from inscriptions, from scattered documentary sources, and above all from archaeology, they have illuminated many facets of its cultural history, and have established much concerning the sequence of its art-styles and the extent of its territorial influence. Yet much remains obscure: we do not know the names of its kings, its political boundaries, or the exact dates of its rise and fall. Furthermore, the precise nature of the Indian influences on it is still unclear; and there are many other topics, as well as many archaeological sites, which have yet to be explored. On the other hand, there are some questions which it may be improper to ask at all, or which at least need to be phrased with care. Some years ago M. Jean Boisselier remarked:

> The name Dvāravatī, traditionally assigned to what was long assumed to be the earliest school of art in Thailand, is but a convenient designation of questionable historical significance. Indeed, the kingdom of Dvāravatī may enjoy a celebrity far greater than is deserved, or at least greater than can be supported at present by the factual record. (Boisselier 1975: 73)

I shall not enter into these controversies and the problems of definition which they imply; but at least there is no doubt that there *was* a kingdom of Dvāravatī, and that the name can be applied to some distinctive and beautiful sculpture, most of which is Buddhist. Having admired the Dvāravatī Buddha type for many years, and having other interests besides in the art, archaeology, music and dance of Thailand, I was naturally intrigued to discover that

Toragaku, one type of court music in eighth-century Japan, was apparently introduced from Dvāravatī. I have never seen this evidence cited by any scholar of Southeast Asia, and I believe that no account of it has hitherto appeared in a Western language. However, Japanese descriptions of it are all quite summary; and in my opinion the theory needs to be re-evaluated, not least in the light of our present understanding of Dvāravatī.

Several kinds of foreign music were brought to Japan during the seventh and eighth centuries, mainly from the three Korean kingdoms and from China. Two of them, however, are supposed to have come from Southeast Asia, whether directly or indirectly: *Rin'yūgaku*, or 'Music of Lin-yi'; and *Toragaku*, 'Music of Tora'. Lin-yi is simply the Chinese name for Campā, in what is now Southern Vietnam; and *Rin'yūgaku* has attracted attention from Japanese musicologists ever since Takakusu Junjirō (1898) pointed out that some of its dances can be related to the Vedic horse-sacrifice, as well as to Buddhist themes. It is interesting to consider how this music was transmitted to the Far East and to Japan, but I shall not pause here to discuss this problem in detail.

Toragaku has been much less thoroughly studied, and there is much less evidence for it. In 731 there were no fewer than 62 performers of *Toragaku* in the Court Music Bureau; it was among the various types of music and dance performed for the Eye-Opening Ceremony of the Great Buddha of Tōdaiji, Nara, in 752; but by 809 there were only two performers of it left, and as a distinct art-form it apparently died out altogether during the ninth century. None of the dances has survived today, although the titles of four of them are preserved, together with a few other details; and Tōdaiji and its famous repository, the Shōsōin, still have some masks and other apparatus used in *Toragaku*.

1 Theories concerning the origins of Toragaku

There have been five different theories about *Toragaku*:
1. that it came from Chejudo, the island off the south coast of Korea;
2. that it came from Tukhāra in Central Asia;
3. that it came from Doulu, a place of uncertain location mentioned in Chinese sources of the Han period;
4. that it came from the Tokara Islands, off the southern tip of Kyūshū;
5. that it came from Dvāravatī.

I shall examine each of these theories in turn before discussing in detail my own tentative solution, which is syncretic in character.

The *Nihon shoki*, which was completed in 720 A.D. and is one of the two oldest Japanese chronicles, tells us that the kingdom of Tanra first sent an embassy to Japan in 661 A.D. (Iida 1940: IV, 3379); and between then and 678 it sent some six further embassies. In 679 a Japanese embassy returned from Tanra, and that is the last we hear of it in the *Nihon shoki*. It is clear from these references that Tanra corresponds to Korean T'amna, an old name for Chejudo which is still used in Korea today. The earliest reference to it in the *Nihon shoki* is actually for the 12th month, 508, reporting that the people of T'amna in the Southern Ocean for the first time had dealings with the country of Paekche (one of the three Korean kingdoms); and some of the other references give the names of the envoys: Prince Si-yŏ, the Minister Chŏn-ma, and Princes Kumaki, Kumaye, Tora, Uma and Koyŏ. (The exact readings of some of these names are conjectural.) T'amna is referred to in other Japanese and in Chinese sources (Iida 1940: V, 2591-2), sometimes written with variant phonetic characters (see glossary); but it has been assumed by Japanese scholars that the Nara-period reading for the name was Tora (or Dora), and that this was the country which gave its name to the music and dance known as *Toragaku*. This assumption goes back to the eighteenth century at least, since the earliest commentary on the *Nihon shoki*, by Tanikawa Kotosuga (1709-76), the *Nihon shoki tsūshō* (1762), simply says 'Tanra, that is to say, Tora' (Kikkawa 1965: 43).

If this is correct, *Toragaku* will have come from Chejudo; and it happens that one of the *Toragaku* pieces was called Kan to So to onna wo ubau mai, (Dance of the Korean and the man of Chu kidnapping women). (Chu was a kingdom in south central China, which flourished during the second half of the first millenium B.C.; and was known in later times above all for the *Chuci*, (Songs of Chu), a poetic anthology compiled in the second century A.D.) Chejudo today retains a distinctive culture and music of its own; so that this hypothesis cannot be dismissed out of hand, as it has been by modern Japanese musicologists[1]; and I shall return to it presently.

The second theory, put forward by Saeki Ariyoshi (1940-1: III, 233), identifies Tora as a corruption of the name Tukhāra, ancient capital of the city-state of the Tocharians, in west Central Asia. In 654, according to the *Nihon shoki*, two men and two women of Tukhāra (Japanese, *Tokara*), together with one woman from Śrāvasti (Japanese, Sha-e), were driven by a storm to Hyūga Province, in southern Kyūshū (Iida 1940: V, 3311; Aston 1896: II, 246). They appear to have stayed several years, and we learn from an entry for 659 that the Indian lady was in fact the wife of one of the Tocharians (Iida 1940: V, 3348; Aston 1896: II, 259). In the autumn of the following year this Tocharian, whose name is given as Katsuhashitatsua, wished to return to his native country, and requested an escort, saying: 'At a later date I desire to pay respects to the court of your great country, and therefore in token of this I shall leave my wife with you.' He then took a course through the Western Sea, with several tens of men (Iida 1940: V, 3360; Aston 1896: 266).

It is naturally of interest to find that a Tocharian with an Indian wife was in Japan in the middle of the seventh century: but there is no suggestion in the *Nihon shoki* that any of these unusual visitors was a musician. Tukhāra had quite close diplomatic ties with China in the seventh and eighth centuries; and the name *Tokara* appears also in the *Shoku Nihongi*, a continuation of the *Nihon shoki*, completed in 797 under the editorship of Sugano Mamichi (741-814) and others; but the association between it and *Toragaku* depends entirely on the similarity of the names, and has little else to recommend it.

The third theory identifies Tora as equivalent to the Chinese name Doulu, a principality mentioned in sources of the Western Han period and later. Doulu would be Toro in Japanese pronunciation, and Toro could have been corrupted to Tora. This theory, which would locate Tora in southern China, was first put forward by Harada Kōichi (1928)[2] and has been given sympathetic attention by Kikkawa Eishi, who describes it as 'an interesting alternative explanation' of *Toragaku* (Kikkawa 1965: 42-3). However, I believe that it can definitely be disproved.

---

[1] The theory was apparently first stated clearly by Iba (1928: 552). It is rejected with little or no comment by Kishibe (Geinōshi Kenkyūkai 1970: 11), Kikkawa (1965: 42) and others.

[2] I have not seen this book, and rely mainly on the summary by Kikkawa (1965: 42-3).

Doulu is known from the Chinese sources to have been famous for its acrobatic dances; and this led Harada Kōichi to regard *Toragaku* too as having been a species of difficult acrobatic performance, akin to the contemporary Chinese acrobatics (*sanyue*) which greatly influenced medieval Japanese performing arts. There is no other reason to believe that *Toragaku* had such a character, although the evidence is inconclusive enough to permit this interpretation. But Doulu was not in southern China, as Harada Kōichi seems to have thought: the Japanese archaeologist Harada Yoshito has shown that it may be identified as Dura-Europos, which was founded in about 300 B.C. by Seleucus Nicator as a Greek military base, and was placed under Parthian rule in the second century B.C. (Y. Harada 1966: 209-21).[3] Thereafter Merv was the Eastern outpost of the Parthians along the Silk Road, and Dura-Europos was on the West side of their domain. Both cities flourished on the silk trade; but Dura-Europos was captured by the Romans in about 165 A.D., and again became a military base. It later fell under Sāsānian rule; and by the seventh and eighth centuries had lost all its former importance.

Thus chronology alone makes it hard to identify Tora as Dura-Europos. Furthermore, *Toragaku*, as we shall see, was partly Buddhist in character; and Dura-Europos was not a Buddhist city, even though some of the early Buddhist missionaries in China came from Parthia. Mr. Bernard Goldman has identified a group of stair-risers from Gandhāra as depicting Parthians, some of whom are playing musical instruments or dancing. Their foreign appearance is immediately apparent; and he concludes that 'professional dramatic groups – actors and musicians – were active in the Parthian sphere of influence, performing Hellenic as well as native epics and sagas; that the Iranians had a formal, native type of dance and musical accompaniment, neither Indian nor Graeco-Roman; and that these dance-dramas they performed were sufficiently wide-spread and well-known that one or two significant episodes from a scene of a play were sufficient to recall the entire drama to the mind of the pilgrim in Gandhāra' (Goldman 1978: 202). None of this pictorial evidence squares with what is known about *Toragaku*; and I do not think it necessary to pursue this theory further.

A fourth theory is mentioned in two places by Dr. Kishibe Shigeo (GeinōshiKenkyūkai 1970: 11; Sōshisha 1973: 242); but he does not discuss it, and he does not seem to place credence in it. This is that Tora may be identified as referring to the seven Tokara Islands, one of the archipelagoes lying to the south of Kyūshū. This theory, like the identification with Tukhāra in Central Asia, relies mainly on the similarity of the names; the *Nihon shoki* passage would then imply that one of the islanders had an Indian wife, which is highly unlikely. Moreover, the name Tokara is written in the *Nihon shoki* with the usual Chinese characters for Tukhāra.

I can think of only two arguments in favour of the last-mentioned theory. The first is that the Tokara Islands are close to Japan: but the Japanese court music repertoire included other items that came from far away in Central Asia. The second is that it allows for a southern element which some scholars have detected in the surviving remains of *Toragaku*: but this also applies to the fifth theory, and should be discussed in conjunction with it.

---

[3] Thanks to its position on the trade routes, Parthia (Anxi in Chinese sources) had some cultural influence in China. Harada points out that Parthian costume and motifs have sometimes been wrongly identified as Scythian.

This theory, to which I therefore turn, is that Tora was Dvāravati, and it has been accepted as the most likely one by several distinguished Japanese musicologists, including Tanabe Hisao (1951: 27); Kikkawa Eishi (1965: 42), Hayashiya Tatsusaburō (Geinōshi Kenkyūkai 1970: 33) and Hayashi Kenzō (Shōsōin Jimusho 1967: 177). Only Kishibe Shigeo has recently cast doubt on it (Sōshisha 1973: 242), drawing parallels with *Rin'yūgaku*, the music of Campā. He regards the latter as an Indian music and dance form, which passed through Central Asia to China, and was then introduced to Japan by the South Indian monk Bodhisena (Japanese *Baramon Sōjō* (The Brahman Monk)) and the Campā monk known to the Japanese as Buttetsu (Phật Triệt in modern Vietnamese). On these grounds he thinks it would be unlikely that *Toragaku* came from Southeast Asia at all, even if it turned out to have Southeast-Asian elements in it.

This argument by analogy is acceptable only in part. We are told that Bodhisena came from South India (perhaps from a region under Pallava control). He decided to go to China because of the reputation of Wutaishan (in Shanxi Province) as the earthly abode of the Bodhisattva Mañjuśri (apparently since the sixth century); and it is known (as Kishibe himself recognises in a later publication (1982: 15)) that he took the sea route via the Malay peninsula. He seems to have spent little time in China before teaming up with Phật Triệt and accepting the invitation to go to Japan. In the circumstances there can have been little Central Asian influence on the original *Rin'yūgaku*; and Kishibe does not allow for the strong Indian influences on the culture of Campā (as of elsewhere in Southeast Asia) from the fourth century A.D. onwards.

There is no doubt that Dvāravati is mentioned in Chinese sources of the Tang period, and so its existence might be known to educated Japanese who had access to those sources and took the trouble to read them, or to Japanese in any walk of life who had heard of it by word of mouth. However, the name does not seem to appear in older Japanese sources in any of the forms used by Chinese writers. If the Tora of *Toragaku* does correspond to Dvāravati – and in that case the word should probably be pronounced Dora[4] – the Japanese are likely to have known of it independently. We have already seen that the references to Tanra in the *Nihon shoki* have to be taken as implying T'amna, off the coast of Korea. Another entry, for 657 (Iida 1940: V, 3325; Aston 1896: II, 251), apparently describes the same party of Tocharians mentioned earlier, although it says there were 'one man and four women', not two men and two women. They reported that they had drifted first to the Amami Islands; on the 15th day of the 7th month the Ullambana Festival (Japanese *Urabon*) for dead souls was celebrated; and in the evening 'the people from Tukhāra were entertained'. A note in the received text of the *Nihon shoki* then adds: 'Some texts say "people from Dora"'; and in this case Dora is written with the same first character as for Dvāravati, implying that this was actually meant.

It is clear that these other texts, whatever they are, were wrong. Apart from anything else, the Ullambana, which later became a major festival in Japanese Buddhism, was associated with Yogācāra Buddhism; and it would not have been particularly apt as entertainment for worshippers from Dvāravati, a Hinayāna country. Tocharians, on the other hand, would

---

[4] *Do* is more likely than *To* to have been the normal eighth-century reading of the first character.

probably have been familiar with it already. The note in the *Nihon shoki* does however show that confusion between Tukhāra and Dvāravatī goes back a long time in Japan; and both may have been confused with the Tokara Islands as well as with T'amna.

Before examining in more detail the evidence for *Toragaku* itself, I think it is worth citing one further passage about Tora, which seems to have been overlooked by musicologists. In *Konjaku monogatari*, a large collection of tales from India, China and Japan, compiled at the beginning of the twelfth century by somebody who was probably in court circles, occurs the following passage:

> To the south-west of Kyūshū, and at a great distance, it is said that there is a large island. This is certainly the place known as the island of Tora. The men of this island are human in shape, but it is a fact that they eat human beings. On this account people do not go to this island unless they have somebody to guide them. In fact I have heard that they gather together, seize people, then simply kill and eat them. That is the kind of country it is. (Iida 1940: IV, 2591)

This terrifying place cannot have been Dvāravatī; and, although the writer is only speaking from hearsay, we may imagine that if he is not referring to Chejudo itself he must be describing some other island where headhunting, if not actual cannibalism, was practised. Taiwan at once springs to mind; but Borneo, or even somewhere in another part of the Indonesian archipelago, could have given rise to such stories.

However Chejudo, a volcanic island still populated by thousands of dangerous spirits who have to be appeased and manipulated by the local shamans (*sinbang*), has myths of divine snakes, Dragon Kings and one-eyed monsters who devour fishermen; these, together with other evidence, have led modern Korean scholars to postulate a partly Southern ancestry for its culture (Chin Sŏng-gi 1983: 143). *Sinbang* rituals incorporate various archaic forms of song and dance, centred on the *Tangsin* (altar deity). One song-myth, from the Yongdong altar of Hansu-ri, Hallim, is particularly pertinent. The story

> imagines some island country across the far seas. Once upon a time, three fishermen in Hansu-ri went over the sea in a sailboat. A terrible storm blew up and they drifted into the land of the one-eyed monsters. They were saved by a man who hid them under a great rock. Soon after the one-eyed monsters followed with hunting dogs. 'Where are the fishermen we were chasing?' they demanded. 'I don't know. I'm looking for them myself,' he lied. Later, when they discovered the truth, they cut the hero into three pieces. The fishermen, forever grateful for his benevolence, have since worshipped him as the guardian deity of sea accidents. (Chin Sŏng-gi 1983: 151-2)

Even though this refers not to Chejudo itself but to somewhere reached from it, the moral for Japanese travellers would be the same. Munakata Taisha, the venerable Shintō shrine in Northwest Kyūshū, together with the uninhabited sacred island of Okinoshima, ancillary to it, has served since at least the fifth century to protect fishermen and others venturing out into the open water towards Korea. Lastly, the description of Tora in *Konjaku monogatari* certainly fits the title of the dance-piece mentioned earlier, Dance of the Korean and the man of Chu kidnapping women.

It will be becoming apparent that I do not accept the identification of Tora with Dvāravatī (see Appendix I); and that I am inclined towards the old theory that *Toragaku* came in the first instance from Chejudo. However, the problem is not quite so simple. Since Japanese have long been vague about the exact location of Tora, but were aware that it lay somewhere in the so-called 'Southern Ocean', they might naturally have incorporated into *Toragaku* various elements of music and dance which could be associated with the Southern regions; and this might include things which actually come from Dvāravatī or were at least similar to what was practised there.[5] Although there is no real evidence of diplomatic relations between Japan and Dvāravatī, we cannot rule out the possibility of more informal or indirect contacts. By the sixteenth century there were Japanese Christian mercenaries and merchants in many parts of Indo-China, including Siam; and some Siamese trading vessels reached Japanese waters (Boxer 1963: 29, 51, 146). In the seventeenth century these activities continued unabated: for example, the Japanese adventurer Yamada Nagamasa (d.1630) is said to have helped quell a rebellion in Ayudhyā with 800 Japanese soldiers, and later he subdued Ligor, taking one of the king's concubines as his wife.[6]

In connection with the Korean theory, another hypothesis, not mentioned by any previous commentator, deserves consideration. It will be remembered that the *Nihon shoki* names some of the envoys from T'amna, and that they included Princes Uma and Tora. The word *uma* in Japanese means 'horse'; and another old Japanese name for Korea was Koma, meaning 'Pony'. We shall return to the subject of horses presently. *Tora*, on the other hand, means 'tiger'; and Korea was famous in Far Eastern folklore for its tigers, who are indeed often depicted in Korean painting. *Toragaku* might, then, be 'Tiger music', that is, music and dance which incorporated tiger symbolism, or which was associated with countries where tigers were commonly found. This would in ancient times have included China and many parts of Southeast Asia, as well as India itself.

2 Dances of *Toragaku*

a   Bari mai

The musical evidence for *Toragaku* provides a few hints of Southern, as well as of Korean, connections. According to an early Heian source,[7] one of the dances was called *Bari mai*, 'Bari dance'. It was apparently for six dancers, two of them holding swords and shields, and the other four holding halberds. One straight sword, identified as a large sword for *Barigaku*, is preserved in the Shōsōin at Nara (Tanabe 1926: 222). Another source says that it was in the mode Sada-chō; that there were ten (or sometimes nine) measures; and

---

[5] Compare the contemporary Chinese image of the Southern regions, as elucidated by Edward Schafer (1967).

[6] I owe my initial awareness of Japanese in seventeenth-century Southeast Asia to Prof. John E. Wills, Jr. (University of Southern California), in a privately circulated conference paper. Recently some doubt has been cast on the legend of Yamada Nagamasa.

[7] The four dances of Toragaku are briefly described in a passage from *Ryōshūge* (40 vols.), a commentary on and translation of the Yōrō legal code (promulgated in 718). This work, which was published only in 1872, was compiled by Koremune no Naomoto (881–after 907). The passage is quoted in Jingūshichō 1936: XIV, 845-6.

that in some manuscripts it was transcribed into Banshiki-chō.[8] This second source is a treatise compiled by the court musician Koma Tomokazu (1247-1333) between 1270 and 1322. He does not mention any of the other dances of *Toragaku*, or even that *Bari mai* had been part of such a genre, and we cannot be sure that the dance was still being performed in his day.

Tanabe Hisao, in a book originally published in 1940, stated flatly that *Bari mai* was a dance from the island of Bali, and that the masks used in it were the same as Balinese masks (Tanabe 1951: 27). This idea is not as far-fetched as it sounds. There is enough evidence to suggest that Buddhism (probably with Hindu elements) was then practised in Bali, as well as probably shamanic trance rituals akin to those of today, and at Tōdaiji *Bari mai* was part of a Buddhist ceremony. Chinese sources mention that Poli (written phonetically with various other second characters, but all corresponding to Japanese *Bari*) sent embassies to China in the first quarter of the sixth century, and it even attracted a few Chinese visitors down to the late seventh century: but the old assumption, first made by Pelliot (1904: 283), that this remote Southern country was Bali has been challenged by modern scholars. Coedès (1968: 53) tentatively favoured an identification with Borneo; but Wolters (1967: 200-1) has shown conclusively that the kingdom of Poli must have been in Eastern Java. Furthermore, the supposed resemblance to Balinese masks adds up to very little. In fact, among the surviving masks at Tōdaiji, none is specifically labelled as being for *Toragaku*,[9] even though some probably were. Those which do resemble Balinese masks might also be taken to resemble sea-dragon or monster masks from many other parts of Southeast Asia, including Ceylon, Java and perhaps Dvāravati as well.

However, Tanabe was right to draw attention to the Southeast-Asian look of the Tōdaiji masks, and a more satisfactory explanation of the name *Bari mai*, as well as the character of the dance, can be found. One of the reliefs at Borobudur in Central Java (c.800) shows a battle dance with swords, shields and halberds, much as described by Koma Tomokazu. Significantly the same kind of martial dance in Bali today is called Baris. The knot can be drawn tighter if we further interpret the names Bari, Bali and Baris as all being variants of the original Indonesian equivalent for Poli (Boli in one Chinese source).

The island of Bali was undoubtedly settled from Java, and was frequently under the control of Eastern Javanese rulers. The East Javanese empire of Singhasāri invaded it in 1284, and its successor, Majapahit, invaded in 1343. Both these empires were Hindu-Javanese, and at the beginning of the sixteenth century many Majapahit princes and their retinues moved to Bali to escape from Islam (Ramseyer 1977: 55-6). As a result, over the centuries many Javanese court and ritual customs entered Bali and enriched its culture. The word *baris* in modern Indonesian means 'row', 'line', 'to drill', 'marches and parades'; and the Baris, which is nowadays usually performed as a solo war dance, is listed separately by lexicographers (Echols & Shadily 1963: 37; Schmidgall-Tellings & Stevens 1981:33), but formerly it might have had ten or twelve male dancers, and it is easy to see how folk etymology could have added a final -*s* to the name, by analogy with the word *baris*. Thus the Baris dance could literally be a survival of the old martial dances of East Java in

---

[8] *Zoku Kyōkunshō*, Book 3. See Masamune 1935: I, 168.
[9] See Nara Roku Daiji Taikan Kankōkai 1968-73, *Tōdaiji*, Vol.2, which describes all the extant masks at Tōdaiji.

the eighth century. The older history of the name 'Bali' is unknown. Crawfurd in 1856 wrote of it that 'The name in Malay and Javanese signifies "to return", but how or why imposed is unknown' (Crawfurd 1856: 28).[10] This too sounds like folk etymology, since the Malay and Javanese word he has in mind must be *balik*, meaning 'the reverse', 'the contrary', 'to change', 'to turn back', 'to return'; and the loss of final -*k* demands an explanation. The fate of Poli is unknown[11]; but, just as Hindu princes later sought refuge on Bali, Buddhist rulers of Poli may have done likewise, bequeathing the name of their kingdom to the island.

Similar dances to the Baris are found in other parts of Indonesia, notably Sumatra and Borneo (Holt 1939: 25-6; 1967: 98-9, 110-1); and can be related to the various systems of self-defence which are native to Southeast Asia, especially the *pencak silat* of Java, Sumatra and Bali, the *bersilat* of Malaysia, and the *kali* and *arnis* of the Philippines. We may extend the list further, to include Burmese *banshay* and Thai *krabi-krabong* (Draeger & Smith 1969: 177-90). Most of these martial arts have come under influence from South China, especially during the last few centuries, and, although their ostensible purpose is different from that of dance, they share something with it as ritual and from an aesthetic point of view. All of them may also be inter-related historically, if in complex ways which will never be unravelled completely. Southeast-Asian and Southern Chinese combat systems further share a number of features with those of Japan.

b   Kuta mai

Another dance in *Toragaku* was called *Kuta mai*. We know that it was performed by twenty dancers, and the only other clue to its identity is the name, which, as written in Chinese characters, is clearly a loan word. Japanese scholars offer no suggestions as to its derivation; so that, given an empty field, I shall perhaps be excused for examining the possibilities at some length.

I begin with what Prof. Kikkawa would no doubt call 'an interesting alternative explanation'. In many parts of Indonesia there are hobbyhorse dances or folk plays using a hobbyhorse, which are clearly survivals from ancient times. In Java these folk plays are known by various names, but always including the word *kuda*, 'horse'. Among the Toba Batak in Sumatra the hobbyhorse dance is called *hoda-hoda*; among other Batak tribes it is *kuda-kuda* or *huda-huda*, and is associated with funerary rites. Both the plays and the dances may involve a large number of performers, some of them masked; and frequently they go into trance. The type of hobbyhorse varies from place to place, and the Batak have substituted hornbill masks. Claire Holt, who describes these dances, concludes:

> Did the horse supplant the hornbill when a horse cult was introduced perhaps from or via India? Are the hobbyhorse dancers of the Javanese folk plays, with the accompanying masked dancers (whose presence is as ghostly as that of the ancestral masks of Batak funerary rites), unknowing perpetuators of ancient and fertility rites? And are they and the Sumatran riders of horses and hornbills both descendants

---

[10] Crawfurd had visited Bali as early as 1814, when serving in Java under Raffles.
[11] The last mention of it seems to be in an early Song dynasty gazetteer, the *Taiping Huanyuji*, compiled in the period 976-983.

of some more widespread death and fertility rites still echoed in the folk plays of other lands on the Eurasian continent? (Holt 1967: 106)

Kuta mai was a group dance; and there is actually evidence from Japan which is consistent with the idea that it may have been a hobbyhorse dance. At the present day hobbyhorse dances survive especially in Northern Japan, in Iwate, Aomori and Akita Prefectures, where they are performed by groups of up to twelve hobbyhorse dancers, accompanied by others armed with swords, quarterstaffs and shields (Gunji 1977: 160). These dances can be traced back only some two hundred years; but were probably preceded by other hobbyhorse dances in various parts of Japan. At certain Shintō shrines in Kyōto, notably the Gion Shrine and the Iwashimizu Hachimangū, it is or was the custom to perform hobbyhorse dances at festivals (Nakayama 1941: I, 610), and in the extreme south of Japan, in the Yaeyama archipelago, there are hobbyhorse dances (known as *ungunja*). Hobbyhorses were already a Japanese children's toy in the middle of the eighteenth century, and this in itself suggests they may have had a longer history as ritual implements. In the 1750's a kind of stick-horse toy became popular in Japan, and is often seen in *ukiyoe* prints of the period. This was probably copied from imported Dutch toys, and was frequently used in the *harugoma*, 'Spring Pony', a New Year dance which came into the Kabuki theatre at the end of the seventeenth century but probably has earlier roots.[12]

The horse is, to be sure, a northern animal, and reached Japan in prehistoric times via northern China and Korea; but that is not to say that a hobbyhorse dance would be associated in the Japanese mind with the steppe lands of Northern Asia. In the late eighteenth century, bean-cake sellers dressed as hobbyhorse dancers began to appear in Japan. They wore a tall Chinese or Korean hat, played a conical oboe of the kind used then in Chinese, Korean and Malay bands, and advertised their presence by crying *Honihoro! Honihoro!* It has been suggested that this was originally a Dutch word: but the Dutch word *hobbelpaard*, which would be the closest equivalent, refers to a rocking-horse rather than a hobbyhorse. Might *honihoro* represent a Chinese corruption of Malay *kudakuda*? Koreans, South Chinese and Malays all came from regions to the far southwest of Japan, and we need not expect ordinary Japanese to have kept the distinction between them entirely clear. Koreans were famous in Japan as horsemen, above all for their ability to perform acrobatic tricks on horseback (*kyokuba*), which were regularly demonstrated by members of Korean embassies to Japan in the Tokugawa period (Waterhouse 1986). Since at least the Mongol occupation in the thirteenth century Chejudo itself has been famous for horses.

The above evidence is consistent; but it may appear to be largely irrelevant to a court dance of the eighth century. Moreover, horses themselves (as opposed to sea-dragons, snakes and other exotic creatures) would naturally be associated with a Northern culture, and this is not in keeping with the generally Southern character we have posited for *Toragaku*. On the other hand, in the eighteenth and nineteenth centuries Koreans and elephants (an undoubtedly Southern animal) were mysteriously associated in the Japanese mind, and both horse-riding Koreans and Southeast Asians share further a

---

[12] I have discussed these and other points in a forthcoming publication (Waterhouse *n.d.*, *ad* No.555).

predilection for shamanism – which in turn suggests another, more attractive interpretation of *Kuta mai*.

It happens that the common Korean word for shamanic ceremony or exorcism is *kūt*, which G.J. Ramstedt connected with Tungusic *kuta*, meaning 'happiness, fortune', Manchu χ*utu*, 'the soul of a departed, a ghost'; Mongolian *qutug*, 'the happiness or glory given by the destiny, the majesty – of a ruler'; Kirgiz *qut*, 'a mythological substance like a dark red jelly, falling from heaven on to the hearth and signifying happiness; amulet; soul, strength of life'; and other words (Ramstedt 1949: 132).[13] Unlike some others proposed by Ramstedt, this etymology has been accepted by modern scholars. However, his definition of *kūt* itself as 'sorcerer's practise, magic' is unsatisfactory, since, as Michele Stephen has recently pointed out, shamanism and sorcery, though similar, differ in emphasis. Both may use ritual magic, but shamans are above all healers, while sorcerers attempt to injure or destroy other human beings (Stephen 1987: 73-5). We may add that they are probably separate historically. We may extend Ramstedt's list with Turkish *kut* ('luck, prosperity' (Alderson & Iz 1959: 206)) and Lessing's definition of Mongolian *qutug* as 'sanctity, holy rank; dignity, distinction; happiness, bliss, benediction' (Lessing 1982: 992). If loss of the initial *k-* can be explained, there may be further connexions to Mongolian *uduɤan*, Ryūkyūan *yuta*, Japanese *itako*, and so on, all meaning 'female shaman' (Lessing 1982: 861; Hori 1978: II, 653).

If we treat *Kuta mai*, then, as a shamanic dance, introduced from Chejudo, it would in the first instance have been a royal rite of benediction, apt both for the Nara court and for the sanctification of Tōdaiji. The fact that it was basically non-Buddhist would matter less than the fact that it was religious. At the present day, *kūt* are of various kinds: they embody music, dance and song; ecstasy; myth; cycles of human life and cycles of agricultural production. At the core of a *kūt* sequence (which may have twelve or more components) are the *chesŏk-kŏri*, prayers for longevity, which are Buddhist; but the cosmological framework of *kūt* is pre-Buddhist, invoking the deities of Heaven and Earth, and the instinctual forces which govern physical life. As such, it is the Korean equivalent of *kagura* and would readily have been understood in this light by Japanese of the Nara period.

The text of one *kūt* song, as presented in translation by Yu Tong-sik, embodies imagery of riding:
> There goes the dragon-horse on the way.
> There goes *Sin-sŏn* the Immortal on the back of the dragon-horse.
> (Yu 1983: 63)

This passage is from a hymn to the mountain god (*San-manura*), and casts Sin-son not simply as a Taoist Immortal, or *xian*, but also as a Korean shaman riding his horse to the realm of the spirits, in this case in the mountains, which have traditionally been regarded as the realm of the dead across a wide region embracing Japan, Korea, Taiwan, Java, Borneo and parts of Oceania (Blacker 1975: 328-29). From this point of view, therefore, our earlier interpretation of *Kuta mai* as a hobbyhorse dance, with the horses serving as symbolic vehicles for female shamans, may not be entirely fanciful, even if the immediate source of the name was the Korean word *kūt*.

Before abandoning these speculations, I shall discuss another possible etymology for *Kuta mai*, one which is phonetically plausible but otherwise fits the evidence less well. It similarly involves a cluster of words drawn from

---

[13] I am obliged to my colleague Dr. Eung-jin Baek for showing me this reference.

various languages, and all related in sound and meaning. In Ottoman Turkish, *kut* might mean 'fort, fortified place' (Özön 1965: 395); and it happens that in both Balinese and Tagalog *kuta* has the same meaning (Anandakusuma 1986: 100; Panganiban 1976: 95). At first sight one might imagine that this was pure coincidence; but a link is provided by Sanskrit *koṭa* or *koṭṭa*, meaning 'fort, stronghold' (Monier-Williams 1899: 312). Malay *kota* ('fort' (Winstedt 1952: 36)), Indonesian *kota* ('city, town' (Echols & Shadily 1963: 199)), Mongolian χ*ota(n)* ('city, town, village; enclosure; fortress; citadel; city wall' (Lessing 1982: 972)), and Ottoman *kut* are therefore all loan words from Sanskrit.

Sanskrit *koṭa* and *kuṭi* can also mean 'hut', 'cottage' and 'curvature, curve' (because ancient Indian huts – as seen in early *stūpa* reliefs, for example – and city walls were circular or curved in plan?), and there are several other related words in Sanskrit, such as *koṭi* ('curved end of a bow or of claws, etc.; end or top of anything, edge or point (of a sword), horns or cusps (of the moon); the highest point, eminence, excellence'); *kuṭa* ('a house, family; water-pot, pitcher; a fort, stronghold; a tree; a mountain'); *kuṭ* ('to become crooked or curved, bend, curve, curl...'); and *kuṇḍa* ('a bowl-shaped vessel, basin, bowl, pitcher, pot, water-pot...') (Monier-Williams 1899: 288, 289, 312). These in turn are connected with Tamil *kōḍu* ('horn'); Tamil *kutai* ('notch at end of bow to secure loop of bowstring'), Malayalam *kuṭa* ('notch of bow or arrow'), etc.; also *kudakuṭṭu* (the pot dance of Kerala); and probably also Korean *koca* ('either end tip of archery bow'); Arabic *kūkh* ('hut'); English *cottage*, etc.; and ancient Greek κότταβος ('a Sicilian game, of throwing heel-taps into a metal basin...') (Clippinger 1984: 17; Liddell & Scott 1940: 985; Vatsyayan 1968: 358-59 & pl.99; Wehr 1974: 845). In all these cases the primary notion (perhaps originally from an ancient Dravidian language) is apparently that of containment within a circle, giving defensive strength: hence also Tamil *kattu* ('to harden, congeal') and *katti* ('clod'); Kannada *kadugu* ('to become hard or solid'); Telugu *gaddu* ('hard'); Japanese *katashi* ('hard'); Turkish *kati* ('hard; violent; dry'); Mongolian χ*ata-* ('to dry, dry up; to become hard'); etc. (Clippinger 1984: 30; Lessing 1982: 943-45).

From this extraordinary extended family of words and meanings we can extract a number of possibilities for *Kuta mai*. Thus, the name could have denoted a circle dance (of strong or protective character?); a martial dance using bows; or a dance in which they balanced on or carried pots. However none of these assorted solutions carries as much conviction as that proposed previously, and it is hard to relate them to the other evidence for *Toragaku*.

Lastly, it should be mentioned that there is actually a tiny island off the west coast of Kyūshū called Kutajima. The name is written with phonetic characters, though not quite the same as those for *Kuta mai*. The same phonetic characters appear in Kuta, the name of a district in Sakyō-ku, Kyōto, which is the home of a dance cycle of over 130 pieces known as *Kuta hanagasa odori*. These dances, of uncertain age, are associated with two small Shintō shrines in the district; are performed at the time of the Bon festival in August; and use distinctive parasols decorated with several kinds of flowers (Nakai, Nishitsunoi & Misumi 1981: 160). Under Kabuki influence, *hanagasa* dances proliferated in the Edo period (being frequently depicted in *ukiyoe*), and *prima facie* it is unlikely that either of these Kuta is connected with our *Kuta mai*. Nevertheless Kutajima could have taken its name originally from a tradition there of Korean-style shamanic ritual.

The upshot of this prolonged discussion is that when we cast about from Turkey to Bali for the etymology of the innocent-seeming word *kuta*, some unexpected word-groups and cultural patterns emerge, from which it is possible to select a likely solution. For many of the languages which have been mentioned, including even Japanese, serious study of historical etymology has scarcely begun, and the reader will be tempted to resist the notion of word-groups which violate the frontiers between distinct language-families (Altaic, Indo-European, Dravidian, Malay). Nevertheless, the evidence presented above for the two main word-groups (connecting *kuta* with Korean *kŭt*, etc., on the one hand, or with Sanskrit *koṭa*, etc., on the other) cannot be gainsaid, and has not been noticed previously. Thus, the negative conclusion to be drawn from the *koṭa* group only tends to reinforce the connection with the *kŭt* group. At the present stage of our knowledge it is impossible to say whether Malay *kuda* too may somehow be connected, suggestive though its shamanic associations are, and the same applies (if in different ways) to Kutajima and the other Japanese evidence. In the absence of historical documentation for *Kuta mai*, the procedure which has been followed is a last resort, but it is designed to conform to scientific criteria.[14]

c *Kan to So to onna wo ubau mai* and *Jakin-jo mai*

There is less reason to speculate about the other two dances of *Toragaku*, although it is impossible to identify or characterise them in detail. One of them, *Kan to So to onna wo ubau mai*, has already been mentioned. Like *Kuta mai*, it was apparently for twenty female dancers, of whom five wore helmets and were girded with swords. Even though this dance too probably came from Chejudo, it is tempting to compare it with the *Serimpi* of Java, a court dance formerly performed only by high-born girls, and culminating in a mock battle with daggers and bows and arrows. In Java at least the tradition of female warrior dances can be traced back to the early tenth century, since a female dancer with a sword and shield is depicted in the Rāmāyaṇa reliefs at Prambanan; and such dances may once have been quite widespread.

It is significant that in the title of this *Toragaku* dance, Korea and Chu are linked, since both countries were famous for shamanism. For Chu, indeed, there is abundant evidence, both archaeological and literary. The archaeological material, especially from Changsha and its vicinity, in what is now the province of Hunan (South Central China), mostly belongs to the last

---

[14] An underlying hypothesis by which I have been guided is that any word embodies a root idea or meaning (defined ultimately by its use). Sometimes this meaning will not be stated even in good dictionaries of the language, so that one has to infer it from a disparate set of derived meanings. The same principle applies when one is comparing words which are apparently related in sound and meaning, either within the same language, or across a number of languages. In the latter case, the language which is the original source of the word may be unknown, or extinct, or both. In Eastern Asia, there are substantial bodies of written material datable to before c.600 A.D. only for Chinese, Sanskrit and Pali (perhaps Tamil should also be included). In the absence of written records, however, much can be done, by applying what the late Bernhard Karlgren called 'retrodiction', to reconstruct earlier forms and even proto-languages. Conclusions drawn in this way, which are necessarily tentative, should be checked against data from other kinds of cultural history, including the evidence of material culture. Analogous considerations apply, in the absence of notations or recordings, to re-constructions of the history of early music – such as that attempted in the present essay.

four hundred years B.C. and includes bronzes, lacquer objects and paintings. For example, one group of bronze vessels, datable to the first half of the 5th century B.C., is engraved all over with pictorial subjects, including scenes of shamanistic ritual with, in two cases, musicians playing the *sheng* mouth organ. There has been controversy about the sources of this type of bronze, since many of the tombs containing them are in Northern China. As Prof. Michael Sullivan has pointed out, however, the landscape and other details suggest a Southern origin (Weber 1968; Sullivan 1962). The participants are often depicted wearing fantastic headdresses, as on the bronze religious drums from the otherwise separate (and later) culture of Đông-sơn in North Vietnam. The *sheng* too was a Southern instrument.

We now know that Chu shamanic drums were hung vertically in wooden frames. Some impressive lacquered drum stands, carved in the form of addorsed cranes standing on coiled serpents or crouching tigers have been preserved in the Cleveland Museum of Art, the Museum of Fine Arts, Boston, and elsewhere (Fontein & Wu 1973: 66-9). Other lacquered wooden objects from Chu with shamanic associations include: ritual palladia in the shape of a grotesque antlered head with a long protruding tongue (Salmony 1954); a beautiful shaman's staff (in the Honolulu Academy of Arts), decorated in red and black lacquer, and having a deer-head finial (with a crouching monkey instead of the second antler). Thus deer symbolism was a feature of Chu shamanism – though not necessarily one which was represented in the Nara court dance. Lastly, of the extant paintings, the most celebrated, since its discovery in 1972, is a silk banner found in the tomb of Princess Dai (1st century B.C.) at Mawangdui, near Changsha. It is covered with motifs which symbolise stages in the soul's journey and has been discussed at length by several scholars (Hunan-sheng Bowuguan & Zhongguo Kexueyuan Kaogu Yanjiusuo 1973; Loewe 1979; Pirazzoli-t'Serstevens 1982: 59-60). Another important source is the so-called Chu Silk Manuscript, in the former Sackler collection (Barnard 1972). Space prevents us from describing any of this material in detail.

Apart from the modern archaeological discoveries, Chu has been famous since ancient times for the *Chuci*, a beautiful and highly distinctive anthology of poetry, compiled by the scholar Wang Yi (d.158 A.D.). The poems, which range in date from the 3rd century B.C. onwards, are in Chinese. Chinese sources tell us, however, that the men of Chu were regarded as foreigners, half-barbarian, for whom this must originally therefore have been an alien tongue (as it later was for Korean and Japanese poetasters). From our point of view, the most interesting poems in the collection are *Li Sao* ('On Encountering Sorrow'), which narrates a mystical journey through the sky, in search of the perfect woman, and *Jiuge* ('The Nine Songs'), a group of shorter songs intended for performance rather than reading. Both *Li Sao* and *Jiuge* are pervaded with the imagery of shamanic flight. In *Li Sao* the hero is ultimately advised to pursue his lady unaided and departs for the holy Kunlun Mountains. The *Jiuge* poems are literary adaptations of shamanic ritual verses, in some ways reminiscent of those for *kūt*. To quote Hawkes's characterisation of the sequence:

> Male or female shamans – it is not always clear which – having first purified and perfumed themselves and dressed up in gorgeous costumes, sing and dance to the accompaniment of music, drawing the gods down from heaven in a sort of divine courtship. The religion of which these songs are the liturgy is a frankly erotic one...

My own view is that it [*Jiuge*] was written for a court which enjoyed the performance of religious masques in much the same way as European courts once enjoyed religious music composed by talented laymen... (Hawkes 1959: 35-36)

We may add that the dancers also take up flower-offerings, brandish swords, beat drums, and sing to the accompaniment of mouth-organ and zither – reminding us that the Mawangdui tombs also contained examples of these and other instruments.

The relevance of this to the dance *Kan to So to onna wo ubau mai* is plain, and the reader is urged to consult the translations of *Jiuge* by Prof. Hawkes and by Arthur Waley (Waley 1955). Although Chu had disappeared from the map by the eighth century, memories of it lasted, and there were even short-lived dynasties which attempted to revive the name. One of these was founded in 617 A.D. by Lin Shihong in the Jiangnan-Lingnan region, but was crushed five years later by the new Tang rulers. Chu and the *Chuci* itself would certainly have been familiar to literate Japanese in the eighth century, though evidence on this last point is hard to come by.

Kan to So to onna wo ubau mai sounds like a story-telling piece, but, as with the *Li Sao* and the *Jiuge* poems, perhaps it was intended to be taken on more than one level. Thus, the woman who was kidnapped (or robbed, either interpretation is possible) could have been Xi Wang Mu, the Queen Mother of the West, who was Keeper of the Peaches of Immortality. We shall never know, but at least the shamanic character of this dance, as of others in *Toragaku*, seems to be confirmed.

The remaining dance in *Toragaku* was *Jakin-jo mai*, 'Dance of the women who interdict wickedness (or falsehood)'. It was performed by five people, of whom three were dancers and two held flowers. The name suggests that it was an apotropaic dance of shamans, though it is just possible also to interpret *jakin* in a Buddhist sense as referring to the Five False Views. In Korean it would be *sagŭm*.

3 Musical instruments

Hardly any information is preserved about the musical instruments used in *Toragaku*. One source[15] tells us that in 809 there were two performers of *Toragaku* in the Court Music Bureau, who were 'masters of drumming, dancing, etc.', but we might have inferred anyway that *Toragaku* was accompanied by drums, since at least three of its pieces were martial and vigorous in character. Perhaps the drum was the main instrument, and was used as it is today in *pencak silat* and some other Asian martial arts, to provide a stimulating rhythmic framework for the performers' movements. If, as we have argued, it also had a strongly shamanic character, the drum (supplemented by the mouth organ, another shamanic instrument) would be most apt for the purpose. As Eliade remarks, 'The drum has a role of the first importance in shamanic ceremonies' (1964: 168). It happens too that the oldest and most general Japanese word for drum, *tsuzumi*, derives from Sanskrit *dundubhi*: and though in this case a Central Asian transmission is

---

[15] The *Nihon kōki*, compiled in 840 A.D., in 40 vols, cover the period from 792 to 833. The passage is quoted in Jingūshichō 1936: Vol.14, 846. Hayashi Kenzō (in Shōsōin Jimusho 1967: 177) wrongly gives the source as *Ruijū kokushi*. The same information is repeated in *Ryōshūge* (see note 7 above).

likely, the mainland and shamanic associations of drums for early Japanese people are suggested even by this. We do not know what kind of drum was used for *Toragaku*: but a two-headed hourglass drum, of the type which is represented in the Shōsōin, or one of the other types which are depicted on the famous ink-painted bow in the same collection, would have been suitable (Shōsōin Jimusho 1967: CPl 26; Pll 192-9).

One last clue to the nature of *Toragaku* is a reference in *Tōdaiji yōroku*, a manscript chronicle of Tōdaiji compiled in 1134 or slightly earlier by a monk of the monastery. As part of the festivities for the Eye-Opening of the Great Buddha in 752 there was '*Toragaku* at the four monasteries for a *gyōdō*, twice round completely. Left and Right divided, and stood in front of the hall'. A note adds that 'The Minister of the Left and his subordinates beat on the drum, and went up to the dais' (Tsutsui 1944: 49). The four monasteries in question are apparently Daianji, Yakushiji, Gangōji and Kōfukuji, all at Nara; *gyōdō* was a Buddhist religious procession, during which some of the monks taking part would chant *sūtras*, and others might be dressed as Bodhisattvas, with special masks. This type of ceremony still survives at some monasteries in Japan. Thus we learn that *Toragaku* might be used to accompany a Buddhist ceremony and that distinguished amateurs might assist with it. Various other types of court music and dance were performed on the same occasion, and the Minister of the Left also played the drum for some kind of martial dance with shields – which again sounds like a *Toragaku* piece.

4 Conclusion

Of necessity, the above discussion has been largely speculative, but it does enable us to draw some tentative conclusions concerning *Toragaku*. As a type of Japanese court music it must have had a vaguely Chinese character, and, like other types of Japanese court music, especially *Gigaku* and *Rin'yūgaku*, it had Buddhist overtones, or at least could be performed in a Buddhist context as well as at court. Basically, however, it seems to have been shamanic. The repertoire was no doubt larger than the four pieces whose titles are preserved, and in the second and third quarters of the eighth century it enjoyed a considerable vogue, but it was never as important as *Rin'yūgaku*, and certainly far less important than other Japanese court music of Chinese and Korean derivation.

I have examined the various theories which Japanese musicologists have put forward about the original home of *Toragaku*, and have shown that there is good reason for favouring the traditional theory which locates it in Cheju Island, off the south coast of Korea. The generally accepted theory that it came from Dvāravatī will not stand serious scrutiny, and in support of the theory, Japanese musicologists cite only an article published in 1943, by Yamamoto Tatsurō (Yamamoto 1943).[16] This article, a well-informed piece of work, is based on a study of ancient Chinese sources for Dvāravatī, and it proposes interesting identifications for Tanling, Tuoyuan, Bola and other mysterious places mentioned by them in the same contexts: but Yamamoto

---

[16] Recently, following Yamamoto, one Japanese art historian has sought to identify certain figures on the base of the famous image of Yakushi (Bhaisajyaguru) at Yakushiji, Nara, as being of men from Dvāravatī (Itō 1979). The argument depends on accepting the *Nihon shoki* references to Tokara (see above p.75) as implying Dvāravatī rather than Tukhāra; but on iconographic grounds alone it is quite unconvincing.

says nothing at all about *Toragaku*, and nothing either about music and dance. Nevertheless, I do suggest that there was a Southern and specifically Southeast-Asian colour to *Toragaku*; and I have cited analogues particularly from Indonesia for three of the dances. Japanese spectators, however, would have identified it in the first instance as Korean – even if visitors from Chejudo (or from Poli) might have regarded it as a pastiche.

The tantalising puzzle of *Toragaku* reminds us that music and dance are the most fleeting of art-forms; that there are yawning gaps in their history which can never be filled. Nevertheless, candour obliges us to acknowledge the gaps, and there is nothing wrong with taking calculated risks in the attempt to bridge them. The problem of disentangling influences is complicated when similar motifs, techniques, words and so on turn up everywhere from India to Japan and beyond: but they do have a history, and the excesses and errors of early diffusionists should not dissuade us from trying to reconstruct it. In the process, we must often draw on linguistic, literary, archaeological and artistic evidence, as well as purely musical sources. In this paper 'tentative solutions' (in Sir Karl Popper's sense (Popper 1972)) have been proposed to a specific set of problems, and previous suggestions have been challenged or modified, but the possibilities have not been exhausted, and new evidence may also come to light. Popper's model allows for 'error elimination', leading to further 'tentative solutions'; and it is to be hoped that this will occur. Meanwhile, as Sir Thomas Browne remarked in a similar context, 'With what difficulty, if possibility, you may expect satisfaction concerning the Musick, or Musical Instruments of the Hebrews, you will easily discover if you consult the attempts of learned men upon that Subject'.[17]

---

[17] Sir Thomas Browne, 'Of Cymbals, Etc.' in *Certain Miscellany Tracts* (1684) (Browne 1912: III, 301).

Appendix: Music and dance of Dvāravatī

In discussing the Dvāravatī theory for *Toragaku*, we have not considered the musical evidence from Dvāravatī itself. Unfortunately this evidence is even more meagre than that for *Toragaku*; but, as our understanding of the cultural situation of Dvāravatī improves, it should be possible to interpret it with more confidence. The Buddha image of Dvāravatī, for example, now seems to derive not so much from that of Gupta India, as from intermediate types which were modelled directly on the style of Amarāvatī. Further, a bronze Buddha of Amarāvatī type has been found in Western Sulawesi; and another, from Kota Bangun in Borneo, looks as if it was imported from Dvāravatī itself.[18] This being so, we may hypothesise that the music and dance of Dvāravatī were not derived directly from Gupta court music and dance, or by implication from such a canonical text as the *Nāṭyaśāstra*, but rather from regional post-Gupta forms of Eastern India, especially Andhra and Orissā; that directly or indirectly they influenced court music and dance in the Indonesian archipelago; and that they also incorporated what Dr. Quaritch Wales liked to call 'local genius'. Secondly, we can postulate that during the ninth century there was an influx of influence from Srīvijaya, which is another blank on our musical map but which had cultural connexions with Pāla Bengal; and that in the eleventh century there was some influence of another kind from Khmer music and dance. We may also expect to find similarities with the music and dance of Môn Burma, as well as with that of the Pyū kingdom just to the north of it.

So far as I am aware, there is no text, in Chinese or any other language, which throws light directly on the music and dance of Dvāravatī; and the archaeological evidence is quite scanty. The most fruitful sites are Ku Bua and Kok Mai Den; but the former is untypical, since its Buddhism was apparently Mahāyāna. Dr. Quaritch Wales has speculated that it represents a settlement of 'gifted Mahayanist monks from Western India' (Quaritch Wales 1969: 62), so that it must be treated with some caution.

On the other hand, in the *Xin Tang shu* ('New Tang History'), there is a very detailed description of a Pyū orchestra which went from Burma with a delegation to China in 802; and several other references to it appear in Chinese sources. The Pyū practised Hīnayāna, and we learn that the twelve pieces played by the orchestra of thirty-five musicians were all on Buddhist themes. We are also given descriptions and tunings of all the instruments (Twitchett & Christie 1959; Picken 1984).

It has been pointed out that many of these instruments differed from those of modern Burmese music, and also from those of medieval Burmese music, so far as its nature can be determined from inscriptions and reliefs at Pagān. Nevertheless, there is some continuity, and it is interesting to find that one or two of these instruments appear in the art of Dvāravatī. At Wat P'ra Pat'on, for example, was found a small bronze bell; the *Xin Tang shu* speaks of 'four small bells (*ling-ba*) arranged like those of the Kucha section [of the Court orchestra]. They were three inches in circumference and were threaded on leather thongs. They were struck in time with the rhythm of the music' (Twitchett and Christie 1959: 185).

Wat P'ra Pat'on also yielded small bronze jingles, perhaps part of a dancer's equipment; a stirrup-shaped jingle, probably the finial of a Buddhist

---

[18] Both bronzes are in the National Museum, Jakarta (Bernet Kempers 1959: 24, 97).

staff; and a pair of hand-cymbals, such as are still commonly used in Thai music to keep the time. These hand-cymbals are seen again in two almost identical stucco reliefs from Ku Bua, which also show a five-stringed short lute. The latter is of exactly the same type as is seen at Amarāvatī, in the second century A.D., and again at Pawaiya in Gwalior State in the fifth century, and it is supposed to have been introduced into North China from Kuča, probably in the sixth century. Kuča, like Dvāravatī, practised Hīnayāna: but, apart from the fact that Ku Bua was a Mahāyāna site, we cannot conclude that the five-stringed lute was specific to Hīnayāna Buddhism, and the Pyū orchestra did not possess one. In the seventh century the five-stringed lute found its way to Japan (from China or Korea), and a magnificent eighth-century example is preserved in the Shōsōin. There is no evidence that it was used in *Toragaku*.

Another musical instrument which had Buddhist associations and which very probably existed in Dvāravatī was the arched harp. This instrument, which can be traced back to Sumeria, appears in early Indian Buddhist art, for example at Bhārhut (second century B.C.), Bhājā (first century B.C.) and Amarāvatī, and is played together with the five-stringed lute at Pawaiya. It spread beyond India to Pyū territory by A.D. 300 (Becker 1967: 18-9), is seen at Anurādhapura in Ceylon, at Borobudur and Kediri in Java, and at Angkor Thom in Cambodia; today it is something of a national instrument in Burma. The modern Thai version is the *p'in* (see Kunst 1968: 9f). No clear representation of such an instrument has turned up from Dvāravatī, but one stucco from Ku Bua seems to show a harpist.

We can be fairly confident that the musical instruments of Dvāravatī might also have included a three-stringed short lute, a mouth-organ, some kind of flute, and some kind of waisted drum. All these were in the Pyū orchestra, and were common in other parts of ancient Southeast Asia and Indonesia. It is also likely that there was some kind of zither, but probably not the sets of tuned gongs and xylophones which are associated with later Southeast-Asian court music. Some of the instruments in the Pyū orchestra are too unusual to permit any generalisation but the Chinese descriptions convey a strange mixture of sophistication and savagery, which may also have been the impression created by the music of early Dvāravatī.

As for the dance of Dvāravatī, there are occasional figures which show dancers, but it is hard to draw any conclusions from them. Dupont illustrated a small bronze (in the National Museum, Bangkok) of a dancing Buddha in Dvāravatī style, which he considered to be a faulty casting (Dupont 1959: pl.467; 221, 225-26). Prof. Subhadradis Diskul, however, has informed me that this piece, which looks so much like a prototype of the Sukhodaya 'Walking Buddha' image, is in fact an archaistic piece of the latter period. It can therefore be eliminated.

References

Alderson, A.D. & Fahir Iz 1959: *The Concise Oxford Turkish Dictionary*, Oxford: Clarendon Press

Anandakusuma, Sri Reshi 1986: *Kamus Bahasa Bali. Bali–Indonesia,Indonesia–Bali*. Den Pasar: CV. Kayumas

Aston, W.G. 1896: *Nihongi. Chronicles of Japan from the Earliest Times to A.D. 697*, (2 vols. in 1). Repr. Rutland, Vermont, and Tokyo: Charles E. Tuttle Company, 1972

Barnard, Noel, ed. 1972: *Early Chinese Art and Its Possible Influence in the Pacific Basin*, New York: Intercultural Arts Press

Becker, Judith 1967: 'The Migration of the Arched Harp from India to Burma', *Galpin Society Journal*, XX (March 1967), pp.17-23

Bernet Kempers, A.J. 1959: *Ancient Indonesian Art*, Cambridge, Mass.: Harvard University Press

Blacker, Carmen 1975: *The Catalpa Bow. A Study of Shamanistic Practices in Japan*, London: George Allen & Unwin, Ltd

Boisselier, Jean 1975: *The Heritage of Thai Sculptures*, New York & Tokyo: Weatherhill

Boxer, C.R. 1963: *The Great Ship from Amacon. Annals of Macao and the Old Japan Trade, 1555-1640*, Lisboa: Centro de Estudos Históricos Ultramarinos

Browne, Sir Thomas 1912: *The Works of Sir Thomas Browne*, ed. Charles Sayle (3 vols.), Edinburgh: John Grant

Chin Sŏng-gi 1983: 'Tangsin: Cheju Shamanism', *Korean National Commission for UNESCO* 1983: 141-64

Clippinger, Morgan E. 1984: 'Korean and Dravidian: Lexical Evidence for an Old Theory', *Korean Studies*, VIII: 1-57

Coedès, George 1968: *The Indianized States of Southeast Asia*, ed. Walter F. Vella, translated by Susan Brown Cowing, Honolulu: East-West Center Press

Crawfurd, John 1856: *A Descriptive Dictionary of the Indian Islands and Adjacent Countries*, London: Bradbury & Evans. Repr. Varanasi: Chaukhambha Orientalia, 1974

Draeger, Donn F. & Robert W. Smith 1969: *Asian Fighting Arts*, Tokyo & Palo Alto: Kodansha International Ltd

Dupont, Pierre 1959: *L'archéologie mône de Dvāravatī* (2 vols.), Publications de L'Ecole Française d'Extrême-Orient, Vol.XLI, Paris: Ecole Française d'Extrême-Orient

Echols, John M. & Hassan Shadily 1963: *An Indonesian-English Dictionary*, Ithaca & London: Cornell University Press

Eliade, Mircea 1964: *Shamanism. Archaic Techniques of Ecstasy*, Princeton: Princeton University Press

Fontein, Jan & Tung Wu 1973: *Unearthing China's Past*, Boston: Museum of Fine Arts

Geinōshi Kenkyūkai, ed. 1970: *Gagaku*, Nihon no koten geinō, Vol.2, Tokyo: Heibonsha

Goldman, Bernard 1978: 'Parthians at Gandhara', *East and West*, New Series XXVIII, Nos.1-4: 189-202

Gunji Masakatsu 1977: *Nihon buyō jiten*, Tokyo: Tōkyōdō

Harada Kōichi 1928: *Kinsei Nihon engeki no genryū*, Tokyo: Shibundō

Harada Yoshito 1966: *Tō-A ko bunka ronkō*, Tokyo: Yoshikawa Kōbunkan

Hawkes, David 1959: *Ch'u Tz'u. The Songs of the South. An Ancient Chinese Anthology*, London: Oxford University Press. Repr. Boston: Beacon Press, 1962

Hayashiya Tatsusaburō 1970: 'Gagaku no haikei', in Geinōshi Kenkyūkai 1970: 27-42

Holt, Claire 1939: *Théâtre et danses aux Indes néerlandaises*, Paris: Librairie C.-P. Maisonneuve 1967: *Art in Indonesia. Continuities and Change*, Ithaca: Cornell University Press

Hori Ichirō 1978: *Waga kuni minkan shinkō-shi no kenkyū* (2 vols., 13th printing), Tokyo: Tōkyō Sōgensha (first published 1953)

Hunan-sheng Bowuguan and Zhongguo Kexueyuan Kaogu Yanjiusuo, eds. 1973: *Changsha Mawangdui yihao Han mu* (2 vols.), Beijing: Wenwu Chubanshe

Iba Takashi 1928: *Nihon ongaku gairon*, Tokyo: Kōseikaku Shoten. Repr. Tokyo: Gakujutsu Bunkan Fukyūkai, 1969

Iida Takesato 1940: *(Zōho seikun) Nihon shoki tsūshaku* (6 vols.), Tokyo: Unebi Shobō (originally published 1902-09)

Itō Shōji 1979: 'Yakushiji no Dovāravatei-jin', *Tōhōgaku* 57, 1-16

Jingūshichō, ed. 1936: *Koji ruien*, Tokyo: Koji Ruien Kankōkai

Kikkawa Eishi 1965: *Nihon ongaku no rekishi*, Osaka: Sōgensha

Kishibe Shigeo 1970: 'Gagaku no genryū', in Geinōshi Kenkyūkai 1970: 7-26

1982: *Kodai Shiruku Rōdo no ongaku. Shōsōin, Tonkō, Koma o tadotte*, Tokyo: Kōdansha

Korean National Commission for UNESCO, ed. 1983: *Korean Folklore*, Seoul: The Si-sa-yong-o-sa Publishers, Inc., & Arch Cape, Oregon: Pace International Research, Inc.

Kunst, Jaap 1968: *Hindu-Javanese Musical Instruments*, The Hague: Martinus Nijhoff
Lessing, Ferdinand G. et al. 1982: *Mongolian-English Dictionary*, Bloomington: The Mongolia Society, Inc.
Liddell, Henry George & Robert Scott 1940: *A Greek-English Lexicon*, 9th edition, ed. Sir Henry Stuart Jones & Roderick McKenzie, Oxford: Clarendon Press
Loewe, Michael 1979: *Ways to Paradise. The Chinese Quest for Immortality*, London: George Allen & Unwin
Masamune Atsuo, ed. 1935: *Zoku Kyōkunshō*, Nihon koten zenshū series, Tokyo: Nihon Koten Zenshū Kankōkai
Monier-Williams, Sir Monier 1899: *A Sanskrit-English Dictionary*, new edition, Oxford: Oxford University Press
Nakai Kōjirō, Nishitsunoi Masahiro & Misumi Haruo 1981: *Minzoku geinō jiten*, Tokyo: Tōkyōdō Shuppan
Nakayama Tarō 1941: *Nihon minzokugaku jiten* (revised edition, 2 vols.), Tokyo: Gotō Shoin
Nara Roku Daiji Taikan Kankōkai, ed. 1968-73: *Nara roku daiji taikan*, Tokyo: Iwanami Shoten (14 vols.)
Özön, Mustafa Nihat 1965: *Buyuk Osmanlica-Turkçe Sözlük*, 4th edition, Istanbul: Inkilap ve Aka
Panganiban, Jose Villa 1976: *Diksiyunaryong Pilipino-Ingles*, 2nd edition, Manila: Bede's Publishing House, Inc.
Pelliot, Paul 1904: 'Deux itineraires de Chine en Inde à la fin du VIIIe siècle', *Bulletin de l'Ecole Française d'Extrême-Orient* 4: 131-413
Picken, Laurence 1984: 'Instruments in an Orchestra from Pyū (Upper Burma) in 802', *Musica Asiatica* 4: 245-70
Pirazzoli-t'Serstevens, Michèle 1982: *The Han Dynasty*, New York: Rizzoli International Publications, Inc.
Popper, Karl R. 1972: *Objective Knowledge. An Evolutionary Approach*, Oxford: Clarendon Press
Quaritch Wales, H.G. 1966: 'Dvāravatī in South-East Asian Cultural History', *Journal of the Royal Asiatic Society*, 40-52
   1969: *Dvāravatī. The Earliest Kingdom of Siam (6th to 11th Century A.D.)*, London: Bernard Quaritch, Ltd
Ramseyer, Urs 1977: *The Art and Culture of Bali*, Oxford, Oxford University Press
Ramstedt, G.J. 1949: *Studies in Korean Etymology*, Helsinki: Suomalais-Ugrilainen Seura
Saeki Ariyoshi, ed. 1940-1: *Zoho Rikkokushi* (12 vols.), Tokyo: Asahi Shimbunsha
Salmony, Alfred 1954: *Antler and Tongue. An Essay on Ancient Chinese Symbolism and Its Implications*, Ascona: Artibus Asiae
Schafer, Edward H. 1967: *The Vermilion Bird. T'ang Images of the South*, Berkeley & Los Angeles: University of California Press
Schmidgall-Tellings, A. & Alan M. Stevens 1981: *Contemporary Indonesian English Dictionary*, Chicago, Ohio University Press
Shōsōin Jimusho, ed. 1967: *Shōsōin no gakki*, Tokyo: Nihon Keizai Shimbunsha
Smith, R.B. & W. Watson, ed. 1979: *Early South East Asia. Essays in Archaeology, History and Historical Geography*, New York & Kuala Lumpur: Oxford University Press
Sōshisha, ed. 1973: *Gagaku*. Tokyo: Sōshisha
Stephen, Michele, ed. 1987: *Sorcerer and Witch in Melanesia*, Carlton, Victoria: Melbourne University Press
Sullivan, Michael 1962: *The Birth of Landscape Painting in China*, Berkeley and Los Angeles: University of California Press
Takakusu Jungirō 1898: 'Nara-chō no ongaku koto ni 'Rinyū hachigaku' ni tsuite', *Shigaku zasshi* XVIII, No.6: 1-15; No.7: 53-92
Tanabe Hisao 1926: *Nihon ongaku no kenkyū*, Tokyo: Kyōbunsha
   1951: *Nihon ongaku gairon*, Ongaku Bunko 32, Tokyo: Ongaku no Tomosha
Tsutsui Eishun, ed. 1944: *Tōdaiji yōroku*, Osaka: Zenkoku Shobō
Twitchett, D.C. & A.H. Christie 1959: 'A Medieval Burmese Orchestra', *Asia Major*, New Series vol.VII, parts 1-2: 176-95
Vatsyayan, Kapila 1968: *Classical Indian Dance in Literature and the Arts*, New Delhi: Sangeet Natak Akademi
Waley, Arthur 1955: *The Nine Songs. A Study of Shamanism in Ancient China*, London: George Allen and Unwin, Ltd
Waterhouse, David 1986: 'Korean Music, Trick Horsemanship and Elephants in Tokugawa Japan', in Tokumaru Yosihiko & Yamaguti Osamu, eds., *The Oral and the Literate in Music* (Tokyo: Academia Music Ltd.): 353-70
   (n.d.): *The Harunobu Decade. A Catalogue of Woodcuts by Suzuki Harunobu and His Followers in the Museum of Fine Arts, Boston*, typescript, 6 vols., not yet published

Weber, Charles D. 1968: *Chinese Pictorial Bronze Vessels of the Late Chou Period*, Ascona: Artibus Asiae
Wehr, Hans 1974: *A Dictionary of Modern Written Arabic*, ed. J. Milton Cowan, 3rd printing, Beirut: Librairie du Liban, & London: Macdonald & Evans, Ltd.
Winstedt, Sir Richard 1952: *Dictionary of Colloquial Malay (Malay-English & English-Malay)*, Singapore: Kelly & Walsh, Ltd
Wolters, O.W. 1967: *Early Indonesian Commerce. A Study of the Origins of Śrīvijaya*, Ithaca & London: Cornell University Press
   1968: 'Ayudhyā and the Rearward part of the World', *Journal of the Royal Asiatic Society*, 1968: 166-78
Wu Nanxun 1964: *Lüxue hui tong*, Beijing: Kexue Chubanshe
Yamamoto Tatsurō 1943: 'Dawara kō', *Shirin* XVIII, 4, pp.347-68
Yu Tong-sik 1983: 'The World of Kut and Korean Optimism', in Korean National Commission for UNESCO 1983: 48-63

Musico-religious implications of some Buddhist views of sound and music in the Śūraṅgama Sūtra

GREGG W. HOWARD

> This paper suggests that the seventh century Chinese *Śūraṅgama Sūtra* may be relevant in attempting to understand various historical and philosophical aspects of the Japanese Fuke sect of Zen Buddhism and its practice of *shakuhachi* playing as a spiritual exercise. While the *Śūraṅgama Sūtra* cannot be regarded as a direct source of the spiritual practice of *shakuhachi* in Fuke Zen, it nonetheless provides an historically and conceptually relevant basis for understanding some religious and philosophical ideas of the Zen *shakuhachi* tradition. The sutra's historical origins and close identification with the Zen tradition in China and Japan are discussed, and the concept of a meditation on sound expounded in this sutra is examined.

In my studies of the use of the Japanese *shakuhachi* in the Fuke sect of Zen Buddhism, I have been continually puzzled by the tradition which traces the playing of *shakuhachi* as a religious practice back to the T'ang period Chinese Zen (Chinese: Ch'an) figure P'u-hua (read Fuke in Japanese). This tradition, recorded in the middle Edo period source *Kyotaku Denki*[1] but certainly much older, does not attempt to ascribe to Fuke either the playing of *shakuhachi* or any knowledge of it whatsoever. Indeed Fuke's only musical connection was his ringing of a bell as he wandered the streets, the sound of which is said to have been captured after his death by a *shakuhachi*-playing disciple, Chang Po, and turned into the first piece of the Fuke repertoire, *Kyotaku*.[2] It is now generally accepted that this history was largely fabricated in order to legitimize the Fuke sect, by establishing an elaborate genealogy leading back to the very source of the Zen tradition in T'ang period China and to a figure (Fuke) traditionally associated with Rinzai Gigen (Chinese: Lin Chi I-hsüan), one of the great figures of early Zen.

Accepting first, that the Fuke sect, a minor sub-branch of Rinzai Zen, would wish to establish some historical connection with Rinzai himself, and secondly, that in so doing they chose as their patriarch a figure, perhaps the only eligible one, whose way of expressing his Zen included the sounding of an instrument (albeit a handbell), I am still inclined to seek further for some doctrinal or philosophical connection between what we know of the practice of the later Fuke sect in using the *shakuhachi* as an instrument of *dharma* and as a tool of enlightenment, and the Zen of the eighth and ninth centuries in China.

---

[1] An English translation is available in Tsuge 1977: 47-63.
[2] The documents of the Fuke tradition and its history are clearly discussed in Sanford 1977: 411-40.

In this respect, the brief existing historical references to Fuke, notably in the *Rinzairoku* (Records of Rinzai)[3], are of little assistance. They paint for us a vivid picture of Fuke, braying like a donkey in response to a question of Zen, knocking over dinner tables, ringing his bell, and in Rinzai's words, 'go[ing] through the streets acting like a lunatic' (Sasaki 1975: 41). But they do not clarify how a spiritual tradition based in the blowing of *shakuhachi* could grow from this source.

To this end, I believe one might focus with profit on a significant Chinese sutra of the period, the *Śūraṅgama Sūtra*, to which passing reference has been made in the context of discussion of Fuke *shakuhachi* by some other writers, in particular by Blasdel (1984). Chinese tradition regards this work as a sutra of Sanskrit origin translated into Chinese at the beginning of the eighth century by Paramartha (Sangharakshita 1985: 201, 267), however it appears that it is in fact a work of indigenous Chinese origin (Bielefeldt 1986: 154), probably written in the seventh century. No Sanskrit version of the sutra either exists or is quoted in other Sanskrit sources (von Staël-Holstein 1936: 137; Sangharakshita 1985: 201). The *Śūraṅgama Sūtra* (commonly known as The Great Crown Sutra)[4] is frequently confused in the literature with the *Śūraṅgamasamādhi Sūtra* (common title, 'Heroic Marching Sutra'), a Sanskrit work translated into Chinese by Kumarajiva in the fifth century.[5] The two sutras are unrelated.

It is relevant to note however that regardless of its authenticity, which is sometimes questioned even within the tradition itself,[6] the *Śūraṅgama Sūtra* exerted significant influence on T'ang Buddhism, and in particular on Ch'an (Zen), within which tradition it emerged (Mizuno 1982: 117; Sangharakshita 1985: 202). This association with Zen is not surprising in view of the subject matter of the sutra, which is largely concerned with determining the most effective method of achieving meditative absorption and ultimate insight, and the significance of the sutra for the Zen school (and particularly the Rinzai sect) is underlined by the references to this sutra in the specifically Zen literature of the *kōan* collections. In the *Mumonkan*, two Cases (16, 48) quote from the sutra, while Case 16 is obviously based on an episode from the sutra. The *Hekiganroku* quotes the sutra three times (Cases 5, 46, 94), while Cases 94 and possibly 44 appear to be based on episodes from it.[7] Such *kōans* represent the essential literature of Zen and have provided its study and practice environment throughout its history. Further, D.T. Suzuki notes that all the commentaries on this sutra originated in the Zen tradition and he includes it in the four or five most read sutras (1960: 26, 65). It is likely then

---

[3] Translations of the relevant parts of this work are to be found in Sanford 1977: 439-40 and Sasaki 1975: 41-2, 49.

[4] Short Chinese title: *Shou-leng-yen ching*. Japanese title: *Shuryōgonkyō* or sometimes, *Ryōgonkyō*. Full Chinese title: *Ta-fo-ting ju-lai mi-yin hsiu-cheng liao-i chu-p'u-sa wan hsing shou-leng-yen ching*, or 'Sutra of the Foremost Shurangama at the Great Buddha's Summit Concerning the Tathagata's Secret Cause of Cultivation, his Certification to Complete Meaning, and all Bodhisattva's Myriad Practices' (Hua 1977: 1); also 'The Buddha's Great Crown Sutra, being an Elucidation of the Secret of the Lord Buddha's Supreme Attainment, and the Practice of all the Bodhisattvas' (Goddard 1970: 661).

[5] Mizuno, for example, appears to have confused them (1982: 117, 120-1).

[6] Dōgen Zenji doubts its authenticity but not its value. See Mizuno 1982: 120-1, where despite confusion concerning the correct title of the sutra, the reference must be to the *Śūraṅgama Sūtra*.

[7] A useful English edition of these works is Sekida 1977.

that this sutra would have been known to serious practitioners within the Fuke sub-sect of Rinzai Zen and may have influenced the development of that group's special attitude to the playing of *shakuhachi* as a religious practice.

This becomes clearer as one turns to examine the content of the sutra more thoroughly. Firstly, it should be stated that this work makes no explicit references to music at all, in contrast to some other Mahayana sutras, notably the *Saddharma-Puṇḍarīka Sūtra* (Lotus Sutra). In the Lotus Sutra, we encounter music constantly as part of the great decorative canvas on which the whole panoply of Buddhas, Bodhisattvas, Heavenly beings, inhabitants of the various worlds, monks and lay people teach and receive the *dharma*. For example:

> No sooner had he sat on that throne than the Brahma heavenly kings rained down celestial flowers... A fragrant wind from time to time arose, sweeping away the withered flowers and raining fresh ones. Thus incessantly during full ten minor kalpas they paid honor to the buddha and even till his extinction they constantly rained those flowers while the gods [belonging to] the four [heavenly] kings to honor the buddha constantly beat celestial drums and other gods performed celestial music during full ten minor kalpas and continued to do so until his extinction. (Katō *et al.* 1975: 147)

Compared with this the *Śūraṅgama Sūtra* is tame indeed. Ellingson sees such descriptions as providing the Buddhist community with 'symbolic models' for Buddhist ritual practice which clearly distinguish it from the musical and performance practices of lay communities (Ellingson 1979: 162-3). The *Śūraṅgama Sūtra* does not, however, address such issues. Rather it goes to the heart of how one can be liberated from attachment to external worldly phenomena and in particular to the objects of the senses, the processes of sensing, conditioned responses to sense data, and ideas of self. The sutra expresses it thus:

> Therefore ... all sentient beings from beginningless time have always hankered after beautiful sights and musical sounds, filling their thinking minds with thought after thought and causing it to be always active, and never realizing that by nature it was pure, mysterious, permanent, and Essential, thus causing them ... to follow the current of transitory deaths and rebirths ... ever filled with contaminations, impermanency, and suffering. Ananda, if you could only learn to get free from this bondage ... and from this fear of impermanency, and learn to concentrate your mind on its true and permanent nature ... then the eternal Brightness would illumine you and all the individualized and discriminated perceptions of objective phenomena, sense organs, false imaginations, self and not-self, would vanish... (Goddard 1970: 212-3)

This investigation of the nature of phenomena and of the self takes place in this sutra in the context of an incident in which Ananda, the Buddha's closest disciple, has been rescued from being drawn into a sexual liason and from the consequent risk of forsaking his vows. This incident has deeply shaken him and provides an ideal opportunity for the Buddha through the personal teaching in this sutra to further shake him free from his attachments and to bring him to ultimate realization.

However, this context is not purely incidental. The power of attachment to sexual desire (which is of course itself sensuously based), forms (to borrow an earlier term) a dramatic symbolic model of the other attachments, particularly those of the individual senses. Ellingson (1979: 149, 203) points out that in earlier Buddhist sources, music is regarded as powerfully 'attractive' and 'intoxicating' and is also likened to the power of sexual attraction. In this sutra, it is sound and the sense of hearing which feature as the most significant sources of attachment and the ultimate key to realization. The Bodhisattva Maitreya declares, '[t]he five other organs are not perfect, but hearing is really pervasive' (Lu 1966: 147) and '[t]he faculty of hearing, beyond creation and annihilation, truly is permanent' (Goddard 1970: 147).

The length and highly esoteric nature of the *Śūraṅgama Sūtra* prevent a systematic exposition here, but we may generalize by saying that the Buddha leads Ananda step by step through a process of analysis of phenomena and their experience resulting in the demonstration of the essentially illusory nature of them all. In particular, the Buddha focuses on Ananda's understanding of his sense experience. He is not dealing with physiological, psychological, or even philosophical questions here, though at times all three modes of investigation are applied. Rather the process leads directly to the core Buddhistic questions: 'What is the essence of worldly phenomena? What is their source? What is permanent in the midst of universal impermanence?' Indeed the search, rather than focusing on the external phenomena themselves, is to be turned within. In Suzuki's words, '[t]he Essence is to be grasped, not the hearing, nor the sound. To take the latter for reality is the result of confused mentality' (1960: 69-70). In Zen terms, the fundamental question might be reformulated as 'Who hears? What hears?'.

In answer to Ananda's request concerning the manner in which to resolve this question, the Bodhisattva Avalokiteśvara ('The One Who Hears the Sounds of the World') gives an account of the profound practice by which she achieved this realization through meditation on the faculty of hearing. Yet she states, 'I myself do not meditate on sound but on the meditator' (Goddard 1970: 139). As we will see, hearing is but the starting point. Avalokiteśvara relates her experience in one of the most difficult parts of the text:

> I was taught to begin practising by concentrating my mind on the true nature of Transcendental hearing, and by that practice, I attained samadhi [absorption]. As soon as I had advanced to the stage of Entering the Stream, I determined to discard all thoughts discriminating as to where I was or had been. Later I discarded the conception of advancing all together, and the thought of either activity or quietness in this connection... I gradually advanced until all discrimination of the hearing nature of my self-hood and of the intrinsic Transcendental Hearing was discarded. As there ceased to be any grasping in my mind for the attainment of intrinsic hearing, the conception of Enlightenment and enlightened nature were all absent from my mind. When this state of perfect Emptiness of Mind was attained, all arbitrary conceptions of attaining to Emptiness of Mind and of enlightened nature, were discarded. As soon as all arbitrary conceptions of rising and disappearing of thoughts were completely discarded, the state of Nirvana was clearly realized. (Goddard 1970: 246)

In attempting to understand this at some rational level, we must first recognize that the experience in question is fundamentally not amenable to verbal expression or codification. Indeed this is a central tenet of Zen

Buddhism.[8] However we may observe that the experience described involves the successive clearing away of various layers of discriminative thinking, judgment, and reaction which accompany our sensory experience of the world.

Pre-Mahayana Buddhist sources provide a model of human perception and cognition, according to which the perceptual-cognitive process is conceived as involving three steps. The first involves the pure cognition of the object (say, sound) by the ear consciousness. In the second step, the mind consciousness also takes the sound as its object and recognizes it. Finally, the mind consciousness further reflects on the after-image of the sound and discriminates meanings, logical relationships, and reactions pertaining to the experience (Ellingson 1979:151-4). This is schematically set out in Figure 1.

X Consciousness has its Object Y which is Perceived as Z

ear consciousness ⟶ sound ⟶ a pure cognition of sound

mind consciousness ⟶ purely cognized sound ⟶ consciousness of sound

mind consciousness ⟶ conscious image or after-image of sound ⟶ basis for reflection, discrimination judgment etc.

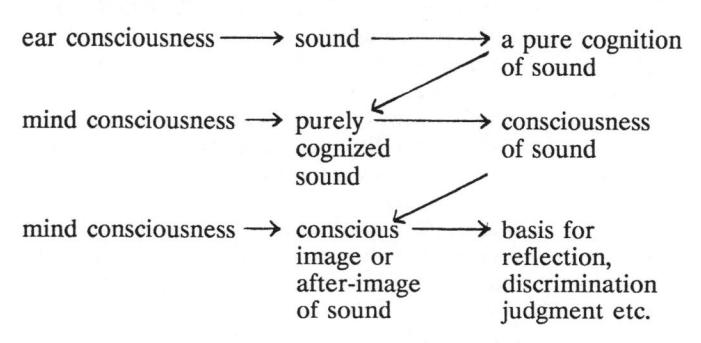

Figure 1. Perceptual-Cognitive Process

In the Zen tradition, this model has its direct analogy in the concept of the three *nen*.[9] According to Sekida:

> Zen theory sees the activity of consciousness as a continuous interplay between a sequence of nen. Thus, the first nen always acts intuitively and performs a direct pure cognition of the object. The second nen immediately follows the first and makes the first its object of reflection... The integrating, synthesizing action of consciousness is the third nen. Reasoning, introspection, and so forth come from the third nen. But this third nen, clouded by its ego-centred activity, often argues falsely and draws mistaken conclusions. (Sekida 1977: 32-3)

The meditative practice described by Avalokiteśvara in the *Śūraṅgama Sūtra* involves the filtering off of successive levels of consciousness related to the second and third *nen*, namely self-consciousness, discriminating consciousness, and consciousness of subject and object. What is left is deep

---

[8] Bodhidharma, first Patriarch of Zen in China, characterized Zen as 'a special transmission outside word and letters'.

[9] 'The word *nen*, which has no equivalent in English, means either a unit of thought or a steadily willed activity of mind' (Sekida 1977: 32). For a fuller discussion of *nen*, see Sekida 1975: 108-27.

absorption in the direct and pure cognition of the first *nen*. In Zen thought, such an experience, if only momentary, is necessary for deep insight.

To return to the starting point of our discussion, how can such ideas be related to the practice of *shakuhachi* in the Fuke tradition? Firstly, if we accept that Fuke Zen had a true spiritual motivation, then the experience outlined above would have a fundamental role to play in its practice and training.

It should be noted however that according to the *Śūraṅgama Sūtra*, sound and hearing do not constitute the only gateway to such experience, although in this sutra they are deemed to be the best gateway. One can speculate that this high evaluation of sound and hearing might have proven convenient to the Fuke sect in arguing the legitimacy of their training methods utilizing the *shakuhachi*. However a difficulty arises. The sutra makes no substantive reference to music, only to sound and the perceptual faculty of hearing. Indeed it would seem that music, in the sense of meaningfully organized sound structures (as in the pieces which seem to have formed the Fuke repertoire), belongs to the realm of the third *nen*, the discriminating, organizing, structuring consciousness which is transcended in the meditative experience. How can this be reconciled with the sutra's seeming advocacy of the abandonment of the third nen in meditative practice? This apparent contradiction might perhaps be overcome by recognizing that despite the 'idealist' tone of this and other Chinese sutras, the Zen philosophy does not advocate withdrawal from the world of activity. Rather it seeks stillness in the very midst of activity. It is therefore consistent with this view that the field of a meditative practice based on sound and hearing should be placed in the very midst of humanly created activity, in this case music. In this way, the optimum conditions not only for realization but also for the subsequent personal integration of that realization are created.[10]

Here, the manner in which the Fuke tradition described its practice is instructive. By describing the *shakuhachi* not as a musical instrument but as an 'instrument of *dharma*' (Japanese: *hōki*), by using the term *okyō*, meaning a sutra, to refer to the pieces of their *shakuhachi* repertoire, by the description of their practice as 'blowing Zen' (Japanese: *suizen*), and by the characterization of direct spiritual insight as 'single-sound enlightenment' (Japanese: *ichion jōbutsu*), the Fuke tradition consciously distinguishes its fundamental purpose from that of secular music making. In so doing, it arguably moves directly into the field of practice defined by the *Śūraṅgama Sūtra*.

In conclusion, it is not the intention of this paper to argue a direct historical connection between this sutra and the Fuke *shakuhachi* tradition. Rather it seeks only to suggest that the *Śūraṅgama Sūtra* provides a conceptual context within the Zen tradition consistent with Fuke philosophy, and a possible source of the ideas of the Fuke sect about spiritual practice based on sound and hearing. In view of the paucity of historical sources connected with the Fuke tradition, it is not possible at present to claim that such a relationship is anything more than circumstantial. Nevertheless, I believe that a study of the *Śūraṅgama Sūtra* expands our limited understanding of the religious content of the Fuke tradition.

---

[10] Case 16 of the *Mumonkan* addresses this. See Sekida 1977: 65-67.

References

Bielefeldt, Carl 1986: 'Ch'ang-lu Tsung-tse's *Tso-ch'an I* and the "Secret" of Zen Meditation', in *Traditions of Meditation in Chinese Buddhism*, ed. Peter N. Gregory (*Studies in East Asian Buddhism* 4: 129-61), Honolulu: U. Hawaii Press

Blasdel, Christopher 1984: 'The Shakuhachi: Aesthetics of a Single Tone', *Japan Quarterly* 31: 214-7

Ellingson, Terry Jay 1979: *The Mandala of Sound: Concepts and Sound Structures in Tibetan Ritual Music*. Diss. Wisconsin – Madison

Goddard, Dwight, ed. 1970: *A Buddhist Bible*, Boston: Beacon Press

Hua Hsüan, Tripitaka Master (comment.) and Buddhist Text Translation Society (Heng Ch'ih, primary translator) 1977: *The Shurangama Sutra*, San Francisco: Sino-American Buddhist Assoc.

Katō, Bunnō *et al.*, tr. 1975: *The Threefold Lotus Sutra*, New York: Weatherhill

Lu K'uan Yü (Charles Luk), tr. 1966: *The Surangama Sutra (Leng Yen Ching)*, London: Rider

Mizuno, Kōgen 1982: *Buddhist Sutras: Origin, Development, Transmission*, Tokyo: Kōsei

Sanford, James H. 1977: 'Shakuhachi Zen: the Fukeshū and Komusō', *Monumenta Nipponica* 32: 411-40

Sangharakshita 1985: *The Eternal Legacy: An Introduction to the Canonical Literature of Buddhism*, London: Tharpa

Sasaki, Ruth Fuller, tr. 1975: *The Recorded Sayings of Ch'an Master Lin-chi Hui-chao of Chen Prefecture*, Kyoto: Institute for Zen Studies

Sekida, Katsuki 1975: *Zen Training: Methods and Philosophy*, New York: Weatherhill
   1977: *Two Zen Classics: Mumonkan and Hekiganroku*, tr., comment., Sekida Katsuki, New York: Weatherhill

Staël-Holstein, A. von 1936: 'The Emperor Ch'ien-lung and the Larger Suramgamasutra', *Harvard Journal of Asiatic Studies* 1: 137

Suzuki, D.T. 1960: *Manual of Zen Buddhism*, New York: Grove

Tsuge, Gen'ichi 1977: 'The History of the *Kyotaku*', *Asian Music* 8(2): 47-63

Composition and improvisation in Satsuma biwa

HUGH DE FERRANTI

This paper examines the sequence of procedures, types of modelling and variation techniques involved in making and performing a piece of music in the tradition of *Seiha Satsuma biwa*, a style of musical recitation accompanied by the *biwa*. Following discussion of the music's history and current performance practice, a scheme for the four stages which lead to a piece's performance is proposed. Through examination of these four stages it is suggested that skill in both compositional and improvisational variation procedures are integral to competence in the *Seiha Satsuma biwa* tradition.

1 Introduction

Satsuma biwa is a style of *katarimono*[1] accompanied by a four-stringed plucked lute, the *biwa*, that is, it is narrative in which the *biwa* plays melodic interludes and brief phrases to punctuate verses of sung text. *Satsuma biwa* is thus similar to *heikyoku*, the recitation of the *Heike monogatari* (Tale of the Heike) with *biwa* accompaniment which has been practised since the 13th century. According to the commonly accepted account of their origins, however, both the instrument (shown in figure 1) and the narrative style now termed *Satsuma biwa* originated in the Sengoku era (1482-1558) in the feudal domain of Satsuma in southern Kyūshū. Shimazu Tadayoshi (1492-1568), a member of the Shimazu family which ruled Satsuma from the 12th to the 19th century, felt that in view of the chaotic social and spiritual conditions of his times, a strict code of ethics and behaviour was needed to guard against the spiritual deterioration of the *samurai* (warrior) class in Satsuma. As well as defining the code of Satsuma *bushidō*[2] in his verse collection called the *Iroha Uta*, Tadayoshi framed regulations which stipulated art forms and pastimes deemed fit for *samurai*, women and children, and the aged, respectively.

Among the arts reserved for *samurai* was the recitation, with *biwa* accompaniment, of Tadayoshi's many poems on themes of Buddhist and Confucianist ethics. The accompanying instrument is said to have been a modified version of the *biwa* used by *mōsō* (blind Buddhist priests) of the Satsuma region, and the vocal and instrumental melodies were probably adaptations of those used by *mōsō* in sutra recitations. It is not known whether the *biwa* had been played in secular contexts in Satsuma prior to this time, but as Tadayoshi is said to have commanded Fuchiwaki Juchōin, the head of the

---

[1] *Katarimono* is a term borrowed from literary theory by Japanese music scholars, who have used it to refer to styles of musical recitation in which the text takes the form of a narrative.

[2] *Bushidō*, the code of the *samurai*, was not a unified body of doctrine; rather, it found various regional interpretations, among which that of Satsuma was distinctive for its particular combination of Zen Buddhist and Confucianist thought.

Satsuma *mōsō* sect, to alter the *biwa* for the specific purpose of making its sound and playing techniques suitable to the tastes of *samurai*, it seems unlikely that any other form of *biwa* had been popular among the warrior class.

The poetry of Tadayoshi was in time supplemented by poems attributed to various of the Shimazu *daimyō* (feudal lords) of the late 16th and 17th centuries, as well as longer narratives about struggles between Satsuma and the rulers of other domains in Kyūshū. Until the late 18th century, *biwa* recitations were performed solely by highly ranked *samurai* and *mōsō*. Sources on the history of the style (Ueda 1912, Yoshimura 1933, and others) relate that from about 1800, however, a small number of the merchant class took up *biwa* recitations as a pastime. It may be surmised that there was a concomitant expansion of repertory, but as there are no known text sources from before 1855,[3] nothing definite can be said in this regard. The adoption of *biwa* among merchants of Satsuma is the basis for the distinction between *shifū* (*samurai* style) and *machifū* (townsman's style), of importance to *Satsuma biwa* players in characterising their individual artistic lineage.

With the movement of many prominent Satsuma *samurai* to Tokyo as statesmen and bureaucrats in the first decades of Meiji (1868-1912), what had been a regional tradition gradually came to be known in the capital. A small number of renowned players from Satsuma began both to teach their art and to write or set new poems on historical and contemporary themes; it was in this period that the term '*Satsuma biwa*' gained currency. During the late Meiji era there also appeared flagrantly nationalistic songs, many of which glorified the exploits of the Imperial forces against China and Russia. Changes in both the repertory and performance techniques of *Satsuma biwa* were symptomatic of a process of popularisation which led in time to the formation in the Taishō era (1912-26) of a new school, the *Kinshinryū*, under the leadership of a native of Tokyo, Nagata Kinshin (1885-1927). Kinshin's singing style showed the influences of *Edo uta* styles such as *shinnai* and *kouta*,[4] and it was largely his immense popularity as a performer, teacher and recording artist which precipitated what *biwa* players even today refer to as a 'golden age'; for two decades from about 1905 *biwa* recitation was a popular form of music among urban dwellers throughout Japan, and by the mid-1920s professional *biwa* teachers numbered in the thousands. Although intellectuals tended to look down upon this music as a recently emerged narrative form which lacked the historical pedigree and literary distinction of *heikyoku* and *nō* (both of which had long been practised on an amateur basis as intellectual pastimes), it found support among those middle-class and working-class people who preferred it to the raucous tones of *Naniwa-bushi*.[5]

During the 1930s and the Pacific War, *Satsuma biwa* maintained a strong (albeit reduced) following, and its repertory was further enlarged by new texts whose content can only be described as propaganda for officially sanctioned ideology. Since the Second World War and Occupation, *biwa* recitation, like

---

[3] The *biwa* player and researcher Shimazu Sei has informed me that a hand-written copy of the text for Toragari (Tiger Hunting) dated 'the second year of Ansei (1855)' is held in Kagoshima Prefectural Library.

[4] *Kouta* and *shinnai* are both *shamisen* song styles which developed in Edo (the name for Tokyo until the Meiji era) in the early 19th century.

[5] *Naniwa-bushi* is a style of narrative accompanied by *shamisen* (and sometimes other instruments) usually performed in *yose* (vaudeville theatres). It was probably the most popular form of narrative in Japan between the World Wars.

many other forms of traditional performing arts, has suffered from relative neglect; this is perhaps because of its association with *bushidō* and values perceived as implicitly supportive of militarism. The 1960s saw the emergence of a new style of *biwa* music – the so-called *Tsuruha* – chiefly as a result of Takemitsu Tōru's and some other modern composers' interest in the potential, as a sound source, of a modified version of the *Satsuma biwa* played by Tsuruta Kinshi. Most young players today are of the *Tsuruha* school. The *Seiha* (orthodox) school, established in the Taishō era by players who claimed fidelity to the original style as it had been brought from Kyūshū to Tokyo, as distinct from the *Kinshinryū* and other new styles formed under the influence of urban vocal genres, is today practised by a total of about 100 people. At present performers and students of the *Kinshinryū* number about 1,000. *Nishikibiwa*, a hybrid style established in the early Shōwa era (1926-89) by Suitō Kinjō, continues to be practised with a level of support comparable to that of the *Seiha* school.

This paper focuses upon the current performance practices of *Seiha Satsuma biwa*, and in particular that of the style's most renowned living performer, Fumon Yoshinori, with whom I studied in Tokyo during 1985-89 (see figure 1). Although Fumon and a few other performers refer to themselves as professionals, today no *Seiha Satsuma biwa* player can earn all of his or her income from performing and teaching. (Since the early years of this century there have been a small number of women practitioners of this predominantly male pursuit.) Opportunities for paid performances are few; most performances in fact take place at monthly or seasonal meetings of *kai* – groups of individual teachers and their students – rather than publicised concerts for which an entrance fee is charged. Among the latter are some annual concerts organised by the Japan *Biwa* Music Association (*Nihon Biwagaku Kyōkai*). Other contexts for performance include festivals at Shintō shrines and Buddhist temples, in which a recitation is performed as a form of offering to the deity, and private celebrations. Among the *Seiha* school's practitioners, at present perhaps only five could be described as fully competent performers by traditional criteria.

It has yet to be demonstrated that the instrument which has been called the *Satsuma biwa* since the Meiji era is in fact the same as that which the priest Juchōinis said to have devised in accordance with Shimazu Tadayoshi's wishes.[6] With the exception of its four frets and plectrum, the *Satsuma biwa* has traditionally been constructed wholly of mulberry wood. For the plectrum very hard materials such as boxwood or black persimmon have been favoured. The strings are of silk twisted in varying gauges and thicknesses. A range of pitches may be sounded at a single fret by applying pressure with the fingers of the left hand at 90 degrees to the plane of the neck and at a slight distance behind the uppermost edge of the fret. By varying pressure in a single position, melodies over ranges as wide as a tenth are produced. This is a characteristic technique which is not used in playing any other of the Japanese lutes, nor any lutes of the classical traditions of China or Korea. A competent player must acquire control of intricate vibrato and glissandi techniques as well as the ability to make extremely subtle adjustments of finger pressure to effect microtonal changes of intonation. The large plectrum is wielded in a

---

[6] The instrument to be described is that used by performers in the Seiha tradition and most performers of the Kinshin school. The Nishikibiwa and Tsuruha schools each use an instrument which is a considerably modified version of the Seiha prototype.

Figure 1: Fumon Yoshinori in performance
(photograph by Hugh de Ferranti, 1988)

range of techniques which regulate the quality of the attack, in particular the presence or absence of percussive elements within the sound. The four strings of the *biwa* are tuned at a pitch appropriate for the singer's vocal range, although usually within the range G – A# for a male, and A – c for a female performer. The strings are always tuned so that the first string (the string which is uppermost when the instrument is held in the traditional manner, as shown in Figure 1) and the third string are a unison, the second string is a major fourth below and the fourth string a major second above. The repeated sounding of the open first and third strings, either separately or as part of rapid cross-string figures between verses of text, has the effect of enforcing the pitch of these strings as a kind of drone; it is always the central pitch of a tonal hierarchy articulated in both the vocal and instrumental melodies.

Both the recitation style and instrumental techniques of *Seiha Satsuma biwa* were formed in accordance with the aesthetic values of *bushidō*. Hence there is an abhorrence of the use of *uragoe* (falsetto) and other vocal techniques which were associated with some styles of *shamisen* and folk music. In the *biwa* interludes too, the striking contrast of intricate threads of melody sounded on the thinnest, top string against a ground of sharp percussive sounds produced by the impact of the large wooden plectrum against the front surface of the instrument seems aptly to embody that combination of compassion and ferocity which has characterised the image of the *samurai*.

2 Compositional and improvisational aspects of performance practice

Studies of the ways in which musicians acquire, conceive of and apply models in making music have distinguished 'compositional' and 'improvisational' modes of variation, and several types of models which embody these activities (Finnegan 1986; Sutton 1987; Susilo 1987; Trimillos 1987). Although in practice the two modes are often complementary, they may be distinguished as, on the one hand, processes of variation which, 'suggest pre-selection and fixity', and on the other, ones which 'suggest an absence of pre-selection and *specific* preparation' (Susilo, 1987: 1; my emphasis). Both processes may involve writing to some extent, and in both cases similar kinds of models can guide the musician's choices of variation techniques; for example, generalised models for the structure of a piece, conceptual models for the aesthetic qualities and uses of particular rhythms or mode forms, and highly prescriptive models for melodic contour, tonality and rhythm can have application in composition as well as in improvisation.

Most forms of traditional Japanese music appear to be structured as sequences of formulaic melodic and rhythmic patterns which some scholars have called *senritsukei*. Such structures have been demonstrated in studies of *nō* (Hoff and Flindt, 1973), *gagaku* (Gamō 1970), *heikyoku* (Kindaichi 1973) and other genres. In many styles of *katarimono* such patterns are accorded names. When these are written onto the text of a recitation they enable it to function as a shorthand score, rather like a song lyric with chord symbols above the text. The sequence of *senritsukei* is generally fixed so that the broad structure of a piece is the same in every performance, yet there is large scope for change to occur at higher levels of structural detail. The identity of each recitation as a unique musical structure is preserved even as individual melody patterns within the structure are subjected to variation from one performance to the next. In the case of *Seiha Satsuma biwa*, the ability to play variations of model forms for the *biwa* patterns, albeit within narrow limitations placed on the choice of melodic materials, has been fostered as a norm of traditional performance practice. A similar degree of freedom is not applicable to the vocal patterns, which exist in multiple forms to suit the conditions of each text but are subject to only slight variation in performance.

The purpose of this paper is to describe the sequence of procedures, types of modelling and variation techniques involved in making and performing a *Seiha Satsuma biwa* recitation. A scheme for the complete process will be proposed, then each of its stages will be demonstrated with reference to the practice of Fumon Yoshinori. This will entail examination of the *biwa* notations employed by Fumon, as well as comparison between the basic model form of a pattern as recorded in notation and two versions of the pattern in performance. It will be suggested that skill in both compositional and improvisational variation is a touchstone of competence in this style.

Four distinct stages lead to the form which a *Satsuma biwa* piece takes in a given performance:

1) **Selection or composition of the text**
   A suitable poem in verses of 12 syllables grouped for the most part in the classical metre of 7 plus 5 is selected or composed.

2) **Distribution of patterns**
   A general musical structure for the poem's setting is devised through a process known as *fushizuke* – the selection and distribution against the text of melody patterns (*senritsukei*) in a fixed sequence, in accordance with the musician's interpretation of the poem's shape and content as a narrative. The names for patterns are written in shorthand form onto a copy of the text, which then functions as a vocal score (*utahon*).

3) **Actualisation of patterns in rehearsal**
   On the basis of such a structural scheme, a recitation is rehearsed. Details of the sequence of vocal melody patterns given in the *utahon* are actualised as the model forms of each pattern are drawn upon and adapted in accordance with the content, syntax and phonology of verses of text. Model forms of *biwa* patterns are also selectively drawn upon.

4) **Variation of patterns in performance**
   In performance the *biwa* interludes are subject to improvisatory variation in response to the conditions of the performance. In the case of the vocal melodies, the rehearsed version of the melody pattern for each line of text is sung with only slight changes of melodic and rhythmic detail.

The four-stage process outlined above may be seen as a sequence of variation procedures, in each of which models of differing degrees of specificity are applied. In examining these stages, I shall explain the nature of each model and the manner in which it is manifested for the performer.

Selection or composition of the text

The first stage, composition of the narrative text, has been bypassed by most performers of *Satsuma biwa* since the time of the style's introduction to Tokyo, if not earlier. Today it is extremely rare for a new poem to be written and set as a recitation; the last player of renown who wrote and set a substantial number of new poems was Nagahama Nanjō, an innovator who died in the 1970s and whose compositions included elegies for those killed in the bombing of Hiroshima and for John F. Kennedy. A standard body of traditional pieces has formed, and continues to form, the repertory of most players; any given piece can, however, be rendered in different settings. New settings may be made only by players of senior status – those who have earned the right to teach (certified on a document received from their own teacher); students always use the setting given them by their teacher. For a small number of texts there is a standard setting by a past master.

The following conditions should be fulfilled before a player is able to carry out *fushizuke* (stage 2 in the preparation of a piece) satisfactorily:

1. The bulk of the poem should be in verses divisible in phrases of 7 plus 5 syllables (*shichigo chō* metre).
2. The content of the poem must be divisible into a clear tri-partite structure as follows: *maeuta*, in which the setting of the narrative and/or its themes are introduced; *honuta*, in which the story is told: and *atouta*, in which the moral of the narrative is stated, either directly in pithy form or else by suggestion through an action of one of the protagonists. The *maeuta* and *atouta* are both quite short (from 3 to 8 verses in length) relative to the central *honuta*. While alternative terms for *maeuta*, *honuta* and *atouta* exist, it seems that all players are aware of this tripartite division.

The first step in making a new setting is to write out the poem from a text anthology (there are many printed anthologies, the most recent of which was published in 1965) using brush and ink, in a scheme of two verses per column. The hand-written text comes to serve as a vocal score during the piece's rehearsal. Symbols for the various vocal and instrumental patterns, as well as graphic mnemonics for some vocal ornaments are written onto it, and it may even be used in performance if the piece is of longer duration than the standard 12-15 minutes. Figure 2 shows the *maeuta* of Shiroyama (Mt. Fortress) in the hand of Fumon Yoshinori. Transliterated and translated versions are provided below.

[*chū*]	*Sore tatsujin wa taikan su*
	Great men have vision
[*jō*]	*batsuzan gaisei no yū aru mo*
	and courage enough to move mountains, to span the world.
[*chūkan nagashi*]	*eiko wa yume ka maboroshi ka*
	And yet, the vicissitudes of this life –
	are they a dream, an illusion?
[*ji no ge*]	*Ōsumi yama no kari kura ni*
	Above a hunters' shelter in the mountains of Ōsumi
[*jō*]	*shinnyo no tsuki no kage kiyoku*
	pure light streams down from the 'moon of Truth'.
[*kiri*]	*munen musō wo kanzuramu*
	Might he see the way to be free of this world?

The *maeuta* here introduces both the general theme of the poem – the pathetic implications of a hero's death – and the setting for the first section of the narrative, Ōsumi Province in Kyūshū. Only the second verse, in which there are two phrases of 9 and 5 syllables, respectively, departs from standard *shichigo chō* metre.

Distribution of patterns

The term *fushizuke* (literally, 'attaching the melody') refers both to the activity of distributing *senritsukei* (melodic patterns) against the text and to the resultant structural scheme itself. In its broadest usage it can also embrace

text →

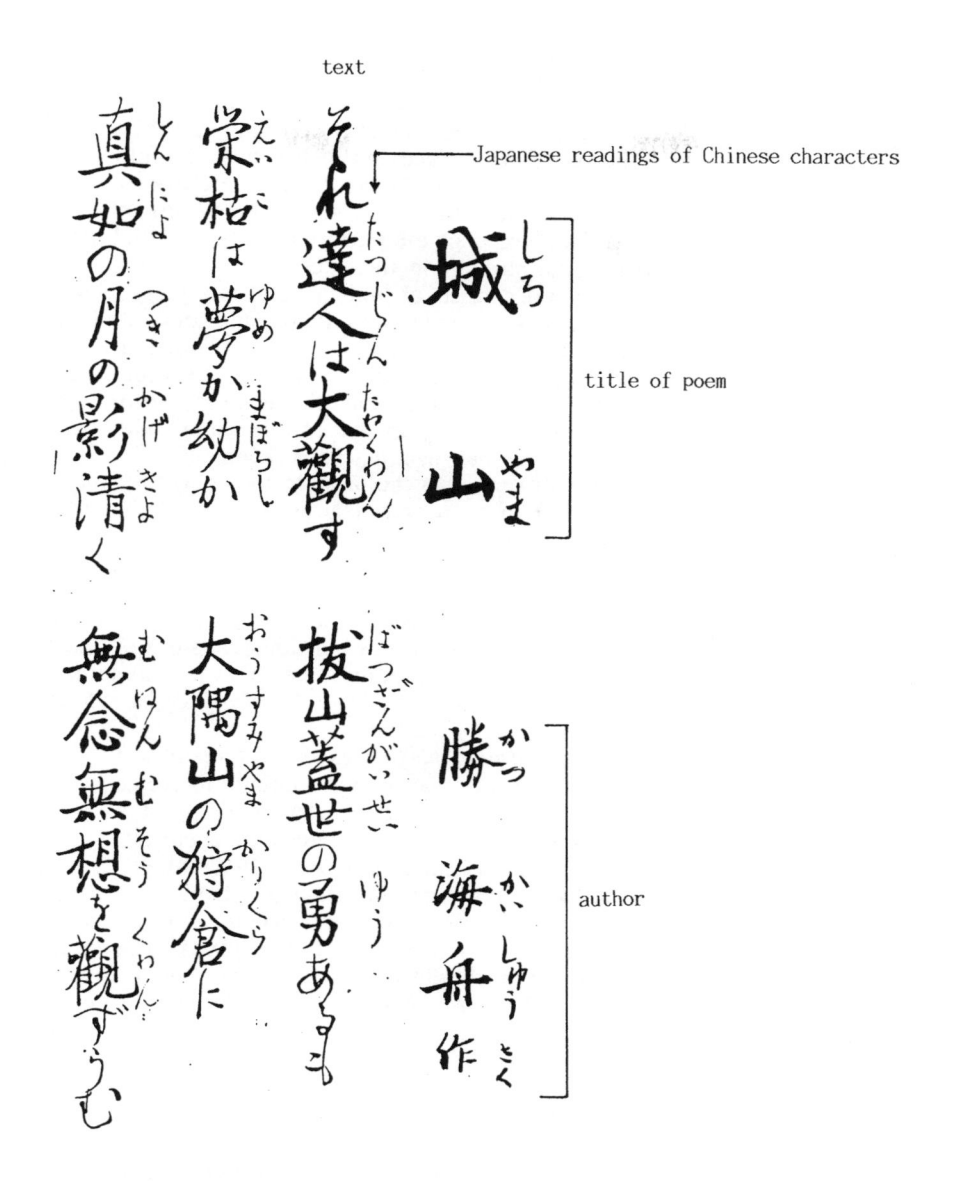

Japanese readings of Chinese characters

城山 (しろやま) — title of poem

それ達人は大観す
栄枯は夢か幻か
真如の月の影清く

勝海舟作 — author

抜山蓋世の勇あるも
大隅山の狩倉に
無念無想を観ずうむ

Figure 2: *maeuta* of Shiroyama (Mt. Fortress)
Text by Katsu Kaishu
Utahon in the hand of Fumon Yoshinori

the working out of melodic details for each *senritsukei* as it is fitted to a single verse of text; this takes place during rehearsal.

To understand the *fushizuke* process, the nature and functions of *senritsukei* in *Satsuma biwa* should first be considered. Like many styles of *katarimono*, *Satsuma biwa* has a vocabulary of a relatively small number of melody patterns which appear in rather similar orderings as the basic structural units for the *fushizuke* of every piece. Distinction must first of all be made between patterns for the *biwa* and for the voice. There are two reasons for this. Firstly, as in *heikyoku*, the *biwa* and vocal elements are always separated; at no point within a piece does the performer both sing and play the *biwa*. Apart from occasional strokes on the open strings to punctuate single verses of text, the *biwa* part consists of preludes and interludes which function both to articulate large format divisions in the narrative, and to reinforce the content of the lines of text with which they are associated. A common expression of this aesthetic relation is that the vocal and instrumental melodies 'mutually reinforce and enhance one another'.[7] Secondly, performers commonly trace their own singing and playing styles to different sources or influences. Most performers identify their own teacher's singing as the source for their vocal patterns, but with regard to the *biwa* melodies as they have been played during the last 100 years, it is widely acknowledged that the playing of a blind priest named Myōjū, who probably lived until the early Meiji era, was the most significant single source. Yet to some extent all players of renown have developed their own versions of the *biwa* melodies by reworking and adding to those of their predecessors. Players today who knew the styles and lineages of the pre-War masters still refer to individual versions of *biwa* patterns as being in the 'Myōjū' style, the 'Kodama Tennan' style, and so on. Ikeda Tenshū, one of the leading performers of the 1920s and 1930s, wrote that

> If the true spirit of *Satsuma biwa* lives on ... then it is a matter of course that master players will continue to create new and distinctive ways of playing. What is more, if a player's *biwa* melodies do not reflect his individual character, then by no means can he be called a master. (1959: 40)

In the practice of *Seiha Satsuma biwa* since the time of Myōjū there have existed nine principal types of *biwa* patterns, most of which are referred to by the names of the vocal patterns which precede them in recitations.[8] The vocal patterns are more numerous and are broadly divided into two types. In the terminology of Fumon Yoshinori, they are: *hiragin*, which are for the most part syllabic and confined to a single reciting tone; and *utagin*, which involve more melodic motion and the use of *kobushi*, a kind of rapid melisma. With the exception of the pattern *utaidashi*, a prelude played at the start of all recitations, *biwa* melodies are played only as interludes after *utagin* patterns. Most *biwa* pattern types are paired with a single *utagin* pattern type, although some (for example, the pattern called simply *ai no te* (interlude) may be played after several different types of *utagin* pattern).

The traditional terms for the vocal patterns which have had currency at least since the late Meiji era in some cases describe the patterns' function in

---

[7] Fumon Yoshinori has described the relationship between the vocal and instrumental elements in this way: '*o tagai ni hikitatseru*' (oral communication).

[8] In *heikyoku* the principle for pairing vocal and instrumental patterns is the opposite; a given *biwa* interlude is always followed by its corresponding pattern for the voice.

articulating the structure of a recitation; for instance, *kiri* (cutting) has the function of dividing off the largest divisions of the narrative, while *utaidome* (song ending) brings the entire recitation to an end. *Hiragin* patterns are named according to the position of their central reciting tone within one or other of the two vocal registers, *kangoe* and *jigoe*; for example *ji no jō, ji no chū, ji no ge, chūkan no jō* and *taikan*. '*Ji*' and '*kan*' denote *jigoe* and *kangoe*. '*Jō*', '*chū*' and '*ge*' mean upper, middle and lower, respectively, while '*tai-*' and '*chū-*' are used as prefixes to designate the 'middle' and 'top' regions within the *kangoe* register. In figure 3 *hiragin* pattern names are shown in alignment with their corresponding reciting pitches, termed according to the three systems of pitch nomenclature which Fumon uses when teaching: solfege, Arabic numbering and *gosei* (see below, p.114).[9] The limits of *jigoe* and *kangoe* are also shown. The words '*ji no*' are given in parentheses as they are often omitted from the names of patterns sung in the *jigoe* register. '*Saige*' refers to a *hiragin* pattern centred upon the lowest available pitch for the voice. Apart from *ai no te* and the prelude *utaidashi*, all *biwa* patterns bear the name of the vocal pattern which they follow.

solfege term	gosei term	Fumon's numerical scheme	hiragin patterns with corresponding responding tone	vocal register
do	kyū	$\dot{1}$		
la#	ei u	#$\dot{6}$		
la	u	$\dot{6}$		
sol#	ei chi	#$\dot{5}$	taikan	
sol	chi	$\dot{5}$	chūkan no jō	kan-
fa#	ei kaku	#$\dot{4}$		goe
fa	kaku	$\dot{4}$	chūkan no ge	
mi	rōkaku	$\dot{3}$		
re#	ei shō	#$\dot{2}$		
re	shō	$\dot{2}$		
do#	ei kyū	#$\dot{1}$	(ji no)jō hari	
do	kyū	1	(ji no)jō	
la#	ei u	#6	(ji no)chū	
la	u	6		ji-
sol#	ei chi	#5		goe
sol	chi	5	(ji no)ge	
fa	kaku	4	(ji no)ge no ge	
re	shō	2		
do	kyū	1	saige	
sol	chi	$\d{5}$	(used in *biwa* part only)	

Figure 3. Pitch resources and vocal registers of *Satsuma biwa*, as conceived by Fumon Yoshinori

For each pattern type there are a number of variant forms used only in songs which have a certain text structure or express a particular sentiment. Although no standard divisions of the repertory according to text content are in use, two broad characterisations are commonly referred to and figure as criteria for choices between versions of a given pattern: there are *eiyūteki* (heroic) and *hageshii* (severe) songs, which usually describe renowned feats of arms, as distinct from *aishūteki* (sorrowful) and *shizukesa no aru* (tranquil) songs, which propound Buddhist and Confucianist teachings or recount literary and

---

[9] As intonation used in *Satsuma biwa* is not based on equal temperament, representation in terms of the relative pitch values of the solfege system (as given in figure 3) or pitches on the Western stave (as given in the transcriptions) is at best an approximation.

historical episodes without reference to martial conflict. This binary division of the repertory is similar to the division of *heikyoku* recitations into *hiroimono* and *fushimono*. As in *Satsuma biwa*, these categories reflect a distinction between narratives which consist largely of descriptions of battle, and ones which relate and comment upon non-martial historical episodes.

The first step in making the *fushizuke* is to decide the points of division between *maeuta, honuta* and *atouta*. When these have been fixed, convention dictates the assignment of patterns which serve to denote the divisions. The pattern *kiri* ends both the *maeuta* and *honuta*, and in especially long recitations may also mark off major points of changes in content within the *honuta*. By convention, too, the *maeuta* and *atouta* must both begin with the pattern sequence *chū – jō*, while the *honuta* always begins with the sequence *taikan – chūkan*. With these patterns in place, the allocation of *utagin* patterns (other than *kiri*) is next to be considered. Musically they stand out as phrases of increased melodic motion in contrast to their surrounding sequences of *hiragin* patterns, and because they are followed by *biwa* interludes. Textually they serve to complete an idea or action within the narrative. For example, in the *honuta* of Chiki (Friendship), a poem which recounts a legendary episode in the life of the Chinese *guqin* master Bo Ziya,[10] Bo Ziya's avowal that only his friend Zhong Ziqi can understand the sentiments expressed in his playing is set as a sequence of four *hiragin* patterns on reciting tones in the upper register, followed by the *utagin* pattern *chūkan otoshi* in which the melody falls sharply down to the lower register.

Transliteration and translation	Pattern name	Melodic framework (taking G as the pitch of the *biwa*'s open first string)
Koto no aruji no ieru yō The *guqin* master said,	*taikan*	$eb^1 - d^1$
waga koto no ne wo taenari to 'Though there are many who	*chūkan no ge*	c^1
tataeshi hito wa kazu aredo praise the wondrous sounds of my *qin*,	*chūkan no jō*	d^1
danzuru kokoro sanagara ni the spirit of the one who plays	*chūkan no ge*	d^1
kimi nomi hitori kore wo shiru is known to you alone.'	*chūkan otoshi*	$eb^1 - d^1 - g^1 - eb^1 - d^1 -$ $c^1 - ab - g - c^1 - ab - g$

Figure 4. Excerpt from the *honuta* of Chiki. Text by Harada Kenji. *Fushizuke* by Fumon Yoshinori

After assignment of the *utagin* patterns, the *hiragin* sequences which link them (other than those at the beginning of the *maeuta* and *atouta*, which are fixed by convention) are decided. Although here again constraints on the choice of patterns exist – for example, in the above extract from Chiki, the choice of *taikan* as an initial pattern is determined by the use of *kuzure*[11] patterns in the preceding segment, and in turn determines that the following three *hiragin* patterns be in the middle register – the choice of *hiragin* patterns is subject to

---

[10] This episode is well known in the history of Chinese classical traditions. Van Gulik (1940) refers to it several times in his study of the *guqin* and its place in Chinese history and philosophy.

[11] *Kuzure* is a type of *biwa* pattern characterised by its quick tempo and the use of tremolando strokes with the plectrum.

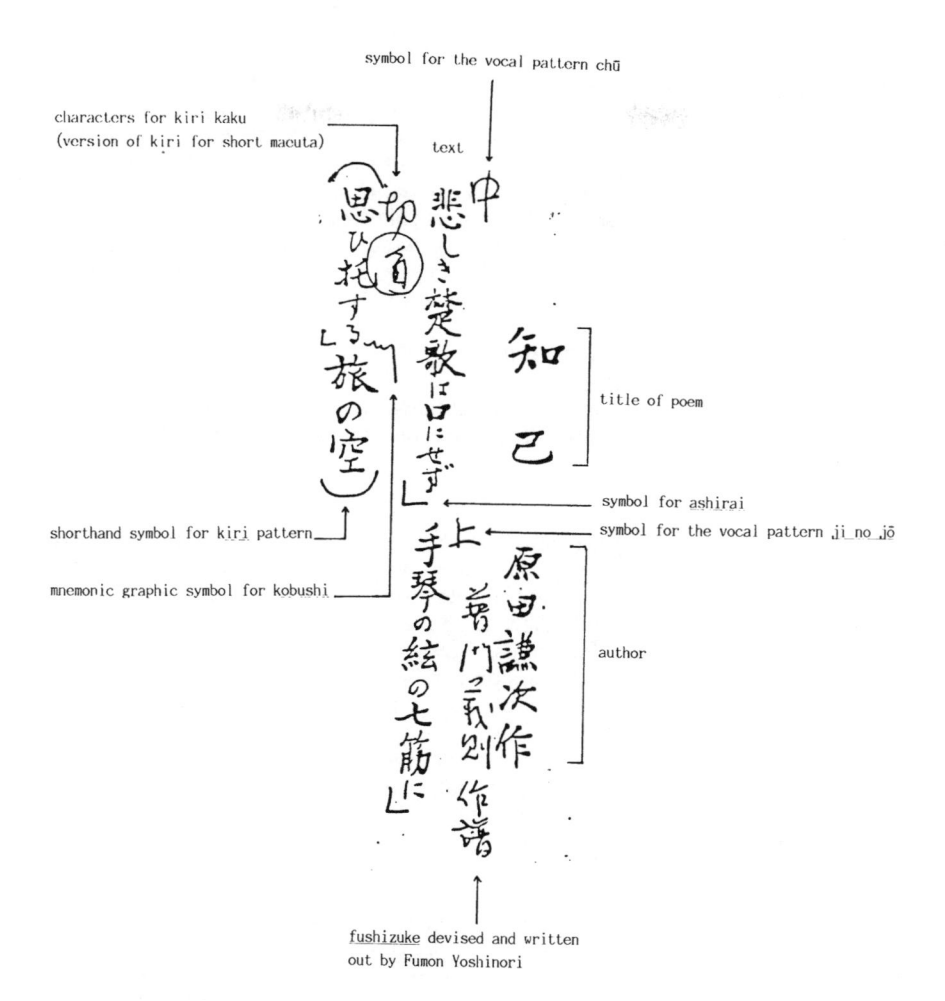

Figure 5: *maeuta* of Chiki
　　　　Text by Harada Kenji
　　　　Fushizuke by Fumon Yoshinori
　　　　Utahon in the hand of Fumon Yoshinori

change in both rehearsal and performance. Of the *senritsukei* sequence written onto the *utahon*, only *hiragin* patterns may be changed in this way.

The *utahon* as it appears at the end of this initial stage (see figure 5) is in one sense a score which documents the distinct identity of a recitation. Yet as it includes no representation whatsoever of most aspects of the piece's realisation, it is in effect merely a fragmentary diagram or simple map of the piece produced during the early stages of its elaboration, primarily for use as a mnemonic aid during rehearsal. Although most players do not refer to the maker of a *fushizuke* as a composer (*sakkyokuka*), this activity is certainly one of compositional variation in that it entails selection and distribution of a set of melody patterns in a unique sequence which remains for the most part unchanged in every performance of the piece. A compositional process, however, continues throughout the rehearsal of a piece.

Actualisation of patterns in rehearsal

The model forms for vocal and instrumental *senritsukei* which are selected and applied during rehearsal are of contrasting nature and may be treated separately.

a) Biwa patterns

Since the early years of this century there have existed notational systems for representing the *biwa* patterns. These notations, called *danpōfu* (see figure 6), are gathered together in a manual in sets – one for each of the nine types of pattern – within each of which there are several versions arranged in order of increasing difficulty. *Danpōfu* are used only during lessons and as references when the detail of a particular version has been forgotten, but their contents, after being memorised, function as source materials for the realisation of patterns in specific recitations.

Common to all the diverse notational systems now in use is a horizontal four-line 'staff' which represents the four strings of the *biwa*, and triangular symbols which, by their position on the horizontal axis, specify the number, type (up or down stroke) and approximate rhythmic relation of plectrum strokes. In a few sources, there are also indications of the degree of pressure to be applied by the left hand, or of the resultant pitch, expressed in terms of scale degree. Figure 6 shows a version of the pattern *chūkan otoshi* in two notational systems developed by Fumon Yoshinori.

In system A the height of each triangle is suggestive of the pitch played, so that the notation functions graphically as an illustration of the melodic contour. Moreover, pitch designations have been added using the *gosei* (five-tone) scale system based on the moveable five-tone grid of traditional Chinese music theory. The symbols for each degree of the *gosei* system are as follows: 宮 *kyū*, 商 *shō*, 角 *kaku*, 徵 *chi*, 羽 *u*. (Figure 3 indicates approximate solfege pitch equivalents for the degrees of the *gosei* system as applied by Fumon.) The symbol *ei* 嬰 (♯) is used to denote raising a pitch by a half-step. *Gosei* symbols are also written at the right-hand end of each line of the staff to show the *biwa*'s tuning. Reading from bottom to top these are *kyū* – *chi* (in the lower octave, as indicated by a subscript dot) – *kyū* – *shō*. A single dot over a symbol denotes that the pitch is sounded in the octave above that of which the pitch of strings 1 and 3 is the lowest tone, while two dots denote the next octave above. At the left-hand end of the staff the two characters for *gedan* (lower position) are written to indicate that the pattern is played on the third and fourth frets of the *biwa*. Apart from the diagonal lines drawn across the

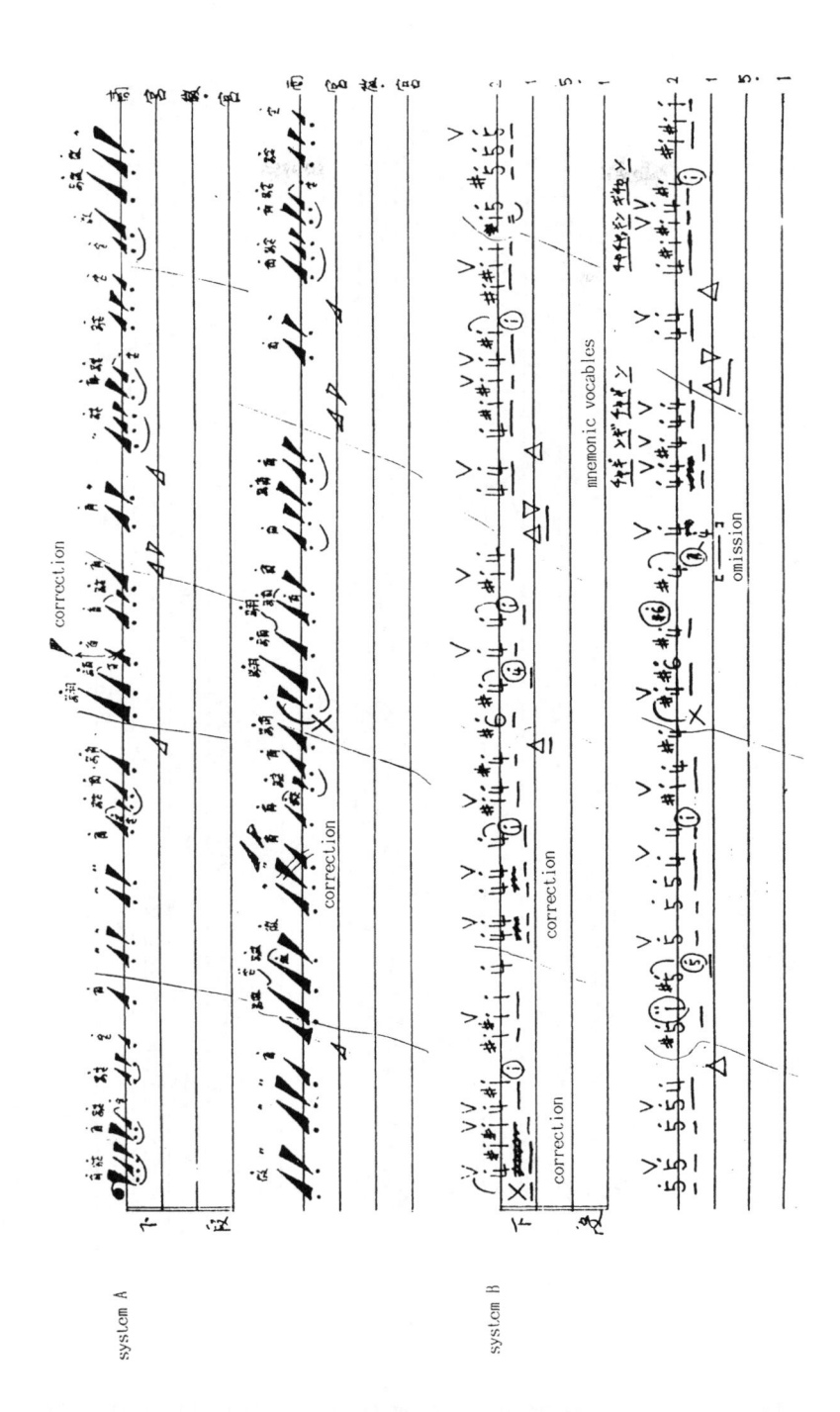

Figure 6: One version of the *biwa* pattern *chūkan otoshi*, in two systems of notation used by Fumon Yoshinori

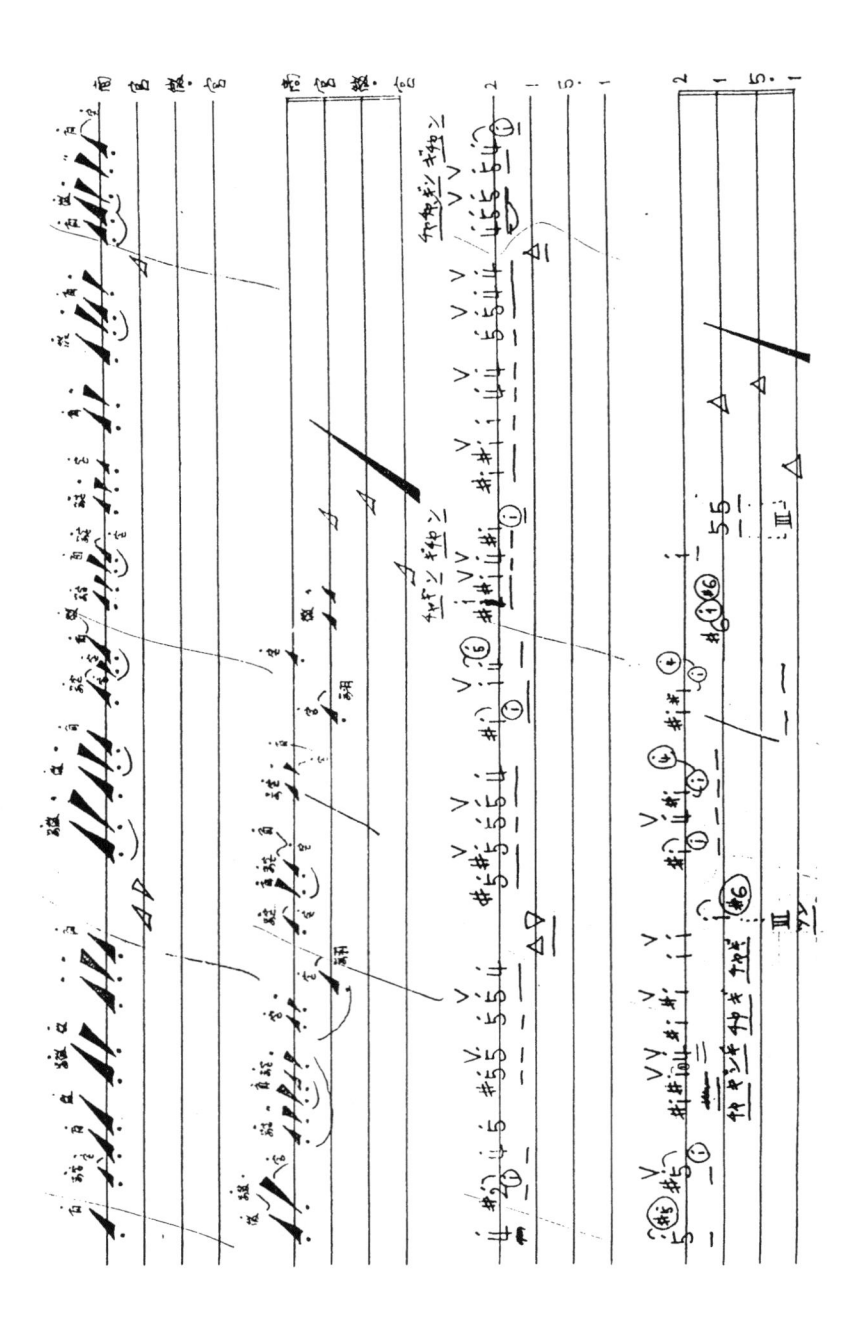

Figure 6: One version of the biwa pattern chūkan otoshi, in two systems of notation used by Fumon Yoshinori

staff, which will be explained below, the meanings of other symbols in this notation system are as follows:

◢	pitch sounded at the third fret
◢̇	pitch sounded at the fourth fret
✗ and ⌒	*kara bachi* (empty stroke); a percussive stroke on the front face of the *biwa*, without sounding a string
△	open string
◢ᵛ	*yoin no henka* (change of the aftertone); glissando motion to the next pitch
‿	play the group of notes in quick succession (the only rhythm notation in system A)

In system B Arabic numerals conflate the two functions of the pitch symbols and the triangular plectrum-stroke symbols. The number system used is based on Chevé numerical notation, which was widely used in Japan in the early decades of this century for teaching school songs and popular instruments such as the *taishōgoto*. As in system A, dots above a pitch symbol indicate the octave in which the pitch is sounded. The first string of the *biwa*, which provides the central pitch of a recitation, is tuned in accordance with the performer's vocal range and is always an octave below the pitch notated as 1̇. Other symbols not found in system A are as follows:

v	upstrokes (symbol borrowed from Western string-writing)
4̄	short duration (relative to 4)
4̄ 5	the first stroke is of very short duration
✗⌢	*yoin no henka*; glissando motion to the pitch shown
⑨	inside the circle

The diagonal lines drawn across the stave in both of these notations are not included in the original form which is photocopied and given to each student. Rather, Fumon draws these lines onto the student's copy during lessons.[12] They indicate the divisions of discrete melodic phrases which Fumon calls *fushigata*, and in practice they are interpreted either as short pauses or as points at which a stroke on the open first or third string may be inserted to articulate the end of a phrase. Their significance for the production of variants will be discussed below.

It seems that from about the turn of the century, most *Satsuma biwa* players have been allowed to use such notations from the early stages of their training. Though they are ambiguous in many respects, *danpōfu* notations should be viewed as visual representations of the basic models for the *biwa* melodies which are acquired by players during their first few years of tuition and which function as sources for the elaboration of each pattern type.

---

[12] When asked why he did not draw such phrase markings onto his original versions of the notation, Fumon replied that these phrase divisions can and should be varied, and he wishes to avoid giving students the impression that they have fixed positions. In his own renditions of 'the same' version of a given pattern, melodic figures are often re-grouped to form new phrase structures.

b) Vocal patterns
Unlike for *biwa* patterns, no notations for the basic forms of the vocal patterns have been adopted in traditional practice. Apart from the names of vocal patterns written beside the text, the only notations for the vocal part are graphic symbols which serve as reminders of the shape of *kobushi* figures, usually drawn at the end of a verse or at its mid-point, on the final syllable of its first phrase (see figure 5). In working up a *fushizuke* for performance a player refers not to a graphic representation of the general shape or structure of each vocal pattern, but to the set of varied realisations of that pattern in different literary contexts which he or she can recall. In strict terms all such realisations are variants of the basic form of the pattern. A broad sample of realisations of a single pattern, however, reveals regularities in the application of certain variants to certain kinds of texts, namely, those which Fumon classifies as either *eiyūteki* or *aishūteki* according to their content (see above, p.111). For example, Fumon sings at least four variants of the pattern *taikan*. In all variants the first phrase is centred upon eb^1 in the *kangoe* register for six syllables before descending to d^1 on the final syllable; in the second phrase, however, each variant employs different pitch sequences to ornament d^1. Of these four variants, two are used only in recitations which Fumon characterises as *eiyūteki*, while two are used only in *aishūteki* recitations. In a given recitation by Fumon, the form which the *taikan* pattern has will be affected by the phonology and syntax of the text, so that on one level it may be called a unique variant, but on a broader level it may be identified as one of the four versions. Analysis of the forms taken by all the vocal patterns in a broad sample of recitations might yield a selection of commonly used versions comparable with the sets of model versions for each type of *biwa* pattern provided in *danpōfu*.

No general model for each vocal pattern-type is offered to students when they are learning to recite. Fumon Yoshinori has described pitch frameworks for all of the vocal patterns in a short publication on the history and theory of *Satsuma biwa* (1979). Fumon has derived these frameworks for the purpose of theoretical exposition; he was not given them as a theoretical tool during his training, does not teach them to his own students, and has referred to them as 'mere bones' which lack 'flesh' until they are applied in recitations and thereby take on varied expression in the form of dynamic contour and ornamentation. To become competent in working up a *fushizuke* for performance, then, a student must learn to adapt the vocal patterns to various texts not by gradually building up more complex variant forms from a general model, but by learning a number of recitations in which patterns of the same name appear in different versions with different texts. From this accumulation of patterns in application, learners develop their own models for each pattern. These are not explicit or abstractly conceived, but are inherent in the melodic framework, ornamental figures and dynamic contours which are common to the various ways of singing a particular pattern in various recitations. Such models are acquired over a much longer period of tuition than is the case with the *biwa* patterns (this may have been otherwise before the use of *biwa* notations). A learner must also gradually acquire a conceptual model for the application of each vocal pattern and its variant forms, which entails becoming familiar with their respective affective characters – in other words, their suitability for expressing particular poetic sentiments in particular narrative contexts – as well as the extent of their dependency upon the surrounding environment of patterns.

In rehearsing the *fushizuke*, the player shapes a fixed melodic setting for each verse by adapting his or her internalised model for each pattern to the text in question. Unlike the *biwa* patterns, however, the forms of vocal patterns tend to develop a high degree of fixity during rehearsal; most variations which occur in performance involve little change from the rehearsed model in terms of the distribution of prolonged and short syllables within phrases and pitches of prolonged tones. The results of the process of adapting the model form of vocal patterns to the text can be illustrated by a comparison of the forms which vocal patterns of the same name take in two different recitations. In example 1 the three vocal patterns *chū*, *jō* and *kiri*, as they were sung in performances of the *maeuta* of Chiki and Shiroyama, respectively, are shown in transcription.[13] Intervals have been rationalised in accordance with equal temperament, and the pitch notated as 1̇ by Fumon is represented by g^1. The text for the *maeuta* of Shiroyama was given above (see p.108). The *maeuta* text for Chiki is as follows:

[*chū*]   *Kanashiki Soka wa kuchi ni sezu*
Rather than sing the sad songs of Chu
[*jō*]   *tegoto no ito no nanasuji ni*
on the seven strings of the *guqin*
[*kiri*] *omoi wo takusuru tabi no sora*
[the traveller] gives life to his thoughts.

As shown in figure 3, *chū* and *jō* are *hiragin* patterns in the *jigoe* register centred on the reciting tones #6 and 1̇. *Kiri* is an *utagin* pattern which effects a downward motion from either 4̇ or 5̇ respectively in the *kangoe* register to 4 in the *jigoe* register. When the two forms of these patterns transcribed in example 1 are examined, the following points of difference are apparent:

(i) The number and placement of pauses within a verse (mabyōshi)
Pauses within patterns which can be sung in a single breath tend to be more frequent in pieces which Fumon classifies as *hageshii* or *eiyūteki* (see p.111). This practice appears to be based on the perception that individual words or phrases within a verse gain in expressive power by being separated from one another, as a distinct, strong attack can be made at the start of each. In the example the first line of each text is structured as seven syllables (the last of which is the topic marker *wa*) followed by five syllables ending in a verb in the present tense. In Chiki a pause is made only after the first lexical unit, the four-syllable adjective *kanashiki*, whereas in Shiroyama (a *hageshii* narrative) there are pauses after both the two-syllable nominal *sore* and the topic marker *wa*.

(ii) The distribution of long and prolonged syllables
In romanised form, all syllables in Japanese are of equal length apart from vowels written with a macron above them, which are doubled in length. The letter 'n' counts as a syllable when it occurs before a consonant or at the end of a word. While long vowels are never sung as short notes in *Satsuma biwa* recitations, neither are they consistently given longer duration than short syllables.

---

[13] Both performances were for archival purposes.

Example 1: The vocal patterns *chū*, *jō* and *kiri* as performed in two songs. Performer: Fumon Yoshinori. Performance dates: (A) 5/2/88 (B) 23/9/84

Notation symbols:	short syllable	●
	prolonged syllable	o
	half-voiced tone, lacking clear pitch content	x
	yuri	‿
	pause or breath point	ʼ

Although many more factors are involved than may be described here, the distribution of prolonged and short syllables is conditioned primarily by the principle that both of the phrases within a line of text in *shichigo chō* metre (of 7 and 5 syllables, respectively), as well as any discrete semantic unit within the first of the two phrases, must start with one or more short tones. This holds true for both *hiragin* and *utagin* pattern types. For example, in the *jō* patterns as performed in Chiki, the first, fifth and eighth syllables of the line are sung as short tones, while in the *kiri* pattern of Shiroyama, the first, fourth and eighth syllables are short. Both emphasise a tri-partite semantic division of the line. Two other principles which are operative here are that syllables sung immediately after pauses are short (for example, 'tatsu' and the 'ta-' of 'tai' in the first line of Shiroyama) and that the final syllable in a word which contains prolonged syllables must itself be prolonged.

(iii) The use of pitches other than the reciting tone in hiragin patterns
Apart from *kobushi* flourishes made on the final syllables of phrases in some *hiragin* patterns, pitches other than the reciting tone are of two kinds: adjacent tones, most of which are short, and half-voiced tones. The latter are intended to intensify the expressive impact of the phrase in which they occur. Short adjacent tones (transcribed as grace notes) usually occur in pieces classed as *hageshii* or *eiyūteki*, and are accompanied by a volume accent. I have not been able to find general principles for the use of other tones adjacent to the reciting tone, many instances of which may be seen in transcriptions 1 and 2 of example 1. It is possible that the speech intonation patterns of the individual reciter is of significance here. The issue of speech intonation patterns and their relations to pitch patterns in any of the *biwa* narrative styles of the modern era has yet to be dealt with in depth by any writer. The issue is complicated by the fact that until the mid-Meiji era all *Satsuma biwa* practitioners were men of the Satsuma domain (see p.102) who spoke with the very distinctive accent of that region. Even today, some performers cite certain melodic figures in their singing as evidence of their fidelity to 'correct Satsuma intonation'.

(iv) The amount and degree of yuri employed
Yuri is a vibrato technique which effects both pitch and volume fluctuations. It is considered a means of ornamenting a single pitch, in contrast to *kobushi*, which involves melismatic motion through several pitches. In Shiroyama, *yuri* is not only used quite extensively, but also is of a relatively heavy kind in which both pitch and volume fluctuate over a large range. This is in contrast to the predominantly pure tone and light *yuri* applied in the *maeuta* of Chiki. These choices reflect the performer's interpretation of the themes of the two recitations as heroic, on the one hand, and contemplative, on the other. In the former kind of recitation, *yuri* ornamentation can at times become a violent oscillation which tears at the melodic line, distorting it by intervals as large as a fourth.

(v) Modification of the pattern's basic pitch framework
For some *utagin* patterns there exist versions which depart from the basic pitch framework of the standard version and which are used only in certain structural environments. The *kiri* pattern in the transcription from Chiki is such a non-standard version (c^1 (4̇) rather than on d^1 (5̇) is emphasised in its first phase). As described above, *kiri* brings to an end each of the major segments of a recitation, with the exception of the final one. The *maeuta* in

Fumon's *fushizuke* for Chiki is only three verses long (see p.119), so that *kiri* immediately follows the conventional opening sequence of *chū - jō*. Herein lies the reason for the choice of this version of *kiri*: in Fumon's practice, this version is always used at the close of *maeuta* which do not include the *hiragin* pattern *chūkan*, in which $c\#^1$ (4) is the reciting tone. In explanation of this practice Fumon said that in this version of *kiri*, the functions of *chūkan* (to take the voice up into the *kangoe* register) and the *kiri* pattern (to execute a descent from the *kangoe* register down to d (5) in the *jigoe* register) are combined.

The first four of the above categories have origins in the performer's perception of the semantic and syntactic characteristics of the texts. The fifth has its origin in the fact that the choice of a particular version is sometimes dependent upon the sequence of surrounding patterns.

Variation of patterns in performance

Whereas vocal patterns are adapted in rehearsal to suit the structure and context of each text, but vary relatively little between performances of a single text by a single player, an attitude of flexibility in the application of the basic models for the *biwa* interludes has traditionally been encouraged. A fully competent player is required to treat the instrumental patterns not as fixed melodies to be rendered the same in the context of all recitations, but instead as highly volatile and responsive to the content of each poem and the conditions of the performance. The most celebrated player in Tokyo during the Taishō and early Shōwa eras, Yoshimura Gakujō, expressed this as follows:

> although there is a general fixed form for each type of melody, one must become skilled in freely altering this form so as to make it shorter or longer, with the effect that the poem is brought to life (1933: 154)

and,

> the notated forms of the melodies are like textbook examples of grammar, but in practice one shouldn't be restricted by grammar, but should make free conversation. (Quoted in Kikkawa, 1978: 255)

Thus the object of a player's training on the *biwa* is first to become familiar with many versions of each pattern, and then the ways in which a version might be shortened, extended or otherwise varied. A competent player will exercise such variations every time she or he plays a given pattern except when teaching its model form as notated in *danpōfu*.

To illustrate the kinds of variation which may occur in performance, example 2 provides a comparison of the pattern *chūkan otoshi* ('falling from the middle register' (*chūkan*)) as performed by the same player (Fumon Yoshinori) in two performances of the song Chiki, separated by an interval of 11 days.[14] As is the case for all *biwa* patterns, there are several notated versions. The one which corresponds most closely to the form of the pattern as it was played on these two occasions is the version given in Fumon's notations in figure 6. To help illustrate how this model version is related to

---

[14] The performance of February 5th was for archival tape purposes, while that of February 16th was before a gathering of Fumon's students as well as other *biwa* players at the Sanshū Kaikan, a club with function rooms in Meguro, Tokyo.

Notation symbols: ⊗ *karabachi* (front face of *biwa* is struck with plectrum)

♪ *uchibachi* (front face of *biwa* is struck as a string is sounded at the pitch indicated)

Ⓢ slightly shorter than the written value

Ⓛ slightly longer than the written value

Example 2: Transcription of two performances of the *biwa* pattern *chūkan otoshi* with transnotation of the same pattern from a score by Fumon Yoshinori
Performer: Fumon Yoshinori
Performance dates: (A) 5/2/88 (B) 16/2/88

the performed versions, a transnotation of the pattern given in notation system B shown in figure 6 has been provided (see example 2). Note that in the transnotation, the accidentals used in Fumon's system B (see figure 6) have been left as they are, while in the transcriptions accidentals are rewritten so as to point up the tetrachordal structures within the melody, in accordance with Koizumi's theories of tonal structure in Japanese music (Koizumi 1958). The placement of letters A to L corresponds with the phrases (*fushigata*; see p.117 above) shown by the diagonal lines on the notation given in figure 6. The four durations expressed in Fumon's rhythm notation as 4, 4̲, 44 and 4̲ are represented as 𝅝 , 𝅗𝅥 , 𝅘𝅥𝅘𝅥 , and 𝅘𝅥𝅮 in the transnotation.

When we compare the transnotation with the transcriptions of performances, it is immediately apparent from transcription 1 that in performance a large section of the model version – segments E to H inclusive – was omitted. When going over a recitation in a lesson or in a performance for which time is limited (usually because a concert programme is running behind schedule), Fumon often employs this strategy of drastically shortening model versions of patterns by jumping from the end of one phrase (as denoted by the diagonal lines which he draws onto notations during lessons) to the start of a later phrase. A second means of variation is evident if one looks at the material within each segment. The material from letter A to C differs from the transnotated version of *chūkan otoshi*. Rather, it derives from another notated version of the pattern. This is also true of the cadence pattern used in both performances (from the tempo change in segment K). At these points, then, Fumon has departed from a single 'model' version and incorporated material from another of his own notated versions. Thirdly, in transcription 2, the time values of some notes in transcription 1 are halved, while some rests and other notes which occur in the shorter version are omitted (indicated by boxes in transcriptions 1 and 2).

The last of these means of variation, in which some notes are extended, shortened or omitted, involves no re-ordering, expansion or contraction of the overall structure of the *biwa* interlude. The other means of variation, however, namely the shortening of a pattern's model form by omission of an internal phrase sequence, and the production of variant forms by combining phrases from a number of basic model forms, are improvisational strategies for which the model patterns acquired during a performer's training function as source materials. While the transcriptions in example 2 show two performances of only a single *biwa* pattern, *chūkan otoshi*, similar strategies are employed in the performance of all nine types of *biwa* pattern.

3 Conclusion

This paper has looked at relationships between modelling and creativity which are integral to the *Seiha Satsuma biwa* tradition. The roles of model forms in the activities of making a *fushizuke*, rehearsal and performance have been described. Differences have been identified between the nature of these models, including their relative specificity in oral and/or literate forms, and the strategies for their application.

Both the generalised model for the structure of all items in the repertoire and the conceptual model which dictates the suitability of vocal pattern versions for expressing particular sentiments represented in the text delimit the player's choices when devising and working up a *fushizuke*. Modelling of this kind must figure in the compositional process in all styles of Japanese narrative and song for which named *senritsukei* are the basic structural units. The application of orally framed models in the adaptation of each vocal pattern to the structure and character of individual texts is also a common procedure in such styles. The strategy of improvisational variation, using as resources the fully notated models for *biwa* patterns, however, has no counterpart in other styles.

The relative fixity of vocal patterns in performance, despite the absence of notations for their model forms, may be attributable to the fixity of the text itself; modifications of text structure (for example, shortening a text to facilitate its performance within a given time limit) never occur in performance, but are completed before the *fushizuke* is devised. The relative freedom in performance of the *biwa* patterns, despite the widespread use of *biwa* notations since the early years of this century, stems from the status attributed to the notations themselves. Fumon Yoshinori refers to the *danpōfu* as a '*kyōsokuhon*', a reference manual. His analogy aptly expresses its role as a storehouse of melody patterns, the contents of which must be internalised by players if they are to be drawn upon in improvising variant forms. These variant forms may include unique sequences of phrases or materials drawn from several model versions of a pattern.

The relationship between the highly specific models for *biwa* patterns and the variant forms played by fully competent performers is as volatile as the relationship between versions of *shakuhachi honkyoku* given in traditional notation and those used in teaching and performance contexts, as described in Riley Lee's paper in this volume. Unlike *shakuhachi* notations, the notated models for the instrumental melodies in *Satsuma biwa* are not representations of discrete pieces to be rendered in full. Nevertheless, both in the *honkyoku* tradition and in the *Satsuma biwa* tradition, the continuing predominance of oral learning is evident in the frequency with which alterations of notated model forms are made in performance.

In the *Seiha* tradition of *Satsuma biwa*, notation continues to be used to reinforce the traditional attitude of flexibility toward the form of *biwa* interludes. In order to gauge the extent of the practice of improvisational variation referred to in writings by Yoshimura Gakujō and others, and in so doing gain a perspective for interpreting modernday practice, transcriptions from old recordings – in particular 75 r.p.m. records of the Taishō and early Shōwa eras – are necessary. To date, however, it has not been possible to gather enough recordings of a single piece to test the accuracy of the written sources. Today a more compositional approach, whereby variants of the basic model forms are worked out and notated during the preparation of a recitation, is occasionally taken by some younger players, but this is still rare. Notwithstanding the small numbers and generally enervated state of its current practice, the ideal of competency in *Seiha Satsuma biwa* remains one in which compositional and improvisational variation are of equal importance.

Acknowledgements

This paper elaborates one of the themes in my Master's dissertation, '*Seiha Satsuma biwa no kifuhō to sono kinō*', completed at Tokyo National University of Fine Arts and Music in 1988. I wish to thank Tsuge Gen'Ichi, Tokumaru Yoshihiko, Allan Marett, David Hughes and Gary Watson for their helpful suggestions.

References

Finnegan, Ruth 1986: 'The relation between composition and performance: three alternative modes', *The Oral and the Literate in Music*, ed. Tokumaru and Yamaguchi, Tokyo: Academia Music Ltd, pp.73-87

Fumon Yoshinori 1979: *Satsuma biwa no yurai to onchō* (The origins and melodic system of *Satsuma biwa*), Yokosuka: Shintaku Daimon

Gamō Mitsuko 1970: 'Gakuri, senritsu, rizumu', *Gagaku*, vol. 2 of Nihon no koten geinō, Tokyo: Heibonsha

Hoff, Frank and Willi Flindt 1973: *The Life Structure of Noh*, Racine, Wisconsin: Concerned Theater Japan

Ikeda Tenshū 1959: *Gen ni ikite* (A life with the *biwa*), vol. 1, Kagoshima: published by the writer

Kikkawa Eishi 1978: Hōgaku e no shōtai (An invitation to Japanese music), Tokyo: Hobunkan Shuppan

Kindaichi Haruhiko 1973: 'Heike mabushi ni mieru heikyoku no daisenritsukei no shurui (The types of large melody patterns to be seen in the *Heike mabushi*)', *Nihon ongaku to sono shūhen*, ed. Koizumi, Hoshi and Yamaguchi, Tokyo: Ongaku no Tomosha

Koizumi Fumio 1958: *Nihon dentō ongaku no kenkyū 1* (Research on traditional Japanese music, part 1), Tokyo: Ongaku no Tomosha

Susilo, Hardja 1987: 'Improvisation in Wayang Wong Panggung: creativity within cultural constraints', *Yearbook for Traditional Music*, 19, pp.1-11

Sutton, R. Anderson 1987: 'Variation and composition in Java', *Yearbook for Traditional Music*, 19, pp.65-96

Trimillos, Ricardo D. 1987: 'Time-distance and melodic models in improvisation among the Tausug of the southern Philippines', *Yearbook for Traditional Music*, 19, pp.23-36

Ueda Keiji 1912: *Satsuma biwa engenroku*, Nippon Ōgakukan

Van Gulik, R.H. 1940: *The Lore of the Chinese Lute*, Monumenta Nipponica Monographs, Tokyo: Sophia University

Yoshimura Gakujō 1933: *Biwa dokuhon* (A *biwa* reader), Tokyo: Shisoin

Glossary of Chinese, Japanese and Korean terms

aishūteki 哀愁的
Anak 安岳
An-kuo-chi 安國伎
Ansei 安政
Anxi 安息
An-yang 安陽
Araki Kodō 荒木古童
ashirai あしらい
atouta 後歌

ban 板
Banshiki-chō 盤渉調
Baramon Sōjō 婆羅門僧正
Bari mai 婆理(舞
biangongdiao 变宫调（變宮調）
bianzhidiao 变徵调（變徵調）
biwa 琵琶
Bo Ziya 伯子
Bola 波剌
bushidō 武士道
Buttetsu 佛徹 (佛哲)

Ch'an 禪
Chang Po 張伯
Chang Sa-hun 張師勛
Changsu 長壽
Changshanüyin 长沙女引（長沙女引）
changso 長簫
Changxing 长兴（長興）
ch'ang-chio 長角
Ch'ang-ch'un 長川
Chejudo 濟州島
Chen Yingshi 陈应时（陳應時）
Ch'en Shou 陳壽
chi チ
chi 徵
Chi-an-hsien wen-wu
  pao-kuan-so 集安縣文物保管所
Chi-an 集安
Chiki 知己
Chikuho ryū 竹保流
Chikuho Ryū
  Shakuhachi no Tebiki 竹保流尺八の手引き
Chi-lin 吉林
ch'i-pu-yüeh 七部樂
ch'in 琴
ch'in-han-tsu 秦漢子
ch'in-p'ip'a 秦琵琶

Chin 晉
Ch'in (Earlier) 先秦
Chin (Eastern) 東晉
Chiu-pu-chi 九部伎
Chiu-T'ang-shu 舊唐書
chong 重
Chŏngdŏk 正德
Chu 楚
Chu 楚
Chu Yŏng-hŏn 朱榮憲
chüan 卷
Chuci 楚辭
Chu-lin ch'i-hsien 竹林七賢
chū 中
chūkan no jō 中干の上
chūkan no ge 中干の下
chūkan otoshi 中干落
Cui Lingqin 崔令钦（崔令欽）

Dai 軑
daimyō 大名
danpōfu 弾法譜
dierbian 第二遍
Dông-so'n 銅山
Doulu 都盧
Dunhuang 敦煌
Dunhuang yuepu 敦煌乐谱（敦煌樂譜）

e エ
Edo uta 江戸唄
ei 嬰
eiyūteki 英雄的
ershipuzi 二十谱字（二十譜字）

fangdian 放點
fu フ
Fuchiwaki Juchōin 淵脇寿長院
fu ho u e ya i フホウエヤイ
Fuke 普化
Fuke shū 普化宗
Fumon (see Fumon Yoshinori)
Fumon Yoshinori 普門義則
furi 振
fushigata 節型
fushimono 節物
fushizuke 節付

gagaku 雅楽

gaikyoku 外曲
gakki 楽器
gakubiwa 楽琵琶
gakusō 楽箏
Gangōji 元興寺
Gansu 甘肃（甘肅）
gedan 下段
gongchepu 工尺谱（工尺譜）
gosei 五声
guqin 古琴
gyōdō 行道

ha ハ
hageshii 激しい
Han 漢
hankai 半開
hara 腹
Harada Kenji 原田謙次
Hayashi Kenzō 林謙三
He Changlin 何昌林
heikyoku 平曲
Hekiganroku 碧巖録
Heike monogatari 平家物語
heng-ti 横笛
hi ヒ
hiki 引き
Hirade Hisao 平出久雄
hiragin 平吟
hiroimono 拾物
Hisamatsu Fūyō 久松風陽
Hitori Kotoba 独言
Hitori Mondō 独問筒
hitoyogiri 一節切
ho ホ
Hodong 好童
hoengch'wi 横吹
hoengjŏk 横笛
hōki 法器
Ho-nan 河南
honkyoku 本曲
Honte Chōshi 本手調子
honuta 本謡
hoten 放點
Hou-Han-shu 後漢書
hsiao 簫
Hsi-liang-chi 西涼伎
Huan Xisha 浣溪沙
Huang-ho 黃河
Huxiangwen 胡相问（胡相問）
Hwanghae 黃海
hyŏn'gŭm 玄琴

i イ
ichion jōbutsu 一音成仏
iemoto 家元
Ikeda Tenshū 池田天舟
Ikeuchi Hiroshi 池内宏
Ikkyū 一休
in 陰
insen 陰旋
Iroha uta いろは詩
issoku on 一息音

Jakin-jo mai 邪禁女儛
ji 急
ji er 急二
ji no chū 地の中
ji no ge 地の下
ji no ge no ge 地の下の下
ji no jō 地の上
jigoe 地声
Ji:Huxiangwen 急胡相问（急胡相問）
jiaofangbili 教坊㫺策
Jiaofangji 教坊記
Jinchi-yōroku 仁智要録
Jing You 景祐
Jiquzi 急曲子
ji san 急三
Jiuge 九歌
jō 上
jō no hari 上のハリ
Juchōin (see Fuchiwaki Juchōin)
juediaoshi 角调式（角調式）

K'ai-huang 開皇
Kaisei Hōgo 海静法語
kai 会
kaku 角
Kamsin 龕神塚
kana 仮名
kange 巻下
kangoe 干声
Kangsŏ 江西
kanji 漢字
Kan-lung 乾隆
Kao-li-chi 高麗伎
kara bachi 空撥
kari 浮り
katakana 片仮名
katarimono 語物
Katsu Kaishū 勝海舟
Katsuhashitatsua 乾豆波斯達阿
Katsuuru Shōzan 勝浦正山
Kawase 川瀬

kazashi 翳し
kazasu 翳す
kiai 気合
Kikkawa Eishi 吉川英史
Kim Ki-ung 金基雄
Kim Pu-sik 金富軾
Kim Wŏn-yong 金元龍
kin 琴
Kinko ryū 琴古流
Kinshinryū 錦心流
kiri 切り
kirikaku 切角
Kishibe Shigeo 岸辺成雄
kisoku shugyō 気息修行
kōan 公案
Kōfukuji 興福寺
kobushi 小節
koch'wi 鼓吹
Kodama Tennan 児玉天南
Koguryŏ 高句麗
Koguryŏ munhwa 高句麗文化
Kokū 虛空
kumiuta 組歌
kŏmun'go 거문고
komusō 虛無僧
Konjaku monogatari 今昔物語
Koremune no Naomoto 惟宗直本
koto 琴 or 箏
kouta 小唄
ku-ch'ui 鼓吹
Kuei-tzu-chi 亀茲伎
Kungnaesŏng 國內城
Kurosawa Kinko 黒沢琴古
Kuta hanagasa odori 久多花笠踊
Kutajima 久多島
Kuta mai 久太儛
kuzure 崩れ
Kwanggaet'o 廣開土
kyokuba 曲馬
kyōsokuhon 教則本
Kyotaku 虛鐸
Kyotaku Denki 虛鐸傳記
kyū 宮

Lee Hye-ku 李惠求
Lee Ki-baik 李基白
Li Huairang 李怀让 (李懷讓)
Li Sao 離騷
Li Yen-shou 李延壽
Lin Chi I-hsüan 臨濟義玄
Lin Shihong 林士弘

mabyōshi 間拍子
machifū 町風
maeuta 前歌
man 慢
man er 慢二
man san 慢三
Manquzi 慢曲子
Mawangdui 馬王堆
mawashiyuri 回し由り
Meian (Myōan) ryū 明暗流
Meian (Myōan) Shimpō ryū 明暗真法流
Meian (Myōan) Taizan ryū 明暗対山流
Meiji 明治
meri メリ 沈り
mogao ku 莫高窟
mōsō 盲僧
Mumonkan 無門関
Munakata Taisha 宗像大社
Muyongch'ong 舞踊塚
Myōju 妙寿

Nagahama Nanjō 長浜南城
Nagata Kinshin 長田錦心
Nangnang (State) 樂浪國
Naniwa-bushi 難波節
Nara 奈良
Nihon Biwagaku Kyōkai 日本琵琶楽協会
Nihon kōki 日本後紀
Nihon shoki 日本書紀
Nihon shoki tsūshō 日本書紀通證
Nishi Kōkichi 西幸吉
Nishikibiwa 錦琵琶
Nishitani Tadashi 西谷正
nō 能

ohyŏn 五絃
ohyŏnakki 五絃樂器
okyō お経
onyŏn-pip'a 五絃琵琶
ori 折り
oshi 押し
Ōsumi 大隅

Paekche 百濟
pai 拍
P'alch'ŏngni 八淸里
Pan Huaisu 潘怀素 (潘懷素)
Pei-shih 北史
Pinnong 品弄
pip'a 琵琶
p'ip'a 琵琶
pipa pu 琵琶谱 (琵琶譜)

p'iri 피리
p'iryul 篳篥
Poli 婆利，婆黎，婆里
P'u-hua 普化
P'yŏngyang 平壤

qianfodong 千佛洞
qin 琴
Qingbeiyue 傾杯乐（傾盃樂）
quzi 曲子

Rao Zongyi 饒宗頤（饒宗頤）
Ren Erbei 任二北
Rin'yūgaku 林邑樂
Rinzai Gigen 臨濟義玄
Rinzairoku 臨濟錄
ro 口
ro tsu re chi ha (hi, ri) ロツレチハ(ヒ、リ)

Ryōshūge 令集解
Ryōgonkyō 楞嚴經
ryū 流
ryūha 流派

Sada-chō 沙陀調
saige 最下
Sajinsha 撒金砂
Sakai Chikuho 酒井竹保
sakkyokuka 作曲家
sakufu 作譜
Samguk sagi 三國史記
samurai 侍
San An 產安
San-kuo-chi 三國志
San Kyorei 三虛鈴
san paizi 三拍子
sanyue 散樂
Sasinch'ong 四神塚
Satsuma 薩摩
Satsuma biwa 薩摩琵琶
sawari さわり
Seiha 正派
senritsukei 旋律型
shaku 尺
shakuhachi 尺八
Sha-e 舍衛
shamisen 三味線
Shan Hsi 山西
sheng 笙
shichigo chō 七五調
shichisengakki 七絃樂器
shifū 士風

Shimazu Sei 島津正
Shimazu Tadayoshi 島津忠良
shinnai 新内
Shintō 神道
Shiroyama 城山
shizukesa no aru 静けさのある
Shoku Nihongi 續日本記
shō 商
Shōwa 昭和
Shōsōin 正倉院
Shōsōin jimusho 正倉院事務所
Shu-ch'ih-chi 疎勒伎
shugyō 修行
Shuiguzi 水皷（鼓）子
Suitō Kinjō 水藤錦孃
Shuryōgonkyō 首楞嚴經
shu-ti 堅笛
Silla 新羅
so 簫
sō 箏
Song Bang-song 宋芳松
Sugano Mamichi 管野眞道
Sui 隋
Sui-shu 隋書
suizen 吹禪
Sumundang 俗字譜
Sundo 順道
Susanni
suzipu 俗字譜
szu 絲

Taemusin 大武神王
Taean 大安
Taedong 大同
taegak 大角
T'aehak 太學
Taesŏngni 臺城里
Ta-fo-ting ju-lai mi-yin
　hsiu-cheng liao-i chu-p'u-sa
　wan-hsing shou-leng-yen ching
　大佛頂如來密因修証了
　義諸菩薩萬行首楞嚴經

taikan 大干
Taiping Huanyuji 太平寰宇記
T'ai Tsung 太宗
Taishō 大正
taishōgoto 大正琴
tamgo 擔鼓
T'amna 耽羅，耽牟羅，耽浮羅，耽羅，儋羅

tan 彈

131

T'ang 唐
T'ang-shu 唐書
Tanikawa Kotosuga 谷川士清
Tanling 曇陵
Tanra 耽羅
Tanteki Hiden Fu 短笛秘伝譜
tateyuri 立由り
Ta-yeh 大業
Tempyō Biwafu 天平琵琶譜（譜）
tettei on 徹底音
tiao 挑
T'ien-chu-chi 天竺伎
Tōdaiji 東大寺
Tōdaiji yōroku 東大寺要録
tōgaku 唐楽
Tŏkhŭngni 德興里
Tokugawa 德川
Tongmyŏng 東明
Tonkō bunbutsu kenkyūsho 敦煌文物研究所
Tora 度羅
toragaku 度羅樂
Toragari 虎狩
tou 头（頭）
touyan 头眼（頭眼）
Tozan ryū 都山流
Tsuruha 鶴派
Tsurata Kinshi 鶴田錦史
Tukhāra 吐火羅
Tuoyuan 陀洹
Tu Yu 杜佑
T'ung-kou 通溝
Tunhuang 敦煌

u 羽
uchibachi 打ち撥
Ueda Keiji 上田景二
Umehara Sueharu 梅原末治
Urabon 孟蘭盆
uragoe 裏声
utagin 歌吟
utahon 歌本
utaidashi 謡い出し
utaidome 謡い止め

waka 和歌
Wang San-ak 王山岳
Wang Yi 王逸
Wang Zhongmin 王重民
wanham 阮咸
Watazumi Dōso 海重道祖
wei 尾
Wei Cheng 魏徵

Wutaishan 五臺山
Wu Ti 武帝
wu-hsien 五絃
wu-hsien-ch'in 五絃琴
wu-hsien p'ip'a 五絃琵琶

Xi Wang Mu 西王母
Xia 夏
xian 仙
Xiang Da 向达（達）
Xijiangyue 西江月
Xin Tang shu 新唐書
Xinshizi 心事子

ya ヤ
Yakushiji 藥師寺
Yaksuri 藥水里
Yalu 鴨綠
yang 陽
Yang Yinliu 杨荫浏（楊蔭瀏）
yanyue banzipu 宴乐半字谱（宴樂半字譜）
Ye Dong 叶栋（葉棟）
yiban sanyan 一板三眼
yiban yiyan 一板一眼
Yi Hang-sŏng 李恒星
Yi Kyu-bo 李奎報
yin 陰
Yingfu 營富
Ying Youqin 应有勤（應有勤）
Yizhou 伊州
yō 陽
yoin no henka 余韻の変化
Yokoyama Katsuya 横山勝也
yokoyuri 横由り
Yonggang
yose 寄席
Yoshimura Gakujō 吉村岳城
you 又
Youjiquzi 又急曲子
Youmanquzi 又慢曲子
Youquzi 又曲子
Yüan Hsien 阮咸
yüan-hsien 阮咸
Yün-kang 雲岡
yuri ゆり

Zen 禅
Zhang Shibin 张世彬（張世彬）
Zhao Xiaosheng 赵晓生（趙曉生）
zheng 箏
Zhong Ziqi 鍾子期
zokusō 俗箏

Contributors to this volume

Mr Gerald Bennett, Zurich Conservatory and College of Music, Switzerland
Professor Chen Yingshi, Shanghai Conservatory of Music, Shanghai, People's Republic of China
Mr Hugh de Ferranti, Department of Music, University of Sydney, Australia
Dr Andreas Gutzwiller, Basel Academy of Music, Switzerland
Mr Gregg W. Howard, Queensland Conservatorium of Music, Brisbane, Australia
Mr Riley Lee, Department of Music, University of Sydney, Australia
Dr Song Bang-Song, College of Music, Yeungnam University, Korea
Dr David Waterhouse, Department of East Asian Studies, University of Toronto, Canada

Notes for authors

Contributions for consideration by the Editorial Board should be addressed to: The Editorial Board, *Musica Asiatica*, c/o Cambridge University Press, Edinburgh Building, Shaftesbury Road, Cambridge CB2 2RU, England. Articles must be typed, double-spaced throughout, on one side of the paper only, with ample margins. References should be cited in the body of the text according to the author-date system, and set out in full at the end of the text, as in the articles in this volume. Footnotes, music examples and illustrations should be kept to a minimum, and should be presented on separate pages from the text. The article should be accompanied by an abstract (not more than 150 words). Standard scholarly romanization for Asian languages should be adopted; for Chinese, the *pinyin* system should be used. Authors whose contributions are accepted for publication will be asked to supply musical examples, and text if possible, in camera-ready form; for further details consult the Music Books Editor, Cambridge University Press.

Volume 7 of *Musica Asiatica* will be edited by Elizabeth Markham.